Taking Part?

Active Learning for Active Citizenship, and beyond

niace
promoting adult learning

To all ALAC/Taking Part participants, past, present and future

Published by **niace**
promoting adult learning

© 2010 National Institute of Adult Continuing Education (England and Wales)

21 De Montfort Street
Leicester
LE1 7GE

Company registration no. 2603322
Charity registration no. 1002775

NIACE has a broad remit to promote lifelong learning opportunities for adults. NIACE works to develop increased participation in education and training, particularly for those who do not have easy access because of class, gender, age, race, language and culture, learning difficulties or disabilities, or insufficient financial resources.

You can find NIACE online at www.niace.org.uk

Cataloguing in Publications Data
A CIP record for this title is available from the British Library

ISBN 978-1-86201-435-0

Cover design by Book Production Services.
Designed and typeset by 4word Ltd, Bristol, UK.
Printed and bound in the UK.

Contents

Acknowledgements

Very warmest thanks to all those who have participated in this project via Active Learning for Active Citizenship, Take Part and Together We Can. This includes all those who have provided advice and support as critical friends as well as all those who have participated as teachers and learners, organisers, managers and facilitators at different levels across the public, voluntary and community sectors. Particular thanks to the chapter authors for their patience and resilience and to colleagues at NIACE for their support as publishers. In addition, the editors owe a special debt of gratitude to colleagues who provided administrative support in their own institutions. And finally warmest appreciations to colleagues at PRIA, New Delhi, India, for their advice and support, facilitating the collection of the comparative materials that are explored in the final chapter.

John Annette
Marjorie Mayo
December 2009

Introduction

JOHN ANNETTE AND MARJORIE MAYO

Citizenship has emerged centre stage as an issue for policy concern, both in Britain and more widely, internationally. The Empowerment White Paper, *Communities in Control: Real people, real power* (Department for Communities and Local Government, 2008) sets the current policy context for the empowerment of citizens in England, building on a series of previous initiatives focusing upon active citizenship and learning for active citizenship. Citizenship has been an issue of concern for some time, then, stretching back at least a decade, and these concerns have continued. As the Final Report of the Advisory Group on Citizenship argued, there have been growing anxieties about the 'levels of apathy, ignorance and cynicism about public life' (DfEE, 1998, p.8). Since 1997, successive governments in Britain have set out to address these concerns, aiming to transform citizens from passive recipients of public services into mutually dependent individuals, active as members of their communities. Citizens have been the subject of policies to encourage and empower them, based upon the civic approach to citizenship development, engaging with public institutions to 'rectify imbalances of power, maintain decent standards for all, sustain mutual respect, and secure their protection from avoidable misfortune' as Henry Tam, the civil servant responsible for turning these policy aspirations into a practical programme of civil renewal, demonstrates in Chapter One.

There have been significant implications for citizenship education, first in schools and colleges and then, more recently, within communities. As the most recent Take Part local pathfinder programme, launched in June 2008, emphasises, quoting the Empowerment White Paper, 'citizenship learning is also important for adults'. It goes on to explain how the Take Part local

1

pathfinder programme will offer information and training on how to be an active citizen, building on the Take Part network that developed from the previous programme on Active Learning for Active Citizenship. The outcomes of these local pathfinders are envisaged as leading to:

- 'An increase in levels of participation in civic activism, consultation and civic participation: and in community leadership roles.
- Increased skills and confidence for participation among citizens, particularly those from more disadvantaged communities.' (Take Part local pathfinder programme: unpublished Department for Communities and Local Government paper).

There are key issues here, then, for adult learning, with varying implications that need to be unpacked, depending upon the differing definitions, perspectives, approaches and policy agendas involved. This book sets out to explore these debates, drawing upon experiences of community-based citizenship education in Britain and setting these within the context of wider debates and exchanges, internationally. As these experiences demonstrate, in the context of increasing globalisation, diversity and population churn, active citizenship involves engaging with processes and structures of governance at European level and beyond, as well as engaging more locally, within neighbourhoods and communities.

The origins for this book go back to a number of workshops, seminars and conferences, sharing reflections on the Home Office Civil Renewal Unit's programme for Active Learning for Active Citizenship (launched in 2004), the predecessor to the current Take Part programme. These ongoing debates were central to the process, developing community-based approaches rooted in models of active participatory learning. Policy-makers, practitioners and programme evaluators met with learners to reflect upon their varying perspectives and experiences, recognising differences as well as identifying shared conclusions about Active Learning for Active Citizenship (ALAC)'s implications for policy and practice.

While the ALAC programme included diverse methods and approaches, there was broad agreement that processes should be participatory and empowering, drawing upon Paulo Freire's model of experiential learning. This emphasis upon participatory processes continues in the current pilot programme, building upon the experiences of the earlier programme, locally, regionally and as part of the national network that developed through ALAC. The structure of this book follows a similar pattern, linking reflections on theory with reflections on practice – and vice versa. Therefore, Section One explores themes, perspectives and approaches, setting debates within and about ALAC within the context of wider debates on definitions, perspectives and competing policy agendas. As Head of the Civil Renewal Unit at the Home Office, as well as being the author of widely read publications on citizenship and communitarianism, Henry Tam has been uniquely placed to explore the definition and approaches to citizenship that underpinned the development of ALAC, with the aim of developing an authentically civic relationship between state and citizens, delivering community empowerment. John Annette, who chaired the ALAC Steering Committee, as well as teaching on ALAC programmes in London, pursues the differing definitions of citizenship and citizenship education, setting these debates within the context of contemporary theoretical debates on civic and civil renewal and community-based learning for active citizenship in Chapter Two. Chapter Three explores competing perspectives and policy agendas and Tony Breslin's chapter sets these within the context of the lessons emerging from previous programmes, lessons from the classroom and beyond. Finally, in the last chapter in this first section, John Potter focuses upon the importance of 'joining up the dots', identifying the links that need to be developed between different policies and programmes.

Having set the context, in terms of the underpinning debates on competing definitions, perspectives and policy approaches, Section Two moves on to reflect upon the experiences of ALAC in practice, as these developed to underpin current initiatives. Val Woodward, who was the co-ordinator, provides a personal narrative, reflecting upon ALAC's development together with the programme's inherent tensions, as well as offering her conclusions on the programme's ultimate achievements. Alison Rooke's chapter goes on to provide an overview of the different 'hubs' within ALAC and their programme outcomes, overall. This sets the framework for subsequent chapters in this section, each of which reflects upon particular aspects of the hubs' work within the ALAC programme, aspects that are being taken forward in the local Take Part pathfinders. So Ted Hartley and colleagues' chapter discusses learning to empower refugees and asylum seekers in South Yorkshire, John Grayson's chapter reflects on anti-racist popular education in the same region and Zoraida Mendiwelso-Bendek and Rebecca Herron's chapter discusses the approach developed in Lincolnshire, including the work with migrant workers. Jill Bedford and colleagues reflect upon programmes to facilitate women's involvement in public life (based in West Midlands), Peter Mangan and colleagues from the

South-West explore the lessons of learning to enable people with disabilities and their carers to 'speak up' to service providers. The London Civic Forum then discusses learning for active citizenship in the context of the global city. Finally, Carol Packham's chapter reflects upon programmes providing accreditation and progression pathways for activists learning how to undertake community-based audits and evaluations.

Section Three then moves to the wider context, linking reflections from practice back to earlier debates on differing perspectives, varying approaches and competing policy agendas. Juliet Merrifield's chapter explores some of the disconnections and tensions within current policy agendas for learning and for citizenship, raising questions about how it has happened that adult education has actually been so sidelined in practice, in relation to civic participation and the 'democratic deficit', identifying ways ahead for adult educators as learners (learning from international as well as from more local experiences). Rennie Johnston reviews the ALAC model and the implications for the current programme, linking this back to the key concepts which were explored in Section One. And finally, Marjorie Mayo's chapter, looking backwards, forwards – and outwards, raises issues about some of the wider implications, sharing learning internationally in the context of neo-liberal globalisation.

The development of policies to promote community-based citizenship education may be expected to be considerably affected by this wider context, with increasing uncertainties, internationally, with fears of recession compounding fears relating to the so-called War on Terror, in the coming period. Government priorities may shift, and governments themselves may come and go, in any case, as a result of electoral changes in Britain and elsewhere. The lessons from ALAC's experiences suggest that the need for community-based citizenship education may be expected to continue, however, and indeed grow rather than decrease in this context of uncertainty and flux. The Take Part programme builds upon ALAC's experiences, extending active learning for active citizenship to new areas and initiatives.

Chapter One argued for taking citizenship very seriously as the roots of democracy. As other chapters have also demonstrated, active citizenship needs to involve commitments to the resolution of conflicts within and between communities on the basis of social justice, equalities and visible fairness. Active learning for active citizenship can contribute to the development of community cohesion and social solidarity, goals of increasing rather than decreasing value, we would argue, which makes this all the more important in the contemporary global context.

SECTION ONE

THEMES, PERSPECTIVES
AND APPROACHES

CHAPTER ONE

The importance of being a citizen

HENRY TAM

We can tell a lot about a society by its attitude towards the development of citizens. At one end of the spectrum we have the hierarchical traditionalist view that there are rulers and subjects, the former to command and the latter to obey. The term 'citizen' would barely feature except in encouraging voluntary, philanthropic deeds by 'good citizens' who are helpful, caring types – but most importantly, unlikely to challenge the rules and structures laid down by those in positions of power. Then there is the middling position of a contractual conception of citizenship. Here we have a package of entitlements on offer in return for compliance with a set of duties – citizens as customers of state provisions paying what the law asks of them so that they will in turn receive what is promised to them. Neither of these positions takes citizenship very seriously as the roots of democracy.

By contrast, at the other end of the spectrum we have the civic notion of citizenship – celebrated by civic republicans and progressive communitarians. Here, citizens are what constitute the state. They pledge their allegiance to no one except to their common well-being. They see public institutions as their own collective instrument to rectify imbalance of power, maintain decent standards for all, sustain mutual respect and secure their protection from avoidable misfortune. On this understanding, people may at times act charitably as private individuals, they may have demands and obligations as users of services provided by the state, but above all, they are citizens – the shapers of the public realm. To strive for its improvement, and guard against complacency and threats of deterioration, they hold the key themselves.

It is fitting that when David Blunkett launched the civil renewal agenda as Home Secretary in 2003, he should invoke the culture of ancient Athens where citizenship in the third sense outlined above underpinned the political ideal of how they should live. Blunkett was convinced that the symptomatic disengagement of the British public from public policies – as reflected in their belief that they had little influence over those policies and their scepticism over what benefits those policies might bring – could only be tackled if the underlying cause of the problem was addressed. He diagnosed this to be the absence of a civic ethos to help develop and sustain citizens who would ensure they have a real say in public affairs.

Supported by a highly civic-minded Ministerial team which included Fiona Mactaggart and Hazel Blears (who later took on the mantle for this agenda as Secretary of State for Communities), and his adviser, Bernard Crick, an outstanding civic republican thinker, Blunkett set up the Civil Renewal Unit to champion the civic approach to citizenship development. As Head of the Civil Renewal Unit, it was my responsibility to turn this political aspiration into a practical programme. I was well aware of the challenges ahead. Most people in society were inclined towards the outlook of either traditionalists who prefer to have submissive subjects who know their place, or market modernisers who want everything to be modelled along the lines of transactions between slick business operators and their customers. Only a small minority believed that it was important for all citizens to attain some tangible influence over public decisions to help promote the common good.

According to the Citizenship Survey, just under 10 per cent of adults in England and Wales have taken on some form of civic activist role (for example, school governor, magistrate, councillor, or membership in a decision-making group for local services) in any given year. This is the core around which the development of a much more vibrant civic culture would have to be built. If this group grows in strength and number, more people would see it as an integral part of their lives to play a part in determining public affairs. They would help to bridge the gap between remote state bodies and the majority of the public who have yet to be convinced that they would ever be taken seriously by government institutions. But the role of a civic activist, in touch enough with their fellow citizens to articulate their shared concerns without becoming a separate professional political class in the process, is far from easy to carry out.

To provide a platform to launch a series of culture change initiatives to raise the profile and appreciation of genuine citizenship, the Civil

8

Renewal Unit devised the 'Together We Can' campaign to take forward the civil renewal agenda. The campaign was to make the case that citizens should be empowered to have a say about the public policies carried out in their name. In so doing we had to demonstrate that the informed input of citizens would improve public services and increase their confidence in and satisfaction with those services, and that the experience of effective engagement would reconnect people with electoral politics. Most importantly, we wanted to shift the role of the citizen from the margins of conventional thinking to the foundations of a revitalised democracy, where recognition of the citizen-decision-maker is the norm.

Active Learning for Active Citizenship

One of our key initiatives was Active Learning for Active Citizenship (ALAC). Its immediate aim was to promote experimentation with a variety of learning methodologies, in different localities, with people from diverse backgrounds, to demonstrate how active citizenship skills could be acquired. Its broader remit was to establish the practical transmission of citizenship skills as one of the three strands of the overarching 'Together We Can' campaign. The other two strands were the strengthening of community level organisations to provide the civic space for people to come together to cultivate a shared understanding of the problems they faced, and the reorientation of public sector bodies at all levels to give citizens meaningful opportunities to engage in their decision-making.

The three strands needed to be developed together, because each one was necessary to enable an authentically civic relationship to emerge between state and citizens. If public bodies were shutting out citizens from their deliberations, or only engaging with them through superficial and wholly ineffectual mechanisms, it would systematically prevent citizens from having any real ownership of their state. Indeed, it would breed cynicism among those who would henceforth suspect public bodies of never truly seeking to work in partnership with them. If communities lack the social infrastructure to enable people to exchange views and explore common concerns, the bonds of citizenship cannot be forged between people who view one another as total strangers. Even if public bodies were ready to reach out to the public, and community organisations were well developed to provide a basis for citizens to come together, people would still need to have the confidence and skills to find the most appropriate ways to get the perspectives of citizens taken on board.

The ALAC strand was taken forward through seven learning partnerships based in the community sector, with support from educational institutions and government. Each partnership looked at how people from different backgrounds could learn to become more effective citizens in engaging with government bodies. They all shared a common commitment to the values of social justice, participation, equality and diversity, and co-operation. These values meant that participants were encouraged, not to put forward their personal views and demand changes they sought as individuals, but to seek what would be a fair representation of their fellow citizens' concerns, and champion these in discussion with statutory decision-makers.

At the level of theory, there are potentially many forms of obstacle to overcome. Modern public services have complex governance arrangements and highly professionalised decision-making processes. How could citizens acquire the skills to find their way around these different set-ups to get their voices heard? Given the majority of people are not interested in spending too much time on public affairs, how could their views be effectively sought so that the minority who get to express their community concerns reflect a broader perspective and not just their own opinions? Priorities cannot be changed without taking into account their resource implications. How could citizens strike the right balance between what appear to call for their most urgent attention and what is affordable? And there is the very real problem of conflicts between what people value — while much attention has been put on the tension which might arise from religious differences, people's divergent assessments of economic, environmental and cultural factors could also lead to sharply different views on what should be done. How could people be expected to resolve such conflicts?

ALAC took the approach that rather than responding with one general methodology, it should allow, indeed positively encourage, citizens and learning providers to try out different techniques and learn from their experiences. In Lincolnshire, for example, they used variations of workshops, cognitive mapping, and iterative interviewing techniques, to help them address problems for migrant workers and other new arrivals to their communities. They also had to deal with the barriers encountered by young people in overcoming the generation gap in seeking to participate more in decision-making. In Exeter, citizens with learning difficulties and their carers learnt alongside workers and managers from social services how they could help to improve the services provided together. In the West Midlands, women from black and minority ethnic backgrounds learnt from a variety of sources, including through meetings with female MPs, to understand how they could make their views count and put themselves forward for leadership positions. In Greater Manchester, accredited education was provided for citizens to make use of the tool, Community-Based Audits and Evaluations, to enable them to strengthen their knowledge, understanding and ability to bring about change in their own lives and those of their communities.

The findings from the different partnerships were brought together in a national framework which the partnerships, coming together as the Take Part Network, would continue to disseminate and develop. Instead of seeking a single comprehensive answer to the theoretical questions about citizen engagement – most likely an impossible task in any case – the ALAC/Take Part partners produced a range of opportunities from which citizens and developers of courses for practical citizenship skills could learn from on a continuous basis to discover how citizens could critically and sympathetically step forward to bridge the gap between state institutions and the wider public.

Civic fulfilment and democratic vitality

Take Part now offers a flexible but well-grounded starting point for individuals and organisations keen to promote the authentic development of citizens. Far from regarding people who embrace civic activist roles negatively as the 'usual suspects' – always a sign that those using that term are uncomfortable with the presence of citizens who have accumulated experience to question their decisions – it celebrates their emergence as the source of democratic vitality. The key issue is not to limit people's civic fulfilment to a few years, but to enable as many people as possible to pursue civic fulfilment as an integral part of living in a democratic society. Democracy is weakened in direct proportion to the extent the public loses interest in having a say in what the state does in their name.

We are aware of many of the barriers to realising one's potential as a democratic citizen. Currently, people aged forty or over are much more likely to take on civic leadership roles. The percentage of elected councillors who are aged under 40 has steadily declined. Citizenship education in schools needs to be supplemented by civic learning opportunities for school leavers so that they have sustained encouragement and support to take on public responsibilities. Consumerism much more than brute oppression, as George Orwell foresaw, is likely to succeed in deflecting people from their identity as citizens into an inward-looking individualism.

The need for learning is linked to the wider challenges to develop a well-educated public. People with degree-level qualifications (15 per cent) and those with higher education qualifications below degree level (14 per cent) were the most likely to take on active civic roles, while people without any formal qualifications were the least likely to participate (5 per cent). Participation in civic governance positions is in turn strongly linked to a sense of being able to influence public decision-making. If people are to view themselves as a meaningful part of the 'public' dimension of public policies, they need to acquire the confidence and skills to speak for their communities in a reasoned, and where necessary, critical manner.

It is not surprising that people with socio-economic disadvantages, lacking access to the education and training others could take for granted, would find it much more difficult to fulfil their civic potential. This is also reflected in the correlations between occupational advancement and participation in civic roles. According to the Citizenship Survey, those in higher managerial and professional occupations were four times more likely to have taken on a civic activist role than those in routine occupations (16 per cent compared with 4 per cent). However, the concerted efforts in areas such as those with dedicated New Deal for Communities schemes – where local people in some of the most deprived areas were given the support to organise themselves and deliberate over how public investment was to be prioritised to meet their improvement needs – have led to higher rates of civic activism and above-average levels of people who believe they can influence the decisions affecting their areas.

Whatever the barriers – and apathy is not one of them – whenever people are given real opportunities to shape public decisions and the support to do so, they tend to make use of those opportunities and become more effective citizens in so doing. Many of the participants in the ALAC projects went on to take up civic activist roles when at the outset they would not contemplate ever doing so. Civic fulfilment is not only an ideal, it is also a practical reality which can be brought about with the help of active citizenship learning.

Community empowerment

By 2008, five years on from the launch of the civil renewal agenda, the challenge to empower citizens has become a mainstreamed part of government with one Public Service Agreement (PSA) Target requiring the percentage of people who affirm they can influence decisions affecting their localities to increase, and another PSA Target seeking to narrow the civic participation gap between disadvantaged groups and the general population. The *Communities in Control* White Paper on empowerment set out more policy commitments to give citizens real power over public decisions.

Moving on from promoting awareness of the need to strengthen the civic roots of democracy, I now have the responsibility for delivering many of these policy commitments on the ground. One of these commitments is to develop and implement a Take Part programme by building on the work of ALAC and the Take Part Framework. This programme combines the rolling out of local pathfinders and a series of national initiatives to enable more citizenship learning to take place. This will in turn help to underpin other programmes designed to get more citizens to participate in setting priorities for particular public budgets, taking over the running of public buildings or parks, putting forward their views on different public services, or becoming lay governors on public institutions.

By its very nature, no government can enable citizens to have a real sense of greater political efficacy by handing to them a ready-made package of solutions. The solutions must be generated with the involvement of citizens, not merely as service users, taxpayers or even once-every-four-years voters, but as civic decision-makers in their own right.

To succeed, we will need to address three issues in particular. Active citizenship learning has an important role to play in relation to each of them. First, the rigid divide between formally elected politicians and civic activists has to be replaced by a more collaborative relationship. It would be as wrong for any citizen to think that they can somehow take over the whole decision-making role from people who have attained validated authority through an election, as it would be for those elected to believe that they can ignore everyone else until the next election. Citizens do not all have the same amount of time to devote to public affairs, but from those who can at most have a chat with the activist in their neighbourhood to those who virtually engage in politics in a full-time professional capacity, they should recognise their shared interest in cultivating a shared understanding of the communities they serve, and work to support each other in meeting those communities' needs. Elected councillors, for example, should reach out to other civic activists and seek their help with engaging the wider community in meaningful deliberations about their priorities. Non-elected activists in turn should respect the role of their elected counterparts, and far from seeking to bypass them, they should systematically engage them in leading community dialogues. Both sides would benefit from learning the art of co-production in the context of democratic decision-making.

Secondly, government officials, at the national and local level, will need to deepen their understanding considerably about how to empower citizens. *Ad hoc* meetings with 'stakeholders' selected on a 'we know about them' basis, or process-driven consultations seeking responses on detailed text without opportunities for deliberative engagement, rarely lead to anything more than giving the public sector organisers a sense of quasi-legitimacy. They are certainly not likely to give civic participants any enhanced efficacy over the policies in question. There is a wealth of knowledge about what works in community empowerment, and the information relating to effective techniques and case studies is growing by the day. This has to be targeted much more at the public sector to ensure that officials have an adequate grasp of the context of empowerment and know what engagement approaches to adopt to give citizens a real say.

Finally, the role of civic activists needs to be better explained and supported in society. In schools, among employers, and within both the statutory and voluntary sectors, a tacit distinction has arisen which treats people who give their time or money to 'good causes' as worthy of recognition — awards, honours, time-off, etc., but deems others who question public policies and organise to challenge decisions as suspiciously 'political'. This is exacerbated by politicians who feel obliged to add, whenever they are saying something they feel is deeply important, that they are 'not making a political point'. Politics in a democracy is about citizens questioning policy options, and contesting how priorities are set. Charitable support for good causes raises but a tiny fraction of the resources required to help people in need. It is public policy decisions which channel public funds to meet the overwhelming demands from society as a whole. Citizens who give their time and resources to help shape such decisions are volunteers too, and active citizenship learning needs to reach those who do not appreciate why these active members of the community should be given just as much, if not more, support and recognition.

Communities will become steadily more empowered when more citizens believe it is worthwhile to speak up about their communities' needs and how they should be met. But they are not the only ones who need to learn more about being effective citizens in a democratic society. Increasingly others – especially institutions in all sectors with considerable influence over how citizens as pupils, workers and campaigners can express their views on decisions affecting their communities – will need to learn about the importance of having people who can function as citizens in shaping the common good, and the actions they should consequently take to support them.

CHAPTER TWO

'Active Learning for Active Citizenship': community-based learning and democratic citizenship

John Annette

To what extent should citizenship education for lifelong learning be based on a more 'political' or civic republican conception of citizenship as compared to a liberal individualist conception, which emphasises individual rights, or a communitarian conception, which emphasises moral and social responsibility? In what ways are people finding new ways to engage in civic participation which can provide the basis for certificated or accredited lifelong learning? To what extent does an experiential learning practice like community-based learning, as part of a citizenship education for schools, the 14–19 curriculum and adult learning based on the 'Active Learning for Active Citizenship' programme, enable learners to become democratic citizens? These are some of the questions I would like to explore in this chapter.

Citizenship education and the concept of citizenship, everyday politics and civic engagement

It could be argued that the conception of citizenship underlying UK life-long learning should be a civic republican one which emphasises democratic political participation. This reflects the influence of Bernard Crick and the government Minister David Blunkett. One of the key challenges facing civil renewal and the introduction of citizenship education in the UK is the question about whether and in what respects citizenship is 'British'. Elizabeth Frazer has written about the 'British exceptionalism' towards discussing citizenship (Frazer, 1999a) and David Miller has written that 'citizenship – except in the formal passport-holding sense – is not a widely understood idea in Britain. People do not have a clear idea of what it means to be a citizen… Citizenship is not a concept that has played a central role in our political tradition' (Miller, 2000, p.26). The question concerning to what extent British people are familiar or comfortable with the concept of citizenship raises questions about the extent to which the political language of citizenship and civic republicanism can increasingly be seen as a tradition of 'British' political thought which can provide the basis for a transformation of the more dominant liberal individualist political traditions.

In the UK the 'New Labour' government has espoused a programme of civil renewal that links the public, private and voluntary and community sectors to work for the common good. This is informed by a set of beliefs and values involving faith traditions, ethical socialism, communitarianism and more recently civic republicanism. According to David Blunkett when he was Home Secretary:

> The 'civic republican' tradition of democratic thought has always been an important influence for me …. This tradition offers us a substantive account of the importance of community, in which duty and civic virtues play a strong and formative role. As such, it is a tradition of thinking which rejects unfettered individualism and criticises the elevation of individual entitlements above the common values needed to sustain worthwhile and purposeful lives. We do not enter life unencumbered by any community commitments, and we cannot live in isolation from others. (Blunkett, 2003, p.19)

It is this civic republican conception of politics which I would argue animates key aspects of New Labour's policies from citizenship education to its strategy towards revitalising local communities.

Richard Dagger, in his influential study of civic education, argues that a civic republican conception of citizenship can reconcile both liberal individuality and the cultivation of civic virtue and responsibility. He writes, 'there is too much of value in the idea of rights – an idea rooted in firm and widespread convictions about human dignity and equality – to forsake it. The task, instead, is to find a way of strengthening the appeal of duty, community and related concepts while preserving the appeal of rights' (Dagger, 1997, p.58 and cf. Maynor, 2003).

17

The creation of a shared political identity underlying citizenship should also allow for multiple political identities based on gender, race, ethnicity, social exclusion, etc. It may be that the civic republican politics of contestability, as recently argued for by Philip Pettit (Pettit, 1997), may provide a more pluralist basis for citizenship in contemporary Britain than traditional republican politics. Equally, recent theorists of liberal democracy like Eamonn Callan also argue that an education for citizenship must hold fast to a constitutive ideal of liberal democracy while allowing for religious and cultural pluralism (Callan, 1997). A more differentiated but universal concept of citizenship (Lister, 1998), which encourages civic virtue and participation while maintaining individual liberty, and allows for cultural difference, will create a way of understanding citizenship that is appropriate for an education for citizenship and democracy.

It could be argued that the recent establishment of an education for citizenship is based more on a communitarian concern for moral and political socialisation than promoting civic engagement. Following Elizabeth Frazer's distinction between a 'philosophical communitarianism' and a 'political communitarianism' (Frazer, 1999b; cf. Tam, 1998 and 2001), Adrian Little raises some important questions about the apolitical conception of community in communitarianism. He writes:

> As such, the sphere of community is one of contestation and conflict as much as it is one of agreement. Thus, essentially, it is deeply political. Where orthodox communitarians see politics as something to be overcome to the greatest possible extent, radicals argue that the downward devolution of power will entail more politics rather than less. (Little, 2002, p. 154)

Both Little and Frazer in their studies of the political communitarianism consider the revival of civic republicanism as emerging from the debate between liberal and communitarian conceptions of the politics of community. In civic republicanism (cf. Pettit, 1997 and Maynor, 2003) freedom consists of active self-government and liberty rests not simply in negative liberty but in active participation in a political community.

In the USA this debate is also reflected in the writings of Benjamin Barber, Michael Sandel and William Galston, which have been promoting a civic republican conception of citizenship (Barber, 1984, Sandel, 1996, and Galston, 2001). According to Barber, the fundamental problem facing civil society is the challenge of providing citizens with:

The literacy required to live in a civil society, the competence to participate in democratic communities, the ability to think critically and act deliberately in a pluralist world, the empathy that permits us to hear and thus accommodate others, all involve skills that must be acquired. (Barber, 1992)

Joseph Kahne and Joel Westheimer recommend a model of citizenship education based on the principles of social justice, and Harry Boyte a model based on the concept of 'public work' (Kahne and Westheimer, 2003; Boyte, 2004). This debate about what is an appropriate model of citizenship for citizenship education raises questions about the need for students to move beyond an individualistic conception of citizenship and a consumer model of citizenship, and develop a model of 'civic republican' democratic citizenship education.

This reconsideration of the concept of citizenship and citizenship education should also be informed by the recent work on the 'politics of everyday life' which can broaden our understanding of what 'the political' could mean in the lives of all citizens (Crick, 2005; Bentley, 2005; Boyte, 2004; Ginsborg, 2005). We need to have more research into how people understand the 'political' as it relates to their everyday concerns in their communities as compared to the more formal political sphere of voting, political parties and holding public office. This broader conception of the political reflects the decline of formal political participation and lack of trust in formal politics at a time when there is evidence of continuing forms of civic engagement which may escape the radar of Robert Putnam's research into social capital (cf. Joseph Rowntree Charitable Trust, 2006). This also reflects the important distinction that should be made between volunteering which leads to active citizenship and a more political form of civic engagement in community which can lead to democratic citizenship.

In the USA, and now beginning in the UK, academics are viewing service learning or community-based learning as an important part of an education for active citizenship which I would argue can be based either on a more communitarian conception of citizenship (volunteering or community service) or a more 'political' or civic republican conception of citizenship (civic engagement and non-formal political participation).

'Politics' and community involvement

In his short book on democratic theory, Bernard Crick has written:

I remain concerned, though, that the interpretation of 'community involvement' that underpins the Citizenship curriculum will involve a conception of the community that sees it simply as a place or neighbourhood where students are merely 'active': doing good rather than political good (i.e. informed, effective citizens). That is, the new curriculum will result in forms of volunteering that will fail to challenge the students to think and act 'politically' ... . (cf. Crick, 2002, p.115)

In contemporary political thinking the concept of community has become both philosophically and 'politically' significant. Community has also become increasingly the focus of government policy in the UK and the USA. From the 'Third-Way' communitarianism of New Labour or the New Democrats, to the emergence of communitarian-based 'Compassionate Conservatism', the idea of community is now seen as a key to rethinking the relationship between civil society and the state. Government social policy concerning neighbourhood renewal and urban renaissance stresses the role of citizens in inner city areas in designing and rebuilding their communities (Taylor, 2003).

Linked to this challenge is the perceived sense of the loss of community in contemporary British society. This lost sense of community also underlies the idea of social capital, which has recently been popularised by Robert Putnam in his study of the decline of civic engagement and social capital in the USA (Putnam, 2000). The concept of social capital has provided a theoretical basis for understanding the importance of community, which according to the neo-Tocquevillian analysis of Robert Putnam and his colleagues has important consequences for citizenship and political participation. While Putnam and others have analysed the decline of traditional volunteering in the USA it is interesting to note that in the UK there has been a much smaller decline (Hall, 2002).

In contemporary political and sociological theory there has been a renewed interest in the idea of community (Bauman, 2000; Delanty, 2003). The concept of community is an elastic concept which allows for an enormous range of meanings. From virtual communities to imaginary communities, there are conceptual understandings of community to be found in a wide range of traditions of thought and academic disciplines. I would argue that there are at least four main ways of conceptualising community. (There are a number of contemporary writers who offer alternative ways of representing the varying understandings of the meaning of community: cf. ibid; Nash, 2002 and Taylor, 2003.) The first is to consider community descriptively as a place or neighbourhood. The second is to talk of community as a normative ideal linked to respect, solidarity and inclusion, which can be found in the now well-established debate between liberalism and its communitarian critics (Mulhall and Swift, 1996). The third way of understanding community is based on the construction of cultural identities and can be found in communities of 'interest'. This conception is based on a politics of identity and recognition of difference. The fourth way is to consider community as a political ideal which is linked to participation, involvement and citizenship, especially on the level of the community.

It is the case, of course, that these conceptual understandings of community are often elided and combined to produce hybrid conceptualisations of contemporary community. Thus a political understanding of community may be based in a specific neighbourhood where there are public places and may include a variety of communities of identity or interest. It is also the case that political communitarianism can be understood through the analysis of the politics of community in terms of liberalism, communitarianism or civic republicanism. Advocates of both communitarianism and civic republicanism have recently begun to revive the idea of a civic service linked to the ideal of service to the local community. In Britain, a number of authors have argued for a national voluntary Citizen's Service initiative and, more recently in the USA, there has been a renewed interest in establishing a form of national service, which would build on the success of the Americorps programme of the Corporation for National Service (Dionne, Jr, *et al.* 2003). Susan Stroud, based on her previous work for the Ford Foundation, has also been exploring this theme internationally (cf. www.icip.org).

Civil/civic renewal and active citizenship

David Blunkett in his Edith Kahn Memorial Lecture and various publications and speeches called for a new *civic renewal* or *civic engagement* which emphasises new forms and levels of community involvement in local and regional governance. This new democratic politics, which would include referendums, consultative activities and deliberative participation, has found support from organisations as diverse as the Local Government Association and the prominent think tank, IPPR (IPPR, 2004). One outcome of this shift in thinking, which might be termed a switch from *government* to *governance*, is the obligation upon local authorities to establish Local Strategic

Partnerships, a duty arising from the Local Government Act 2000. These partnerships seek to involve local communities in the development of Community Strategies. More recently, the Home Office established a Civil Renewal Unit, which has begun piloting an 'Active Learning for Active Citizenship' programme through which it is intended that adult learners will develop the capacity to engage in deliberative democracy at a local level. This unit is now the Community Empowerment Unit in the Department for Communities and Local Government and the 'Together We Can' cross-departmental strategy is being supported by the new 'Community Empowerment Strategy' (cf. Brannan *et al.*, 2007).

In the USA this revitalised civic renewal movement has led commentators to challenge the assumption of Robert Putnam and others that there has been a fundamental decline in social capital and civic participation. Carmen Sirianni and Lewis Friedland have mapped out the different dimensions of this movement, and while recognising the decline of more traditional forms of civic engagement and political participation – membership of formal organisations, voting and membership of political parties – they argue for new and changing forms of civic renewal and call for greater and more creative forms of civic engagement (Sirianni and Friedland, 2001 and 2005). Internationally, there is evidence of new global networks emerging which promote these new forms of civic engagement and deliberative democracy (Fung and Wright, 2003; Gastil and Levine, 2005).

This recent work on civic renewal also points out the limitations of social capital theory, as bonding and bridging social capital can correlate with civic engagement but cannot explain why it takes place. It also highlights the need to go beyond both bridging and bonding social capital and enable linking social capital through political action. Without vertical political networking, for example, poor communities do not necessarily gain access to new forms of political influence (Woolcock, 2001 and Field, 2003).

Active citizenship, citizenship education and civic renewal

In UK schools, the problem for teachers is to integrate the new Citizenship Education curriculum – including the opportunity to engage in Community-Based Learning – into a National Curriculum, which many view as already overcrowded. And the Community-Based Learning element poses an additional burden: providing the opportunity for students to participate in Community-Based Learning requires strong partnerships with local community-based organisations, educational institutions and sufficient funding. Nonetheless, it is important if Crick's ambitions are to be fulfilled:

> *We aim at no less than a change in the political culture of this country both nationally and locally: for people to think of themselves as active citizens, willing, able and equipped to have an influence in public life and with the critical capacities to weigh evidence before speaking and acting; to build on and to extend radically to young people the best in existing traditions of community involvement and public service, and to make them individually confident in finding new forms of involvement and action among themselves. (DfEE, 1998, p. 7)*

The vision of Crick's Advisory Group is a formidable one and there are, of course, many challenges to be faced if it is to be realised. Terence McLaughlin, among others, has raised a number of issues arising from the Advisory Group's report (McLaughlin, 2000 and cf. Osler, 2000). Here I want to build on these and encourage further debate and discussion about how Citizenship Education through Community-Based Learning might help to bring about the more participative democratic political culture that Crick seeks. It is also the Community-Based Learning which is essential for a model of adult learning for democratic citizenship which was developed by the ALAC programme for adult learning for democratic citizenship.

Given the introduction of the new Citizenship curriculum in England and other developments in the rest of the UK (DfEE, 1998; Crick, 2002; Annette, 2003) and following the subsequent publication of the report of Sir Bernard Crick's second Advisory Group which examined Citizenship provision for 16–19 year olds in education and training (DfEE, 2000), opportunities to develop new models of Citizenship learning across the developing 14–19 phase and into adult and community education are now emerging. In the USA there is a growing concern about political disengagement and academics are beginning to ask what model of citizenship underlies the development of citizenship education (Battistoni, 2002; Crick, 2002; Colby *et al.*, 2003; Levine, 2007).

Crick's second report viewed Citizenship less as a 'subject' for the classroom and more as a life skill for the maturing student, arguing that

23

all young adults should have an entitlement to Citizenship Education based on participation, and that they should all have the opportunity to have this participation academically recognised. As a result, September 2001 saw the launch of a developmental programme of pilot projects centrally co-ordinated by the Learning and Skills Development Agency (LSDA) and managed locally by groups as diverse as Education Business Partnerships, LEAs, LSCs and the Citizenship Foundation. Following the successful completion of the Post-16 Citizenship Development Programme, the Quality Improvement Agency (QIA) commissioned the Learning and Skills Network (LSN) to manage a new support programme for post-16 citizenship. The programme's central aim was to disseminate as widely as possible, and build on, outcomes from the development programme in order to mainstream citizenship provision in post-16 education and training.

Citizenship's place in the National Curriculum, the publication of this second report and the associated pilot programme (and, more recently, the issuing of Crick's third report into the educational needs of new-comers to Britain during 2003) together provide the basis for establishing Citizenship Education as a key component within, not just schooling, but ongoing (or 'lifelong') learning provision. Especially beyond the school the focus is likely to be on active citizenship, civil renewal and regeneration. Indeed, the third Crick report expressly, if controversially, links adult learn-ing, volunteering, community involvement and the process of becoming a UK citizen.

Citizenship education, active citizenship and community-based learning

So, what is the link between Citizenship Education and Community-Based Learning? And what role might community-based learning play in delivering the objectives of Citizenship Education? As readers will be aware, Crick's first and seminal report, *Education for Citizenship and the Teaching of Democracy in Schools* (DfEE, 1998), resulted in the addition of Citizenship to the National Curriculum. This report also recognised the importance of active learning in the community – learning that is, by definition, *experiential* in nature.

This pedagogy of experiential learning is based on the learning cycle of David Kolb and is now beginning to establish itself in schools, colleges and in higher education, and in professional development and training programmes (Kolb, 1998). As a form of learning it is based not just on experience but on a *structured learning experience* with *measurable learning outcomes*. A key element of Kolb's model is that learning emerges from the structured reflection of the learner. Thus, as applied to Citizenship Education, the student learns not just through, for instance, volunteering or civic engagement, but through their reflections on this. Thus, Carnegie Young People Initiative, CSV Education for Citizenship, Continyou, Changemakers, the Citizenship Foundation, Envision and other voluntary sector organisations have highlighted the importance of encouraging the development of, for example, citizenship education through reflective service learning. In the USA one important leader in this area is Terry Pickeral who is director of the National Center for Learning and Citizenship, which provides leadership in the Compact for Learning and Citizenship, a national organisation of chief state schools officers and district superintendents committed to integrating service learning into K–12 schools. The centre has led on the 'Policy and Practice Demonstration Project', which is part of the W.K. Kellogg-funded 'Learning in Deed' national service-learning initiative and the Ford Foundation-funded 'Every Student a Citizen' initiative which focuses on citizenship education and service learning. Many schools in the UK and the USA now provide school students with the opportunity to engage in this kind of Service Learning (to use the prevalent US terminology), learning that derives from the offering of service in the community: 'active learning in the community', 'community-based learning for active citizenship', or 'active citizenship in the community' as different US- and UK-based programmes frame such activity (Wade, 1997, and for the UK cf. Annette, 2000; Potter, 2002). A key challenge facing such programmes is to go beyond traditional volunteering and doing good works and link the service learning with political knowledge, skills and understanding.

While there has been a tradition of community-based internship and experiential education since the 1960s, the new emphasis in the USA since the early 1990s has been on the link between Citizenship Education and Service Learning (Battistoni, 2002). There is also an increasing emphasis on the need for Service Learning programmes to meet the needs of local community partners (Cruz and Giles, 2000). Thus Service Learning helps to build a type of 'bridging as well as bonding social capital' (cf. Putnam, 2000) *and* may also develop the capacity building for democratic citizenship within civil society (Annette, 1999; Kahne and Westheimer, 2000 and 2003). An important research question that needs to be examined, albeit one beyond the reach of this chapter, is: 'what are the necessary elements of a Service Learning programme which can build not only social capital but also active citizenship?' (Eyler and Giles, 1999; Billig, 2000; Kahne and Westheimer, 2000 and 2003; Annette, 2003).

Community-based learning and political awareness: the evidence

Until recently there has been relatively little empirical research in the UK into Citizenship and Citizenship Education beyond some pioneering studies of youth political socialisation. Ivor Crewe and his colleagues noted that much of the debate about Citizenship is 'conducted in what is virtually an empirical void' (Crewe *et al.*, 1997). There has been more recently an increasing amount of research into Citizenship Education and its learning outcomes internationally. In the UK there have been a number of small-scale studies since 1998 and more recently the eight-year *Citizenship Education Longitudinal Study* has been launched. Outlined elsewhere in this text, the study has been commissioned by the Department for Education and Skills (DfES) and is being carried out by David Kerr and colleagues at the National Foundation for Educational Research (NFER) (Kerr *et al.*, April 2003). This will, for the first time in the UK, provide a comprehensive understanding of the outcomes of Citizenship Education as a compulsory core National Curriculum subject at Key Stages 3 and 4, and it will complement the Post-16 Citizenship Education Survey that is also being funded by DfES (now the Department for Children, Schools and Families) and undertaken by NFER. There are a number of contextual factors raised in the first report of the longitudinal study and in other research. Critically, these focus on the competing definitions of Citizenship with which practitioners contend and the lack of a coherent vision for Citizenship Education – but here and elsewhere there are also concerns about the 'definitions, purposes and outcomes' of Citizenship Education, particularly given the competing claims for emphasising 'equality, identity and diversity', global citizenship, etc.

Although research into Citizenship Education in the UK remains in its infancy, there is an extensive range of research studies in the USA into the learning outcomes of Service Learning programmes for students in both secondary schools and higher education. What is especially interesting about this research is the almost universal finding that Service

Learning, where volunteering is part of a formal Citizenship curriculum, is more effective in its link with 'Citizenship' outcomes than with 'Community Service' or volunteering itself. That is, it serves to develop just the type of political awareness and literacy that Crick and his colleagues intended the new UK curriculum to do: A Community-Based Learning, which builds Citizenship knowledge and develops Citizenship skills which can lead to Active Citizenship and Civic Renewal.

In another recent research study, Daniel Hart, Thomas Donnelly, James Youniss and Robert Atkins (Hart *et al.*, 2007) note that:

> *The most striking finding to emerge from our analyses is that high school community service predicted adult volunteering and voting, after controlling for other relevant predictors and demographic variables … Our results strongly suggest that civic participation in adulthood can be increased through community service participation in adolescence, a conclusion contrary to claims by some that service detracts from political involvement. (Ibid., p.213)*

The authors also note that an important part of such a service learning experience, along with a deeper civic identity, is the experience of developing and using civic skills (cf. Kirlin, 2003). Project 540 was a network of 270 high schools that enabled school-wide deliberation and action about issues that students chose. Data from a research survey indicate that the students who participated in Project 540 had a more positive commitment to deliberative democracy, civic action and a greater sense of political efficacy (Project 540). This raises questions about the importance of the theory of deliberative democracy for citizenship education and highlights important issues about the need to enable inclusive voices and to develop the civic skills of civic listening and inter-cultural understanding. It also challenges citizenship educators to learn from the innovations of the practice of deliberative democracy and to apply them to the curricular practice of an education for democratic citizenship.

There is growing research which shows that young people are developing new forms of civic engagement, including wide-ranging social networking and e-civic participation. Based on the National Youth Civic Engagement Index Project funded by the Pew Charitable Trust from 2001 to 2005, Cliff Zukin, Scott Keeter and colleagues have developed a national telephone survey of 3,200 respondents of four generational cohorts. They find that the younger cohort, the 'DotNets', engage in volunteering and community problem-solving activities but lag behind in electoral activities. They then analyse the implications of these findings for future civic participation in the USA. This research is important, not only for distinguishing between civic and electoral forms of civic activity, but also for taking into account lifecycle and generational differences (Zukin *et al.*, 2006). More recently, Peter Levine sees the new forms of youth civic engagement as part of a wider civic renewal movement in the USA and argues that school-based service learning that is based on community-based problem solving and political engagement is an important part of this movement (Levine, 2007). It is interesting to compare these findings with the work of the Youth Electoral Study (YES) Project based at the University of Sydney, which has examined the decline of youth voting and the changing forms of youth participation in Australia (cf. Print and Coleman, 2003). In the UK recent qualitative research studies have considered some of the new forms of civic engagement among young people (cf. Lister *et al.*, 2003 and Weller, 2007).

These research findings and the evidence of new kinds of youth civic participation raise the issue of how we develop through community involvement, especially on the local level, a more deliberative and democratic politics that can also provide a more active and political framework for enriching Citizenship Education. Thus, learning about Citizenship through active Community Involvement should, at least in part, be based on the pedagogy of overtly reflective experiential Service Learning linked to models of public problem solving or more deliberative democracy. There are now an increasing number of academics who are exploring how the theory and practice of deliberative democracy can be an effective way of providing learning for democratic citizenship (for example, Eslin *et al.*, 2001; Gastil and Levine, 2005). Here, the key to success is to be found in asking how community-based or focused learning experiences can best be structured to challenge students to become 'political', such that they become more aware of the political significance of civic engagement in local communities.

'Lifelong learning for active citizenship' and community involvement

In the UK there are increasingly capacity building programmes for people in the voluntary and community sectors who participate in partnership working in Single Regeneration Budget Programmes and New Deal for Communities Programmes. There are also the 'Local

Strategic Partnerships' (LSPs) for the development of local authority 'community strategies', which in key areas of deprivation are linked to Neighbourhood Renewal Programmes. These LSPs that are funded by the Neighbourhood Renewal Programme now have Community Empowerment Networks and funding for community learning. These capacity building programmes and the experiential learning involved in participating in regeneration activities offer an important opportunity for structuring non-formal lifelong learning for active citizenship. The learning theory and practice of service learning, with its emphasis on 'reflective practice' and the development of active citizenship through experiential learning can be adapted to provide a way of learning that best meets the needs of adult learners who are actively involved in their communities. In many of these cases the interest in lifelong learning for active citizenship may be more with building social capital (cf. Putnam, 2000) than with capacity building for democratic political participation (Edwards *et al.*, 2001). While recent research by Charles Pattie, Patrick Seyd and Paul Whitely (Pattie *et al.*, 2004) provides a framework for examining attitudes in the UK towards citizenship, and there is growing research on the nature and forms of political participation (Schlozman, *et al.*, 1994; Seyd and Whiteley, 1996, etc.), much more research is needed to more fully understand the complex political attitudes of people in order to establish more effective forms of political participation. Research in this area also needs to go beyond the limited conception of politics that can be found in the literature of political socialisation.

There is an increasing amount of research into the relationship between volunteering and adult learning. This includes both the formal learning required for the professionalisation of volunteer management and the non-formal and informal learning outcomes of the experience of volunteering on adults (Elsey, 1993; Elsdon, 1995). There is evidence that volunteers are increasingly looking to gain knowledge and skills for employability through volunteering (Elsey, 1993). The types of learning that occur in volunteer settings cross the range of adult learning. At the core of this development is the recognition of reflective learning, which is based on the principles of experiential learning. Elsdon (1995) has found that many volunteer activities produce learning outcomes that involve personal growth, self-confidence and a range of key skills and capabilities. While this research represents an important beginning, it does not match the extensive research into the learning outcomes of service learning referred to above. In particular, it does not address the question of whether volunteer activity promotes, not only bonding and bridging social capital, but also active citizenship (Kahne and Westheimer, 2000).

In *Appendix C* of the second NAGCELL Report, *Creating Learning Cultures* (NAGCELL, 1999), which is entitled 'Building Democracy: Community, Citizenship and Civil Society', John Field argues that:

> *The Social Exclusion Unit ... (should) undertake a major review of all the initiatives that link together the concepts of citizenship, community development and civil society. Learning should be placed at the heart of efforts to build a more inclusive society and the Social Exclusion Unit should expand its membership to include a lifelong learning presence.*

This report affirms the view of the Secretary of State for Education and Employment who in the introduction to the Green Paper 'The Learning Age' argued that learning should be valued for its promotion of active citizenship (DfEE, 1998, p.7). The report also goes on to note that NIACE and the Basic Skills Agency, in implementing the Adult and Community Learning Fund, have provided a stimulus to voluntary sector organisations to become learning organisations and have encouraged lifelong learning activities within the sector. In this report, there is, however, an awareness of the limitations of such efforts and in particular the problem of including more diverse sections of society to benefit from the learning involved in volunteering. This is confirmed by a recent Home Office (Prime *et al.*, 2002) survey entitled 'Active Communities: Initial Findings from the 2001 Home Office Citizenship Survey'. This survey confirms the data linked to political participation that in the most deprived areas in the UK the people living there are the least likely to formally volunteer. Yet, overall, the survey indicates that 'people engage with and participate in their communities in a substantial way' (ibid.).

In a study based in South London including a range of stake holders involved in regeneration partnerships, Anastacio and Mayo (Anastacio *et al.*, 2000 and Mayo, 2002) identified three main views of capacity building for partnership working. These were, firstly, capacity for effective consultation; secondly, capacity for effective community representation; and finally, capacity for community empowerment. The majority of participants in the study regarded capacity building for the representative role as the major need for community leaders. This capacity, although critical of the relationships of power involved in partnership working, nevertheless accepted and worked within established structures and processes of change. Another study by Henderson and Mayo (1998), in partnership with the Community Development Foundation for the Joseph Rowntree Foundation, involved a national review of training and education in urban regeneration. It indicated that there was a need for capacity building, not only for community representatives, but also for professionals (usually local government officers) involved in regeneration partnership boards. Participants in this survey indicated a preference for experiential learning or action-based research learning over formal training. The emphasis on the importance of informal learning for social action highlights the question of how non-formal learning opportunities for participation in partnership working might be provided. Again, I would argue that the pedagogy of service learning provides a useful model for the establishment of such learning opportunities, which might be accredited and could lead to qualifications in community work or community leadership. Marjorie Mayo points out that such experiential learning might be based on negative experiences of partnership working and might result in political alienation and not active citizenship. Henderson and Mayo (1998) argue for the establishment of a national framework for lifelong learning for active citizenship, which would be through participation in community development and community action. Such a framework would provide greater social inclusion and opportunities for accreditation and personal development. It would also allow for much greater research to be undertaken into curriculum development and experiential learning opportunities needed for effective partnership working and community leadership.

In January 2001 the National Strategy for Neighbourhood Renewal was established with the publication of *A New Commitment to Neighbourhood Renewal: National Strategy Action Plan* (Social Exclusion Unit, 2001). This followed on from the Social Exclusion Report *Bringing Britain Together: A national strategy for neighbourhood renewal* which was published in 1998 and the consultation document which was published in April 2000. The strategy called for new approaches to tackling worklessness, crime, low educational achievement, poor health, and housing and the physical environment. It also called for the establishment of 'Local Strategic Partnerships' which would provide more effective local co-ordination and encourage community empowerment. There would be regional support provided by the Government Offices for the Regions and national support provided by the Neighbourhood Renewal Unit, based in the Office of the Deputy Prime Minister. The LSPs would ensure that local residents and local voluntary and community sector organisations would be involved in developing local neighbourhood renewal strategies which would be supported by funding from Community Chests and a larger Community Empowerment Fund. Jane Thompson perceptively notes that:

> ... *The case for adult and community-based learning still has to be made. Its claim to relevance and its presumptions about engagement with local people will be sorely tested. Adult and community learning could be at the heart of neighbourhood renewal but will need to be very clear about what it has to offer residents and activists who want to get involved in turning around their lives and their communities in ways that just might make a difference. (Thompson, 2001, p.3)*

While it is now an established principle in regeneration programmes that local people should be involved in partnership working, it is not clear to what extent they will be able to shape a local or regional learning and development strategy for neighbourhood renewal. The role of the voluntary and community sectors in learning partnerships linked to the LSCs is uneven across the country. According to Regional Action West Midlands (RAWM), for example:

> *Engagement with the learning agenda is not unproblematic for the voluntary and community sector; involvement partnership activity can be perceived as an unequal relationship in which the voluntary and community organisations give access and legitimacy but gain little in return. (RAWM, 2002, p.2)*

In December 2001, the Neighbourhood Renewal Unit published its 'Neighbourhood Renewal Skills and Knowledge Programme' for consultation and in October 2002 it published 'The Learning Curve', which is a learning and development strategy for neighbourhood renewal. The 23-point action plan provides for all those involved in neighbourhood renewal activities. These include 'residents', 'regeneration practitioners', 'professionals', and 'organisations'. It stresses the need for evidence-based policy and practice and the development of accessible knowledge management systems concerning regeneration practice. The report impressively outlines the knowledge and skills required by all participants for effective working in neighbourhood renewal partnerships. The strategy is sophisticated in that it notes the formal, non-formal and informal learning involved in neighbourhood renewal activities. The recognition of the importance of the non-formal learning opportunities through action learning or experiential learning is to be welcomed, but it does not specify in any detail how this might be achieved. As I have argued previously, the pedagogy of service learning can be applied to the learning involved in participating in partnership working and being involved in community leadership (Neighbourhood Renewal Unit, 2002).

It refers to 'leadership skills' necessary for community leadership but does not refer to any 'political' awareness or skills as necessary for effective and equitable partnership working. The learning agenda is about individuals and organisations and their capacity to work in partnership in order to tackle the priority areas of neighbourhood renewal. The document also does not refer to 'citizenship' as a category which entails both rights and responsibilities, nor does it refer to the problem of the competing claims for 'community leadership' between local councillors and representatives from residents associations, and voluntary and community sector organisations. (It does however recognise the importance of capacity building for local councillors and local government officers working in regeneration.) Its frame of reference for 'urban regeneration' is that of urban geography and the study of the built environment, which does not recognise fully enough the political context within which neighbourhood renewal activities take place. This failure or reluctance to appreciate the 'political nature' of community leadership underlies the fact that it also misses the opportunity to consider how involvement in neighbourhood renewal can include the opportunity to provide lifelong learning for active citizenship through partnership working and community leadership.

'Active Learning for Active Citizenship' (ALAC)

In 2004 the Civil Renewal Unit of the Home Office, which was established under the influence of the then Home Secretary David Blunkett, enabled the development of the ALAC programme for adult learning in the community for citizenship education. In a scoping report by Val Woodward entitled, *Active Learning for Active Citizenship* a participatory and community-based pedagogy was proposed (Woodward, 2004). This learning framework is analogous to one which is proposed by Pam Coare and Rennie Johnston, which they argue should be inclusive, pluralistic, reflexive and promote active citizenship (Coare and Johnston, 2003). They emphasise the need to listen to community voices in determining what forms of learning meet the needs of different communities. In the action research-based evaluation by Rooke and Mayo, they recognise that the ALAC programme did not result in a formal national curriculum, but instead provides a learning framework which is participatory, community based, one which recognises difference while enabling a shared political identity of citizenship, and which enables an understanding of global interdependence (Mayo and Rooke, 2006).

An important feature of participatory politics which has recently been emphasised is that of the need to enable the capacity to participate in deliberative democratic engagement. From citizens' juries to community visioning, the deliberative engagement of citizens has become an increasing feature of the new localism and also public service delivery (Lowndes *et al.*, 1998; Fung and Wright, 2003; Brannan, *et al.*, 2007). The work of the Power Inquiry Commission and think tanks like the IPPR, the New Economics Foundation and Involve now promote a more participatory and deliberative form of citizen engagement (cf. IPPR, 2004; Joseph Rowntree Charitable Trust, 2006; Involve, 2005; and Rosenberg, ed., 2008). What has been lacking has been an analysis of what form of capacity building is necessary for citizens to participate in these activities and in what ways does participation in deliberative democratic engagement provide a form of education for democratic citizenship (Gastil and Levine, 2005). We need to know more about how citizens can develop the civic skills necessary for deliberative democratic engagement. A particular civic skill which is necessary is that of 'civic listening' and not just 'civic speaking'. This would include both levels of emotional literacy and intercultural understanding (Kirlin, 2003).

In conclusion, I would like to note how the New Labour government's programme for the modernisation of local government and its community empowerment strategies provide the opportunity for local people to get involved in local government and regeneration partnership boards. This is part of a shift from local government to local governance and such activities provide rich opportunities for non-formal lifelong learning for active citizenship. This non-formal experiential learning would benefit from being informed by the theory and practice of community-based learning as developed in the USA and now growing internationally. Research into the working of the community leadership involved in Single Regeneration Budget partnerships, New

Deal for Communities elected boards and now LSPs has highlighted the need for capacity building programmes for active citizenship and community leadership. This research also recognises the importance of the political context within which these activities take place (Taylor, 2003 and Annette, 2003). The opportunity for lifelong learning for active citizenship through participation in local governance and regeneration partnership working provides for the possible development of a civic republican or participatory democratic conception of citizenship. What is needed is the provision of a lifelong learning for active citizenship that involves participatory experiential learning and an innovative form of 'political' learning.

References

Anastacio, J. *et al.* (2000) *Reflecting Realities: Participant's perspectives in integrated communities and sustainable development.* Bristol: Policy Press

Annette, J. (1999 and new edition, 2003), 'Citizenship and Service Learning in Higher Education.' Gardner, J. *et al.*, *Education for Values.* London: Kogan Page

Annette, J. (2000) 'Education for Citizenship, Civic Participation and Experiential Service Learning in the Community,' in Gardner, J. *et al.* (eds), *Education for Citizenship.* London: Continuum

Annette, J. (2003) 'Community and Citizenship Education' in Lockyer, A., Crick, B. and Annette, J. (eds) *Education for Democratic Citizenship.* Surrey: Ashgate

Barber, B. (1984) *Strong Democracy.* California: University of California Press

Barber, B. (1992) *An Aristocracy of Everyone.* Oxford: Oxford University Press

Battistoni, R. (2002) *Civic Engagement Across the Curriculum.* Providence, RI: Campus Compact

Bauman, Z. (2000) *Community: Seeking safety in an insecure world.* Cambridge: Polity Press

Bentley, T. (2005) *Everyday Democracy: Why we get the politicians we deserve.* London: Demos

Billig, S. H. (2000) 'Research on K–12 School-based Service-learning: The evidence builds.' *Phi Delta Kappan,* Vol. 81, No. 9, pp. 658–664

Blunkett, D. (2003) *Civil Renewal – A new agenda* (Edith Kahn Memorial Lecture), CSV. London: Home Office

Boyte, H. (2004) *Everyday Politics: Reconnecting citizens and public life*. Pennsylvania: University of Pennsylvania Press

Brannan, T., John, P. and Stoker, G. (eds) (2007) *Re-energizing Citizenship: Strategies for civil renewal*. London: Palgrave Macmillan

Callan, E. (1997) 'The Great Sphere: Education against servility', *Journal of Philosophy of Education*, Vol. 31, No. 2, pp. 221–232

Coare, P. and Johnston, R. (2003) *Adult Learning, citizenship and community voices*. Leicester: NIACE

Colby, A. *et al*. (2003) *Educating Citizens: Preparing America's Undergraduates for Lives of Moral and Civic Responsibility* San Francisco: Jossey-Bass/A Wiley Imprint, in partnership with the Carnegie Foundation for the Advancement of Teaching

Crewe, I., Searing, D. and Conover, P. (1997) *Citizenship and Civic Education*. London: Citizenship Foundation

Crick, B. (2005) *In Defence of Politics* (5th edition). London: Continuum

Crick, B. (2002) *Democracy: A very short introduction*. Oxford: Oxford University Press

Cruz, N. and Giles, Jr, D. (2000) 'Where's the Community in Service-Learning Research?' *Michigan Journal of Community Service Learning*, Fall

Dagger, R. (1997) *Civic Virtues: Rights, citizenship and republican liberalism*. Oxford: Oxford University Press

Delanty, G. (2003) *Community*. London: Routledge

DETR (1998) *Modern Local Government: In touch with the people*. London: HMSO

DfEE (1998) *Education for Citizenship and the Teaching of Democracy in Schools: Final report of the Advisory Group on Citizenship*. London: QCA

DfEE (2000) *Citizenship for 16–19 Year Olds in Education and Training*. Coventry: FEFC

Dionne Jr, E. J. *et al*. (eds) (2003) *United We Serve: National service and the future of citizenship*. Massachusetts: Brookings Institution Press

Edwards, M. and Gaventa, J. (eds) (2001) *Global Citizen Action*. London: Earthscan

Elsdon, K. T. (1995) 'Values and Learning in Voluntary Organisations', *International Journal of Lifelong Education*, Vol. 14, No. 1

Elsey, B. (1993) 'Voluntarism and Adult Education as Civil Society and the Third Way for Personal Engagement and Social Change.' *International Journal of Lifelong Education*, Vol. 12, p. 1

Eslin, P., Pendlebury, S. and Tjiattas, M. (2001) 'Deliberative Democracy, Diversity and the Challenges of Citizenship Education,' *Journal of the Philosophy of Education,* Vol. 35, 1

Eyler, J. and Giles Jr, D. (1999) *Where's the Learning in Service Learning?* San Francisco: Jossey-Bass

Field, John (2003) *Social Capital.* London: Routledge

Frazer, E. (1999a) 'Introduction: the idea of political education.' *Oxford Review of Education,* Vol. 25, 1–2.

Frazer, E. (1999b) *The Problems of Communitarian Politics.* Oxford: Oxford University Press

Fung, A. and Wright, E. O. (eds) (2003) *Deepening Democracy.* London and New York: Verso

Galston, W. (2001) 'Political Knowledge, Political Engagement and Civic Education', *Annual Review of Political Science,* Vol. 4, pp. 217–234

Gastil, J. and Levine, P. (2005) *The Deliberative Democracy Handbook.* San Francisco: Jossey Bass

Ginsborg, P. (2005) *The Politics of Everyday Life: Making choices, changing lives.* New Haven: Yale University Press

Hall, P. (2002) 'The Role of Government and the Distribution of Social Capital,' in Robert Putnam, ed., *Democracies in Flux.* Oxford: Oxford University Press

Hart, D., Donnelly, T., Youniss, J. and Atkins, R. (2007) 'High School Community Service as a Predictor of Adult Voting and Volunteering', *American Educational Research Journal,* Vol. 44, pp. 107–219

Henderson, P. and Mayo, M. (1998) *Training and education in urban regeneration: A framework for participants.* Policy Press

Involve (2005) *People and Participation: How to put citizens at the heart of decision-making.* London: Involve

IPPR (2000) *Tomorrow's citizens: Critical debates in citizenship and education.* (Edited by Nick Pearce and Joe Hallgarten.) London: IPPR

IPPR (2004) *The Lonely Citizen.* London: IPPR

Joseph Rowntree Charitable Trust (2006) *Power to the People. The Report of Power: An Independent Inquiry into Britain's Democracy (also known as the 'Power Inquiry').* York: York Publishing Distribution

Kahne, J. and Westheimer, J. (2000) 'Service-Learning and Citizenship in Higher Education: Directions for research.' *Michigan Journal of Community Service Learning.* Special Issue, pp. 42–51.

Kahne, J. and Westheimer, J. (eds) (2003) 'Special Issue on Education, Democracy and Civic Engagement.' *Phi Delta Kappen,* Vol. 85, No. 1

Kerr, D. *et al.* (2003) *Citizenship Education Longitudinal Study: First Cross-Sectional Survey 2001–2002.* National Foundation for Educational Research

Kirlin, M. (2003) *The role of civic skills in fostering civic engagement.* CIRCLE Research Paper

Kolb, D. (1998) *Experiential Learning.* Englewood Cliffs, NJ: Prentice Hall

Levine, P. (2007) *The future of democracy: Developing the Next Generation of American Citizens.* Medford, Mass: Tufts University Press

Lister, R. (1998) 'Citizenship and difference: Towards a differentiated universalism'. *European Journal of Social Theory,* Vol. 1, No. 1, pp. 71–90

Lister, R. *et al.* (2003) 'Young People talk about citizenship: empirical perspectives on theoretical and political debates.' *Citizenship Studies,* Vol. 7, No. 2, pp. 235–253

Little, A. (2002) *The Politics of Community: Theory and Practice.* Edinburgh: Edinburgh University Press

Lowndes, V. *et al.* (1998) *Enhancing Public Participation in Local Government: A Research Report.* London: DETR

McLaughlin, T. (2000) 'Citizenship Education in England: The Crick Report and Beyond.' *Journal of Philosophy of Education.* Vol. 34, No. 4, pp. 541–570

Maynor, J. (2003) *Republicanism in the Modern World.* Cambridge: Polity Press

Mayo, M. (2002) 'Learning for Active Citizenship: Training for and learning from participation in area regeneration,' in *Supporting Lifelong Learning.* Reeve, F. *et al.* (eds) London: Routledge/Falmer

Mayo, M. and Rooke, A. (2006) *Active Learning for Active Citizenship: A report by Professor Marjorie Mayo and Dr Alison Rooke.* London: Home Office

Miller, D. (2000) 'Citizenship: what does it mean and why is it important?' in Pearce, N. and Hallgarten, J. (eds), *Tomorrow's Citizens: Critical debates in citizenship and education.* London: IPPR

Mulhall, S. and Swift, A. (1996) *Liberalism and Communitarianism.* (2nd Edition) Oxford: Blackwell

NAGCELL (1999) *Creating Learning Cultures: Next steps in achieving the Learning Age – Second report of the National Advisory Group for Continuing Education and Lifelong Learning.* London: DfEE

Nash, V. (2002) *Reclaiming Community.* London: IPPR

Neighbourhood Renewal Unit (2002) *The Learning Curve: Developing skills and knowledge for neighbourhood renewal.* London: Neighbourhood Renewal Unit

Osler, A. (2000) 'The Crick Report: Difference, equality and racial justice,' *The Curriculum Journal*, Vol. 11, No. 1, pp. 25–37

Pattie, C., Seyd, P. and Whitely, P. (2004) *Citizenship in Britain: Values, Participation and Democracy.* Cambridge: Cambridge University Press

Pettit, P. (1997) *Republicanism: A Theory of Freedom and Government.* Oxford: Oxford University Press

Potter, J. (2002) *Active Citizenship in Schools.* London: Kogan Page

Prime, D. *et al.* (2002) *Active Communities: Initial Findings from the 2001 Home Office Citizenship Survey.* London: Home Office

Print, M. and Coleman, D. (2003) 'Towards understanding social capital and citizenship education.' *Cambridge Journal of Education*, Vol. 33, No. 1, pp. 123–149

Putnam, R. (2000) *Bowling Alone: The collapse and revival of American community.* New York: Simon and Shuster

Regional Action West Midlands (RAWM) (2002) *Engaging in Learning: Surveying voluntary and community sector perceptions of engaging with the learning agenda within the West Midlands.* Birmingham: RAWM

Rosenberg, S. (2008) *Can the People Govern? Deliberation, participation and democracy.* London: Palgrave Macmillan

Sandel, M. (1996) *Democracy's Discontent.* Cambridge, Massachusetts: Harvard University Press

Scholzman, K., Burns, N. and Verba, S. (1994) 'Gender and the pathways to participation – the role of resources', *Journal of Politics*, Vol. 56, No. 4, pp. 963–990

Seyd, P. and Whiteley, P. (1996) 'Rationality and party-activism: encompassing tests of alternative models of political participation,' *European Journal of Political Research*, Vol. 29, No. 2

Sirianni, C. and Friedland, L. (2001) *Civic Innovation in America: Community Empowerment, Public Policy, and the Movement for Civic Renewal.* Berkeley, California: University of California Press

Sirianni, C. and Friedland, L. (2005) *The Civic Renewal Movement* (2nd Edition). Dayton, Ohio: The Kettering Foundation

Social Exclusion Unit (2001) *A New Commitment to Neighbourhood Renewal.* London: Cabinet Office

Tam, H. (1998) *Communitarianism: A New Agenda for Politics and Citizenship*. New York: New York University Press

Tam, H. (2001) *Progressive Politics in the Global Age*. Cambridge: Polity Press

Taylor, M. (2003) *Public Policy in the Community*. London: Palgrave

Thompson, J. (2001) *Rerooting Lifelong Learning: Resourcing neighbourhood renewal*. Leicester: NIACE

Wade, R. (ed.) (1997) *Community Service-Learning: A Guide to Including Service in the Public School Curriculum*. Albany: SUNY Press

Weller, S. (2007) *Teenagers' Citizenship*. London: Routledge

Woodward, V. (2004) *Active Learning for Active Citizenship*. London: Home Office

Woolcock, M. (2001) 'The place of social capital in understanding social and economic outcomes.' *Isuma: Canadian Journal of Policy Research*, Vol. 2, No. 1, pp. 1–17

Zukin, C., Keeter, S., Andolina, M., Jenkins, K. and Delli Carpini, M. X. (2006) *A New Engagement?: Political Participation, Civic Life and the Changing American Citizen*. New York: Oxford University Press

CHAPTER THREE

Competing perspectives, definitions and approaches

Marjorie Mayo

Introduction

As the previous chapter has demonstrated, in recent years, citizenship has taken centre stage as a public policy concern in Britain. The current Labour government has been committed to developing strategies to transform citizens from passive recipients of public services to self-sustaining individuals, active as individuals and as members of communities. Citizens have been the subject of policies to activate and to empower them, making them the subjects of 'responsibilities as well as rights' (Clarke, 2005, p.447). Citizenship education, starting with citizenship education in schools, has been promoted as part of this wider aim to change the political culture 'for people to think of themselves as active citizens, willing, able and equipped to have an influence in public life ... to build on and to extend radically to young people the best in traditions of community involvement and public service and to make them individually confident in finding new forms of involvement and action' (DfEE, 1998, p.7). So young people in schools, and then also in colleges, were to develop social and moral responsibility, community involvement and political literacy. Parallel aims informed the programme to explore ways of developing community-based citizenship education for adults, Active Learning for Active Citizenship (ALAC), which was set up through the Home Office's Civil Renewal Unit in 2004 and is the subject of subsequent chapters in this book, setting the context for the current Take Part programme, launched in 2008, following the

41

publication of the Empowerment White Paper, *Communities in control: real people, real power.*

As the Home Secretary responsible for launching ALAC, David Blunkett, argued: 'We must aim to build strong empowered and active communities' (Blunkett, 2003). Fiona Mactaggart, the Parliamentary Under-Secretary responsible at the time, stated in her introduction: 'We should therefore work to improve the capacity of individuals and communities to relate to the world around them as active, critical, engaged citizens. If we are to have a healthy democracy we need to support each other in identifying the issues that concern us, and develop the confidence and skills to make a difference to the world around us' (Woodward, 2004). Active citizenship was to be promoted within the framework of strategies for empowerment, addressing existing structures and relations of power in order to promote democratic change. Government departments were aiming to develop and work with active citizens with the confidence to speak about the matters that concern them, to strengthen communities to find shared solutions and to encourage public bodies to be willing and able to work in partnership with local people.

While this commitment to promoting active citizenship has been a central theme for Labour governments, since 1997 citizenship has become a major issue in public policy debates more widely too. Around the world, it has been argued, despite the spread of democratic forms of governance, the relationships between citizens and the institutions that affect their lives have been characterised by a growing crisis of legitimacy (Kabeer, 2005). As the Final Report of the Advisory Group on Citizenship argued in similar vein, more locally, in the British context, 'There are worrying levels of apathy, ignorance and cynicism about public life' (DfEE, 1998, p.8). The report of the Power Inquiry into Britain's Democracy, supported by the Joseph Rowntree Charitable Trust, provides disquieting evidence about this growing crisis of legitimacy. The report explains this, not in terms of public apathy so much as in terms of public scepticism as to whether those with the most power actually listen to those who have less (Joseph Rowntree Charitable Trust, 2006). Governments and international institutions have been concerned to address this 'democratic deficit'. They have been facing increasing pressures for rights-based approaches to development, with increasing challenges to institutional failures to meet the needs of the most deprived groups in society, both locally and globally, as demonstrated, for example, in the Global Campaign to Make Poverty History. There are challenges to be addressed in relation to the planning and the delivery of services, to meet social needs, just as there are challenges to be addressed, in relation to issues of democracy and governance. As Giddens has argued, in the global era, active citizenship needs to engage with processes of structural change as part of a social justice agenda (Giddens, 2000).

This chapter aims to unpack the competing perspectives that underpin these differing concerns. Active citizenship can be promoted as part of varying agendas. The notion of citizenship itself has fluid meanings, and so do notions of civil society and the nation state, in the context of increasing globalisation. Having unpacked these competing perspectives and agendas, the chapter concludes with a focus upon their varying implications for learning for active citizenship in the contemporary context. Are there inherent conflicts between these differing perspectives and approaches? How might strategies be developed to build a more actively engaged civil society AND a more responsive, more democratically accountable and more inclusive state, a state that can deliver public services to meet social needs more appropriately and more effectively?

Competing perspectives: neo-liberalism and its critics

In the context of the continuing ascendance of neo-liberal approaches to development, rolling back the state and shifting the emphasis of service provision from the public towards the private and not-for-profit sectors, there has been widespread emphasis on active citizenship. Active citizens take increasing responsibility for their own health and welfare, it is argued, and they contribute to their communities as volunteers and community activists, thereby reducing the pressures on public provision. There are potential implications here, in terms of the independence of citizen action. There are challenges too for the voluntary and community sectors and for civil society more generally. As Bernard Crick has pointed out: 'There is a real danger that voluntary bodies and charities, sometimes even more informal community groups, can end up tied by grants as virtual agents of the state' (Crick, 2001. 7) rather than as independent organs of civil society. This would be an ironic outcome indeed, given governments' avowed aims to strengthen the voluntary and community sectors as part of the revitalisation of civil society more generally.

Neo-liberalism gained increasing predominance from the late 1970s and early 1980s onwards. As the long economic boom following the

Second World War began to slow down and economic growth became more problematic, neo-liberal economists argued that new strategies were needed in response (Amin, 2001). State intervention had been widely accepted, as a means of tackling the problems of reconstruction and development, in the post-war period, while providing services to meet social needs (the development of the Welfare State in Britain). This acceptance of the need for state intervention represented a middle way, informed by social democratic perspectives (Alcock, 1996).

Far from representing a way forward, however, neo-liberal economists such as Milton Friedman argued that states were intervening far too much, and so interfering with the operations of the free market (Friedman, 1962). Without going into the detail of these arguments here, the point to emphasise is simply this: neo-liberals were convinced that state intervention had grown too much. This was the problem, rather than the solution. Resources were being drained away from productive investments to support ever-expanding public services. And these services were being run by professionals and bureaucrats, according to their own views of people's needs, it was argued (Le Grand, 2003), part of a 'producer-culture', rather than a 'consumer culture' based upon respect for the individual consumer's choice. So this paternalistic state needed to be rolled back, freeing up resources for economic growth – the most effective way of meeting social needs and tackling poverty (Murray, 1984, 1990), enabling individuals to take responsibility for their own welfare and the welfare of their families. In summary then, neo-liberal solutions started with deregulation, to free up market mechanisms, fundamentally shifting the balance between the market and the state. Civil society was to play an enhanced role, with greater scope for voluntary and community sector initiatives, but as part of these wider strategies, promoting the use of market mechanisms within services that had previously been provided more directly by the state, whether locally or nationally.

By the 1990s, neo-liberal perspectives were predominant, not only in Britain and the USA, following the Thatcher/Reagan years, but also internationally. These were the policies that predominated in international bodies such as the World Bank and the International Monetary Fund. And with the collapse of the former Soviet Union, together with a number of states that had formerly been linked to the Soviet sphere of influence, alternative perspectives had become seriously weakened, if not widely discredited, for the time being at least. As Alcock among others has argued, in relation to welfare policies more specifically, this collapse of the Soviet Union and a number of its former allies 'cast a deep shadow over the aspirations of the supporters of Marxism' (Alcock, 1996, p.37).

Neo-liberal perspectives have not been without their contradictions and their critics, however. In summary, critics have pointed to the increasing inequalities that have resulted from the less fettered operations of the market – inequalities within and between countries that have the potential for increasing social tensions and disorders. And neo-liberals' emphasis upon the individual has given rise to concerns, too, concerns that society is becoming too fragmented, losing the social capital that societies need to function effectively (Baron *et al.*, 2000; Fine, 2000). While there has been a particular focus upon policies to strengthen civil society as part of strategies to build these new democracies, these concerns to offset the negative effects of neo-liberalism have featured in older Western democracies such as Britain too – concerns to address the problems of social exclusion as well as concerns to strengthen social capital and to tackle the democratic deficit. These have been central issues for successive Labour governments since 1997 in fact – to combat the growth of excessive individualism, and the consequent fragmentation that has concerned communitarian proponents of the Third Way thinkers (Etzioni, 1998) who had considerable influence in the policy-making process following the election of New Labour. More recently, since the events of 9/11 in New York and 7 July 2005 in London, governments have also been concerned with issues of social cohesion and the so-called 'war on terror'. Without going into detail here, the point to emphasise is simply this: neo-liberal perspectives involve their own contradictions, unintended consequences and challenges, and these include challenges for governments to address. Strategies to strengthen civil society and to promote active citizenship have featured among these attempts to manage these challenges.

Before moving on to explore varying approaches to the promotion of active citizenship, more specifically, feminist, anti-racist and other progressive perspectives need to be outlined, too. As Lister has argued, citizenship is a universalist concept with inclusive and socially progressive potential (Lister, 1997), but citizenship has too often been discussed in gender-blind terms, somehow assuming a level playing field for women and men alike. The reality, however, is very different. The fact of the matter is that women and men experience different pressures, with varying needs as a result. Simply assuming that women are in a position to participate, equally, fails to recognise these underlying structural inequalities. Feminist perspectives raise key theoretical issues then, with significant policy implications, if programmes to promote active citizenship are to challenge structural inequalities and social exclusion. The chapters that follow illustrate these arguments in more practical detail, with a particular focus upon issues of gender in *Chapter Eleven* on *Women active in community and public life.*

There are similar arguments to be made from anti-racist perspectives, too. As Lister has also demonstrated, citizenship can be defined in ways that exclude black and minority ethnic groups, especially relative newcomers, whether these are economic migrants or whether these are refugees and asylum seekers. As Crick has pointed out, 'there are those who would retreat from an expansive idea of Britishness into a constricted shell of right-wing nationalism' (Crick, 2001, p.4). The dangers of a narrow, reactionary approach to citizenship have particular salience in Britain, given the legacy of its imperial past, contradictory policies towards immigration for the former colonies while addressing racism back home (Solomos and Back, 1996), and the more recent experiences of white backlash, challenging the basis of multiculturalism (Hewitt, 2005). These represent issues of continuing concern, whatever the proponents of exclusive notions of Britishness may prefer, given continuing population mobility in the context of increasing globalisation. Here too, subsequent chapters address some of the implications for anti-racist approaches to learning for active citizenship.

While these have represented significant criticisms, the promotion of notions of citizenship has nevertheless retained potentially progressive connotations more generally, as Lister herself recognised (Lister, 1997). Citizenship has been associated with rights-based approaches to public policy, including development policies internationally. And rights-based approaches can include social rights as well as legal and political rights, including the right to basic services as well as the right to be treated equally before the law, the right to participate in decisions that affect our lives as well as the right to vote.

Before engaging with varying definitions of what, precisely, these rights might mean in practice, or how these rights might be utilised, however, there are underlying tensions to be unpacked. How effectively can social, legal and political rights be enjoyed, unless these rights are accompanied by economic rights? And what might be the limits on access to such economic rights, in the context of neo-liberal economic policies (Molyneux and Razavi, 2002). Lister's arguments about the limitations on citizenship rights, given the lack of a level playing field, can be applied to other groups too, all those who, like women and disadvantaged minorities, suffer the effects of structural inequalities that limit their capacities to participate effectively as citizens.

For critics from progressive perspectives, then, the key problem is that liberal rights-based approaches to citizenship do not go far enough. Economic justice issues have to be addressed, as well as social, legal and political aspects of citizenship. Such a view has been associated with left-wing perspectives, including those informed by Marxist approaches. Noonan, for example, points to Marx's critique of approaches to civil and political rights that fail to address the underlying structures of economic power and the social relations that reproduce inequalities (Noonan, 2006). Although he moves outside a Marxist approach, Noonan himself concludes that neo-liberal globalisation needs to be challenged, and that economic democratisation is essential for democratisation in other spheres. Such views are not confined to those drawing upon Marxist perspectives, either. Giddens, for example, an influential thinker and proponent of the Third Way, has also recognised that the notion of respon-sibilities as well as rights has to apply to corporate power, too (Giddens, 2000). There are key implications here for citizenship and social justice agendas, implications that emerge further in the chapters that follow. Before moving on to these, though, the varying definitions that relate to these competing perspectives need to be outlined first.

Varying definitions

The very idea of applying notions of responsibility to corporate power poses fundamental questions for discussion. Neo-liberals start from the position that states have been intervening too much already. Alternative perspectives, such as those informed by pluralist theories of the state, start by accepting the desirability of state intervention, in principle – to pro-mote social democratic agendas for social justice and equalities. Although pluralists define the state in terms of its authority and power, they argue that this power is limited by the presence of different interest groups in modern democracies, with competing groups who negotiate on behalf of the different interests that they represent. These processes take place through elections as well as through processes of lobbying and other forms of citizen participation (Giddens, 1992), thereby providing space for active citizenship.

Critics, in contrast, point to the limitations of pluralist approaches, both in theory and in practice. In summary, critics argue, some interest groups have far greater power and influence than others. As Lister and others have argued, participatory democracy is not being played out on a level playing field. And while women and disadvantaged minorities have less power and influence (and less scope for participating in any case, given some of the practical barriers that they have to face), business interests, typically, have far more power and influence. By definition then, the state becomes part of the problem, rather than simply providing the solution to the 'responsibilisation' of corporate capital.

From a structural conflict perspective, it is not just that the state tends to be swayed by pressures from the most powerful interests. Marxists argue that the state actually represents the interests of the dominant groups in society, although this is not to argue that business interests necessarily rule directly in modern capitalist democracies. On the contrary, in fact, Marxist theorists such as Gramsci have identified the state as a site of contestation and struggle for competing agendas. The development of state welfare services demonstrates precisely such outcomes, with states providing services to meet social needs rather than leaving these services to be provided through the market. But democratic states are not level playing fields, in their view, and there are limits to the extent to which states can be pressured into making demands on business interests in order to meet the needs of the less powerful. Current debates on the changing boundaries of the state and the market illustrate precisely this continuing tension. Defining the state as a site of contestation and struggle provides a framework, then, for understanding the shifts that have been taking place, as the boundaries of the state have been pushed back, in recent years, with increasing marketisation in the provision of welfare.

Alternative approaches vary in the extent to which they would argue that the state could, or even should, provide a counterbalance to market forces. At the libertarian end, the state tends to be viewed with continuing suspicion (with parallels as well as differences with neo-liberal perspectives here). Some feminists and anti-racists have adopted such views, understandably frustrated by paternalism and oppressive bureaucracy too often associated with the provision of state services. But the more typical response has been to recognise the potentially progressive role that the state can play. For all its inherent limitations, the state can be pressurised into intervening, to mitigate the dysfunctions of the market. While the extent to which this can be achieved within capitalist society remains contested, the strategy of a broad range of progressives continues to be precisely this, to organise to persuade the state to do more to meet social needs, working both 'In and Against the State' (to use a redolent phrase that was developed in an earlier period (London Edinburgh Weekend Return Group, 1979). This sets the framework for the strategy to be discussed subsequently, to work 'both sides of the equation', to build 'a more active and engaged civil society and a more responsive and effective state that can deliver needed public services' (Gaventa, 2004, p.270).

Before moving on, however, one further aspect of the state's definition needs to be addressed. This is the association of the state with the 'nation state', an association that has been central to traditional definitions in the past (Giddens, 1992). Neo-liberal globalisation, together with the increased significance of transnational structures of governance, pose major challenges here, leading some scholars to argue that the role of the nation state has been effectively diminished if not actually rendered obsolete (Rosenau, 2002).

Without minimising the impact of globalisation, others have challenged this approach, arguing, in contrast, for the continuing relevance of the nation state as a strategic site of governance in its own right, as well as having the potential for weaving together the multiple channels of governance, locally, nationally and internationally (Keohane and Nye, 2000; Held and McGrew, 2002; Tarrow, 2005). Some of the implications of these arguments emerge in subsequent chapters, as citizens strive to make sense of their capacities for making a difference, locally, exploring ways in which they have been attempting to do this, in the context of neo-liberal globalisation.

So what have been the varying implications of these different perspectives and definitions, as applied to active citizenship and to learning for active citizenship? Active citizenship has been promoted, for a variety of reasons, to offset the dysfunctions of neo-liberalism on the one hand, and to respond to mobilisations for human rights and deepening democracy on the other. In view of the differences that underpin these varying agendas, it is not surprising, then, that 'citizenship', in general, and 'active citizenship', more specifically, have been and continue to be contested terms. There have been, by implication, at least two approaches to defining citizenship education − a minimal definition and a maximal definition, the first formal and didactic and the second values-based, process led and interactive (Tate, 2000).

Writing for the National Council for Voluntary Organisations, Jochum, Pratten and Wilding (Jochum *et al.,* 2005) break these distinctions down further, using three different approaches to the definition of citizenship:

- the liberal approach, defining citizenship in terms of status, with formal rights before the law, such as the right to vote;
- the communitarian approach, which includes a sense of belonging to groups in society, a definition that includes group rights as well as individual rights; and
- the civil republican approach, which includes a wider emphasis upon the group, to include the nation, with a greater emphasis upon rights and responsibilities, leading to the idea of active citizenship in practice.

The seven ALAC hubs explored these differing definitions and approaches as part of their joint discussions, sharing their thinking and reflecting together upon how their own aims, approaches and experiences related to the relevant literature. For ALAC, citizenship was more than a formal status, with rights and responsibilities within a particular nation state. How far, though, was active citizenship about civic engagement – as voters or volunteers, for example? Active citizenship was seen to be concerned with more than learning 'the rules of the game', how to participate within existing models and structures. From ALAC's perspective, active citizenship should be defined more broadly to encompass active learning for political literacy and empowerment, addressing structures and relations of power, and working to change these, where necessary, in the pursuit of social inclusion and social justice agendas (Lister, 1997). Definitions of active citizenship needed to include the pursuit of agendas to promote community cohesion and social solidarity, strengthening civil society, as well as empowering individual citizens. And definitions needed to be compatible with community development approaches to the promotion of active citizenship – 'working both sides of the equation' to build 'a more active and engaged civil society and a more responsive and effective state that can deliver needed public services' (Gaventa, 2004, p.27).

One of the models that hubs brought to these discussions was the typology developed by Westheimer and Kahne. This identifies three separate models of citizenship and citizenship education – 'the personally responsible citizen' (for whom citizenship education increases their awareness of individual rights and responsibilities), the 'participatory citizen' (for whom citizenship education also enhances their knowledge of participatory structures and rights), and the 'justice-oriented citizen' (for

50

whom citizenship education also adds a high level of awareness of collective rights, more widely, and a high level of collective political and social responsibility, including responsibilities to engage with issues of social justice and equalities) (Westheimer and Kahne, 2004). Citizenship education for the 'justice-oriented' concept of citizenship would draw upon critical theory and pedagogy, such as the approaches developed by Paolo Freire, promoting critical thinking, encouraging learners to ask questions, to critically analyse the established system and its power structures. The learning outcomes of courses would include high levels of collective political and social responsibility together with some knowledge of participatory rights and procedures for engaging in formal participatory structures (ibid., 2004).

While this approach stimulated useful discussions, some of the hubs also raised a number of reservations. There was some merit in the notion of a typology that comprised three differing definitions of 'citizenship' and 'active citizenship' in their view:

- the citizen as a 'voter', and 'volunteer';
- the citizen as an individual within a group(s), actively participating in existing structures, taking up opportunities for participation including participation in the planning and delivery of services; and
- the citizen as an individual who also participates within group(s) actively challenging unequal relations of power, promoting social solidarity and social justice, both locally and beyond, taking account of the global context.

The ALAC hubs concluded that frameworks also needed to avoid rigidity. It was important to emphasise flexibility and change. ALAC needed to be conceptualised as a process. So, for example, individuals may become active as volunteers, but this in no way suggests that individuals may not be supported to move on to engage as members of community groups, actively participating in governance structures (such as school governing bodies or local strategic partnerships, for example) or as active members of organisations campaigning on human rights, the environment and social justice issues.

In addition, the hubs explored Westheimer and Kahne's discussion of the potential relationships between these different definitions of citizenship – from the more restricted version to the fuller and more comprehensive definition – to varying approaches to adult learning.

51

The more restricted definition of citizenship could be related to a relatively constrained view of learning in the context of social change, locally and globally. Here learning would focus upon gaining knowledge of the self, in the individual's social, cultural, political and legal context and developing the self-confidence to become active as a responsible citizen. The second and fuller definition could be related to learning that goes on to enable citizens to gain the knowledge and skills to cope, responding to opportunities to participate and engage, in order to adjust and to adapt to social change. And finally the third and fullest definition of citizenship could be related to learning that goes further still, to enable citizens to gain the knowledge and critical understanding actively to shape social change, promoting social solidarity and social justice within the context of globalisation.

There are parallels here with definitions of 'popular education' which has been defined as being 'rooted in the real interests and struggles of ordinary people' critical of the status quo and 'committed to progressive social and political change' (Martin, 1999, p.4). Education for citizenship, as Ralph Miliband defined it, 'means above all the nurturing of a capacity and willingness to question, to probe, to ask awkward questions, to see through obfuscation and lies'. It requires 'the cultivation of an awareness that the request for individual fulfilment needs to be combined with the larger demands of solidarity and concern for the public good' (Miliband, 1994, p.56).

Having reflected upon these different typologies, the hubs concluded that there were differing views – no one typology offered a precise fit – one size did not necessarily fit all. There was widespread agreement that for ALAC, the principles and practices of active learning for active citizenship can cross the boundaries between these differing definitions of citizenship. (Espejo, 2003, Mendiwelso-Bendek, 2002). Each type of learning needs to start from people's own issues and concerns, and each needs to be participatory and reflective, constructed through critical dialogues between learners and learning providers. Each requires long-term, sustainable support structures, based upon relationships of trust. And each needs to be delivered in a variety of ways at differing levels, depending upon the priorities and needs of the learners in question. Subsequent chapters address each of these aspects in turn. Provided in such ways, ALAC would aim to empower citizens to use whatever democratic spaces there may be to maximum effect, in the pursuit of democratic change to promote equalities and social justice agendas.

Such spaces are not neutral, however, as the hubs also recognised. Spaces for citizen participation, it has been argued, on the contrary, are 'permeated with relations of power' (Cornwall, 2004, p.79) within communities, between communities, between communities and states, and between states and communities internationally. Developing a critical understanding of the power relationships that permeate these spaces has been key to the learning for active citizenship at every level, locally as well as globally, opening up spaces for wider reflection on the interconnections between the local, the national and the international, together with the implications for building strategies for democratic social change.

Principles and approaches in practice

ALAC started from the principle that active learning for active citizenship should build upon existing models of good practice across the voluntary and community sectors, working in partnership with different forms of public provision. The hubs were to be located 'where it is known that community-based groups in partnership with others are able and willing to initiate new work on active learning for active citizenship' (Woodward, 2004, p.6). There are two key principles here. Firstly, active learning for active citizenship for adults should be firmly rooted within civil society itself, rather than being simply provided for citizens, as public policy should deem fit. Secondly, active learning for active citizenship was being conceptualised as an ongoing process of learning and reflection, within and between partners within civil society and between civil society and the state. The hubs would 'embrace projects working towards extending democratic activities within civil society as well as offering educational and partnership opportunities for government agencies' (ibid., p.11). ALAC started by recognising and valuing local expertise, knowledge and experience and building upon these, developing partnerships for the longer term. This was a community development-based approach, working towards empowerment, supporting organisations and groups within communities, and pursuing agendas for equalities and social justice.

The hubs or 'learning partnerships' were to be based upon networks characterised by diversity. Equalities issues were to be centre stage and ALAC was to develop models of good practice in addressing issues of equalities, valuing diversity and strengthening co-operation and social solidarity, taking account of issues of gender, race and other aspects of marginalisation, in the pursuit of participation for social justice. As

Active Learning for Active Citizenship argued, 'Providing education for and encouraging active citizenship needs to actively challenge exclusionary attitudes and practices, not just guarding against excluding groups of people' (ibid., p.13).

Most significantly, ALAC was to promote active citizenship, participation and empowerment. This implied that the learning process itself should be participatory and empowering. Citizenship education was to start from people's own perceptions of their issues and their learning priorities, negotiated in dialogue rather than imposed or parachuted in from outside. In common with the Neighbourhood Learning Centres to be developed by the DfES, the hubs were to be local people's provision – *their* provision, based in accessible premises, with a variety of programmes and activities tailored to local people's interests, driven by the priorities and aspirations of the learners themselves. In summary, then, learner participation was to be central at every stage in the process of:

- identifying learning priorities;
- developing the learning programme to be directly relevant to learners' interests and experiences;
- delivering the programme with the active involvement of the learners, with an emphasis upon the links between knowledge, critical understanding and active citizenship – in practice, collectively – and political literacy; and
- evaluating the programme participatively subsequently.

By implication, ALAC learning programmes were to be flexible as well as diverse, to take account of these differing interests and needs. Each hub would negotiate the range of programmes to be offered, and the levels at which they would be provided.

While the original focus was upon ensuring that those most at risk of social exclusion would be enabled to be included, the hubs' experiences soon demonstrated the importance of providing for a wider audience. While it was essential to facilitate the participation of individuals and groups that have been characterised as 'excluded', ALAC programmes were relevant to a broad range of organisations and groups more generally, including service providers, professionals and policy makers – just as ALAC programmes were relevant for the range of activists working for solidarity and social justice agendas. For example, once people with learning disabilities gained increasing self-confidence to 'Speak Up' for themselves, to express their views and priorities, including their preferences in relation to the delivery of health and welfare services, it became clear that their carers were also a group who wished to learn how to 'Speak Up'. Local service providers were equally in need of learning – to learn how to listen and to learn how to respond. This was anticipated in the original ALAC report, recognising that 'government at all levels needs political will and training to cope with active, empowered, sometimes dissenting citizens' (ibid., p.10). The provision itself has been similarly diverse. By definition, negotiating learning provision with potential learners, rather than imposing courses from the outside, results in varying forms of provision. ALAC hubs provide the range from accredited courses through to tailor-made training workshops, visits to key institutions of governance, e-learning, mentoring and one-off training sessions.

While the forms and levels of ALAC provision have varied enormously, however, there are a number of shared principles and approaches. Starting from people's own priorities and needs, ALAC has emphasised experiential learning, processes of critical reflection and dialogue rooted in people's own experiences, both individually and collectively, through collective action. This learning draws upon the methods and approaches developed by the Brazilian educator, Paulo Freire (Freire,1972; Freire and Shor, 1997), facilitating the development of critical consciousness and understanding, through cycles of action, reflection and then further action, informed by these processes of reflection. In this model of learning, defined in terms of collective and critical reflection and dialogue, learners and learning providers learn together. Freire's ideas have, of course, been central to debates on adult learning and the development of critical consciousness, as these have been developed and applied in Britain, and in popular education and social movements globally (Merrifield, 2000).[1]

Summarising the principles and values that should guide local authorities in supporting learning for neighbourhood renewal, Merton *et al.* offer a comparable list. The learning should be driven by the needs and aspirations of learners, and this should be negotiated between participants and providers, beforehand. The learning should be flexible and

---

[1] As Coare and Johnston's collection of essays demonstrates, there is a wealth of experience to draw upon here including, for instance, Allen and Martin, 1992, Brookfield, 1995, Coare and Johnston, 2003, Crowther *et al.*, 1999, Jeffs and Smith, 2005, Tett, 2002.

it should be developed in the context of sustained engagement – as part of continuing relationships between learners and providers, rather than as one-off events parachuted into particular neighbourhoods. And the learning should be based upon a desire for social justice, fairness and respect, with an active view of the learners, respecting and building upon their existing knowledge and skills, rather than a 'deficit model' of individuals and communities as being in some way inadequate and in 'need of treatment' (Merton *et al.*, 2003).

There are parallels here with ALAC's approach, although ALAC provision was not necessarily neighbourhood-based. There are parallels too with approaches to citizenship education in schools. An emphasis upon active approaches combining:

> *Knowledge, understanding and skills with practical action – what is termed a 'political literacy in action' approach was identified as a key factor in the most successful provision together with the involvement of young people in decisions about their learning and the development of a student voice. (Craig et al., 2004, pp.i–ii)*

Approaches to citizenship education in schools were initially criticised on a number of grounds, however, including the extent to which issues of race and racism had been adequately addressed. Was this multicultural education for monocultural citizenship, asked Stuart Hall (Hall, 2000)? Osler and Starkey raised similar questions about the extent to which citizenship education was preparing young people for citizenship in the context of globalisation, including the impact of globalisation on Britain, in terms of migration flows, including the flows of refugees and asylum seekers (Osler and Starkey, 2003). In response, citizenship education in schools has been concerned to take these points on board. ALAC has been able to build upon this. So, for example, ALAC has focused upon the interconnections between the local and the global, from the outset, specifically including hubs with experience of working with migrants, refugees and asylum seekers, as well as working with the white British communities among whom they were living as neighbours. These interconnections between the local and the global represent a recurring theme throughout ALAC's work.

There are, in any case, inherent differences between Citizenship Education in schools and colleges and ALAC in community-based settings. Without getting into debates about the nature of adult learning per se, it is important to recognise the significance of these differences. In particular, adults, unlike school students, do have choices as to whether or not they participate in learning programmes (Jarvis, 1995, Rogers, 2002). Similar points apply to young people outside school settings. Typically adults have other pressures on their time and energy, too, whether these are the pressures of paid employment, or the pressures of childcare and other caring and community responsibilities, or both. As ALAC recognised at the outset, the learning needs to be relevant and seen to be relevant to adults' and to young people's needs as they themselves perceive them, provided flexibly and accessibly to take account of all their other pressures. And the learning needs to be enjoyable as well as useful, building upon the learners' existing knowledge and skills. Realistically, these requirements necessitate a flexible learning framework rather than a core curriculum approach.

To summarise then, the emphasis was upon working democratically and learning collectively, through organisations and groups in communities. ALAC focused upon community empowerment, through learning, enabling organisations and groups to enhance the effectiveness of their strategies for social change. Through increasing their knowledge and their critical understanding of power structures and decision-making processes, ALAC participants would be empowered to intervene and, where necessary work towards changing these, working 'both sides of the equation' in the pursuit of the values of equalities and social justice.

References

Alcock, P. (1996) *Social Policy in Britain*. London: Macmillan

Allen, G. and Martin, I. (1992) *Education and Community: The politics of practice*. London: Cassell

Amin, S. (2001) 'Capitalism's global strategy', in Houtart, F. and Polet, F. (eds) (2001) *The Other Davos: The Globalization of Resistance to the World Economic System*. London: Zed Books, pp. 17–24

Baron, S., Field, J. and Schuller, T. eds (2000) *Social Capital: Critical perspectives*. Oxford: Oxford University Press

Blunkett, D. (2003) *Civil Renewal – A new agenda* (Edith Kahn Memorial Lecture), CSV. London: Home Office

Brookfield, S. (1995 edition) *Adult Learners, Adult Education and the Community*. Buckingham: Open University Press

Clarke, J. (2005) 'New Labour's Citizens' in *Critical Social Policy*, Vol. 25, No. 4, pp. 447–463

Coare, P. and Johnston, R. (2003) *Adult Learning, Citizenship and Community Voices: Exploring and learning from community-based practice.* Leicester: NIACE

Cornwall, A. (2004) 'Spaces for transformation?' in Hickey, S. and Mohan, G. (eds) (2004) *Participation: From tyranny to transformation?* London: Zed Books

Craig, R., Kerr, D., Wade, P. and Taylor, G. (2004) *Taking Post-16 Citizenship Forward: Learning from the Post-16 Citizenship Development Projects.* London: HMSO

Crick, B. (2001) 'Introduction' in Crick, B. (ed.). *Citizens: Towards a Citizenship Culture.* The Political Quarterly

Crowther, J., Martin, I. and Shaw, M. (eds) (1999) *Popular Education and Social Movements in Scotland today.* Leicester: NIACE

DfEE (1998) *Education for Citizenship and the Teaching of Democracy in Schools: Final report of the Advisory Group on Citizenship.* London: QCA

Espejo, R. (2003) 'Social Systems and the Embodiment of Organizational Learning', in *Complex Systems and Evolutionary Perspectives on Organizations – The Application of Complexity Theory to Organizations.* Edited by Mittleton-Kelly, E., pp. 53–70. London: Pergamon-Elsevier Science

Etzioni, A. (1998) *The Essential Communitarian Reader.* Lanham, MD: Rowman and Littlefield

Fine, B. (2000) *Social capital versus social theory.* London: Routledge

Freire, P. (1972) *Pedagogy of the Oppressed.* London: Penguin

Freire, P. and Shor, I. (1997) *Pedagogy for Liberation.* London: Macmillan

Friedman, M. (1962) *Capitalism and Freedom.* Chicago: University of Chicago Press

Gaventa, G. (2004) 'Towards Participatory Governance: Assessing the transformative possibilities' in Hickey, S. and Mohan, G. (eds) (2004) *Participation: From tyranny to transformation?* London: Zed Books

Giddens, A. (1992 edition) *Sociology.* Cambridge: Polity Press

Giddens, A. (2000) 'Citizenship education in the global era', in Pierce, N. and Hillgarten, J. *Tomorrow's Citizens.* London: IPPR

Hall, S. (2000) 'Multicultural Citizens, Monocultural Citizenship?' in Pierce, N. and Hillgarten, J. *Tomorrow's Citizens.* London: IPPR

Held, D. and McGrew, A. (eds) (2002) *Governing Globalization: Power, authority and global governance.* Cambridge: Polity Press

Hewitt, R. (2005) White *Backlash and the Politics of Multiculturalism*. Cambridge: Cambridge University Press

Jarvis, P. (1995) *Adult and Continuing Education: Theory and practice*. London: Routledge

Jeffs, T. and Smith, M. (2005 edition) *Informal Education*. Nottingham: Educational Heretics Press

Jochum, V., Pratten, B. and Wilding, K. (2005) *Civil Renewal and Active Citizenship: A guide to the debate*. London: NCVO

Joseph Rowntree Charitable Trust (2006) *Power to the People. The report of power: An Independent Inquiry into Britain's Democracy (also known as the 'Power Inquiry')*. York: York Publishing Distribution

Kabeer, N. (2005) 'Introduction' in Kabeer, N. (ed.) (2005) *Inclusive Citizenship*. London: Zed Books

Keohane, R. and Nye, J. (2000) *Governing in a Globalizing World*. Cambridge: Cambridge University Press

Le Grand, J. (2003) *Motivation, Agency and Public Policy*. Oxford: Oxford University Press

Lister, R. (1997) *Citizenship*. London: Macmillan

London Edinburgh Weekend Return Group (1979) *In and Against the State*. London: London Edinburgh Weekend Return Group

Martin, M. (1999) 'Introductory Essay: Popular education and social movements in Scotland today' in Crowther, J., Martin, I. and Shaw, M. (eds) *Popular education and social movements in Scotland today*. Leicester: NIACE, pp. 1–25

Mendiwelso-Bendek, Z. (2002) 'Citizens of the Future: Beyond normative conditions through the emergence of desirable collective properties,' *Journal of Business Ethics*, Vol. 39, pp. 189–195

Merrifield, J. (2000) *Learning Citizenship* (Working Paper prepared for the Institute of Development Studies, University of Sussex Participation Group and the Society for Participatory Research in Asia)

Merton, B., Turner, C., Ward, J. and White, L. (2003) *Learning for the Future: Neighbourhood renewal through adult and community learning*. Leicester: NIACE

Miliband, R. (1994) *Socialism for a Sceptical Age*. Cambridge: Polity Press

Molyneux, M. and Razavi, S. (eds) (2002) *Gender Justice, Development and Rights*. Oxford: Oxford University Press

Murray, C. (1984) *Losing Ground*. New York: Basic Books

Murray, C. (1990) *The Emerging British Underclass*. London: IEA Health and Welfare Unit

Noonan, J. (2006) *Democratic Society and Human Needs.* Montreal: McGill-Queen's University Press

Osler, A. and Starkey, H. (2003) 'Learning for Cosmopolitan Citizenship: Theoretical debates and young people's experiences' in *Educational Review*, Vol. 55, No. 3

Rogers, A. (2002) *Teaching Adults* (3rd edition). Buckingham: Open University Press

Rosenau, J. (2002) 'Governance in the Twenty-First Century' in R. Wilkinson (ed.) *The Global Governance Reader*, pp. 45–67. London: Routledge

Solomos, J. and Back, L. (1996) *Racism and Society.* London: Macmillan

Tarrow, S. (2005) *The New Transnational Activism.* Cambridge: Cambridge University Press

Tate, N. (2000) 'Citizenship in a liberal democracy' in Pierce, N. and Hillgarten, J. *Tomorrow's Citizens,* pp. 64–73. London: IPPR

Tett, L. (2002) *Community Education, Lifelong Learning and Social Inclusion.* Edinburgh: Dunedin Academic Press

Westheimer, J. and Kahne, J. (2004) 'What Kind of Citizen: the Politics of Educating for Democracy' in *American Educational Research Journal*, Vol. 41, No. 2, p. 240

Woodward, V. (2004) *Active Learning for Active Citizenship.* CRU. London: Home Office

From citizenship-rich schools to citizenship-rich communities: lessons from the classroom and beyond

TONY BRESLIN

Aspirations and contexts: the recent history of citizenship education in English schools

Since September 2002 secondary schools have been required to teach Citizenship as a Foundation (compulsory) Subject of the National Curriculum. More recently, there have been calls for statutory Citizenship Education to be extended to the primary curriculum (Citizenship Foundation, 2006; Citizenship Foundation, 2008; Goldsmith, 2008; GMG, 2008; Rose, 2009[1]); the wider secondary National Curriculum has undergone a comprehensive review (with new Programmes of Study in each Key Stage 3 and 4 subject from September 2008 – QCA, 2007); and citizenship and the wider curriculum has been the subject of a further specific review, led by Sir Keith Ajegbo, concerned with the particular issues of identity and diversity (DfES, 2007a). Concurrent with these curricular developments have been new initiatives to promote pupil participation (DfES, 2003; Institute of Education-DCSF, 2007), the emergence of the *Every Child Matters* framework (DfES, 2003) and the creation of a new (statutory) 'Duty' on

---

[1] Sir Jim Rose's DCSF commissioned review of the primary curriculum proposes to organise learning at Key Stages 1 and 2 into six subject clusters or 'areas of learning', one of which – 'Historical, Geographical and Social Understanding' – gives equal and statutory status to History, Geography and Citizenship.

schools to promote Community Cohesion (DCSF, 2007), in place since September 2007 and inspected since September 2008.

These school-related developments have taken place against the backdrop of a broader policy agenda that the opening chapters in this collection have drawn attention to. In particular, there have been three concerns: the level of participation in the political system, the functioning of community life and the integration of newcomers into these communities, and the political system. The latter has been given particular impetus because of high levels of immigration, especially from those countries that are more recent members of the European Union (EU), and the apparently entrenched disaffection of some minority ethnic communities, a disaffection seen as articulated through the involvement of young British-born males in the London bombings of July 2005. Against this backdrop, four documents are of special note: *Power to the People*, the report of the Power Inquiry (Joseph Rowntree Charitable Trust, 2006); *Our Shared Future*, arising from the work of the Commission on Integration and Cohesion (CLG, 2007); *Citizenship: Our Common Bond*, emerging from a broader review of citizenship-related issues (Goldsmith, 2008), itself a component in the government's wider *Governance of Britain* agenda (Ministry of Justice, 2007) and the *Path to Citizenship* Green Paper, concerned with possible future developments in the naturalisation process that newcomers to the UK are required to go through to gain 'citizenship' (Home Office, 2008).

In this chapter I want to provide a summary of the current state of play in Citizenship Education in schools and, in so doing, I want to identify gaps in – and lessons from – this for policy-makers and practitioners working in Professional, Adult and Community Education (PACE)[2] and in youth and community settings that have some educative impact and/or intent but which are not always termed *educational* settings, either in the formal or informal sense. My fundamental presumption – and one that my co-authors share – is that to achieve all

---

[2] I use the acronym deliberately to refer to the range of activities usually grouped under the generic (but wholly unhelpful) heading of 'further' education. In particular, I select 'professional' as an inclusive and status-neutral term to embrace the range of activities that reaches from work-related learning and vocational education delivered across the 14–19 continuum to workplace-based training and formal professional education delivered as part of the preparation for membership of chartered and similar institutes in areas such as law, medicine and accountancy.

of our objectives with regard to Citizenship Education in schools is insufficient. To do so will serve the needs of the emergent generation but *not* the greater bulk of other, older citizens. We are right to demand that every young person leaves full-time education with a rich understanding of the knowledge base that is a pre-requisite for *effective* citizenship and the skills and dispositions to act on this. However, we must also ensure that those who have not benefited from such a curriculum can access this knowledge and these skills, when they need to and in a form that works for them.

In this context, the recent efforts of the Public Legal Education and Advisory Support (PLEAS) Taskforce on legal literacy (DCA, 2007) and the Campaign for Learning on political literacy (Alexander, 2007) are to be commended, but this is not enough: one may never be able to ensure that all adults *will* access the PACE programmes provided but, given the failure of our school curriculum to introduce these issues in the past, it is our moral obligation to ensure that any adult who wants to access such provision *can* do so. Nonetheless, professional, adult and community educators have much to learn from the recent experience of schools. In particular, I will focus on four things: the nature of Citizenship as a curriculum subject (for the issues that arise for schools are likely to emerge in PACE settings), the transformation of schools into 'citizenship-rich' environments (the contention being that other settings can, likewise, aspire to become 'citizenship-rich'), the emergence of community cohesion as a key theme – and statutory obligation – in the lives of schools and other organisations and, finally, the emerging view that Citizenship Education programmes are drivers not just of inclusion but of achievement: this agenda is emphatically not about simply the so-called *soft* skills; it is about the *hard* data of educational success and all that flows from that for individuals, their families and their communities.

At the time of writing, there is a stronger suggestion of political change in the air than at any time since 1997. I contend that whatever the next government's complexion, the broader policy concerns that have both emerged from debates about citizenship and Citizenship Education and which frame these debates – about political and community engagement, about rights and responsibilities, about identity and diversity in a globalising world – will still need attention. It is a strength of what I might term the citizenship *perspective* that it can enable us to explore these enduring and multiple challenges, as it is beginning to do in our schools and as it might do elsewhere.

Teaching Citizenship: opportunities for a different kind of subject

Almost six years ago, in an article for the journal *Teaching Citizenship* (Breslin, 2004), I reflected on the challenges that schools were facing in teaching what was then not just a new subject but one in its infancy. I observed that:

- schools were dealing with something that did not have the academic heritage of those subjects that have long dominated our school curriculum;
- schools were struggling to get to grips with how Citizenship as a *National Curriculum* subject might differ from its immediate predecessor, Citizenship the *Cross Curricular* theme;[3]
- curriculum managers were trying to work out, and articulate in curricular terms, the distinction between citizenship and other areas of the social curriculum, notably Personal, Social and Health Education (PSHE);
- school leaders had a sense that citizenship was not just about classroom teaching but about whole-school ethos issues and mechanisms for processes such as pupil participation;
- there was an apparent skills shortage in terms of who might teach this new subject;
- there was genuine confusion about how, or indeed whether, Citizenship should or could be assessed; and
- there was no real sense of where Citizenship sat in relation to the wider policy debate and, in particular, with regard to the so-called standards agenda.

Five years on, significant progress has been made in some of these areas. Concerns over a lack of academic heritage are giving way to an understanding that Citizenship is a composite of a range of highly academic, disciplines (often more traditionally taught post-16) that have much to

---

[3] Shortly after the introduction of the first model of the National Curriculum in the late 1980s, a set of six non-statutory 'Cross-Curricular Themes' were added, one of which was 'Education for Citizenship'. Although pockets of good practice emerged, the themes largely sank without trace, evidence that, sometimes, 'everywhere is nowhere' (Citizenship Foundation, 2006). See Whitty *et al.* (1994) for a discussion of the problems with such approaches.

draw on: sociology, law, politics, economics and history. Indeed, teachers from these traditions have much to offer the Citizenship classroom. Likewise, the assumption that Citizenship programmes can be delivered entirely across the curriculum or by non-specialist form tutors as a part of already low status PSHE programmes are beginning to give way to an understanding that Citizenship is a *real* subject (one strengthened by being based on a composite of disciplines rather than a single discipline) and requires the attendant timetable slot, assessment strategy and specialised delivery team – the paraphernalia of a school subject, not least because of the dominance of 'subjects' in our schooling tradition. Thus, Ofsted (2006), DfES (2007a) and the National Foundation for Educational Research (NFER) (2002–08) routinely report that the best practice is found where appropriately trained and resourced dedicated teams are allocated sufficient timetable space to deliver the Programmes of Study, and although less than half of those currently teaching Citizenship are formally trained to do so (Kerr *et al.*, 2007), the value of specialist delivery is slowly gaining acknowledgement. As Miriam Rosen, Ofsted's Director of Education puts it:

> *Citizenship is still seen as the poor relation of more established subjects, but it requires teachers to be highly skilled and able to deal with contentious and sometimes difficult issues. (GMG, 2006)*

In fact, the growth of GCSE Citizenship Studies in recent years (up from 6,500 candidates in 2003 to over 96,200 candidates in 2009, almost 20 per cent of the student cohort) is as much a sign of schools using the framework provided by an examination programme to give citizenship status as an indicator of contentment with the form of assessment on offer. Finally, head teachers are beginning to see the connections between National Curriculum Citizenship, the wider life of the school and the broader policy agenda. Opportunities for student participation, for instance, enable learners to rehearse and develop their active citizenship skills – applying, and therefore consolidating, their curriculum knowledge in the process – and enable schools to demonstrate their commitment to engagement and consultation, building a clearer experience of inclusion in the process. As I have remarked elsewhere and shall elaborate on later, included students achieve (Breslin, 2007b; Breslin, 2008; NFER, 2002–08) – and the evidence is beginning to support this (Hannam, 2006; Davies and Yamashita, 2007).

Citizenship Education in schools remains, though, in a period of 'subject-building'. A literature is beginning to develop (Huddleston and Kerr, 2005; Breslin and Dufour, 2006; NFER, 2002–2008) and a nationally accredited, DCSF-endorsed CPD certificate for teachers has been developed, but calls for a coherent National Strategy for Teaching and Learning in Citizenship (Citizenship Foundation, 2006) have, as yet, fallen on deaf ears. The most successful schools have identified two lessons, though, from early practice that those involved in the PACE sector and in community settings would be wise to draw on. First, they have come to an understanding of citizenship that sees it not simply as a new subject but as a new and different *type* of subject, based on, as noted earlier, a composite of disciplines rather than a single discipline, and taught both within *and* beyond the classroom. Second, they have recognised that in its evolution from 'Cross Curricular' *theme* to 'Foundation' *subject*, Citizenship has moved from being *less* than a subject to being *more* than a subject, having its proper place on the timetable but finding expression in a range of settings beyond this: the school council, the mock election, the community volunteering programme, the charity project – the Citizenship classroom both lays the foundation for this 'cross-curricular' and 'extra-curricular' activity and draws out the Citizenship lessons from it, about justice, equality, diversity and responsibility. Pattisson and Barnett (2005) articulate this relationship between the curricular and the broader aspects of Citizenship Education neatly, as shown in Figure 1.

At the Citizenship Foundation we have taken this analysis further, developing the concept of the 'citizenship-rich' school (Breslin and Dufour, 2006) and, subsequently, the 'citizenship-rich' community (Citizenship

Figure 1 The 'three Cs' of citizenship

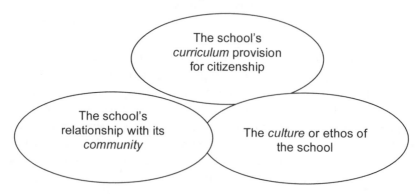

Foundation, 2007). Here, the self-evaluation question is clear – whether it is asked in school, college, youth group, voluntary organisation or workplace – to what extent might this setting be considered as one that is, genuinely, citizenship-rich? It is to our experience in refining and operationalising the idea of the citizenship-rich school that I now turn.

Building the citizenship-rich school

In its earlier years, the nine-year longitudinal study referred to earlier (NFER, 2002–2008) provided a useful typology that has proved instructive both to school leaders and to the inspectorate: 'progressing' schools are providing both a strong taught curriculum and multiple experiences for students to develop their citizenship skills through participation in the life of the school and the wider community; 'focused' schools are offering a sound curriculum, but are less inclined to provide the participation opportunities through which skills and confidence are developed; 'implicit' schools offer much of the latter but do not build this around a clearly identified curriculum entitlement to citizenship learning; 'minimalist' schools have barely got off the launch pad – Citizenship is one more burden and one they hope will pass.

As I have noted elsewhere, the last point needs to be nailed: 'citizenship education', as the report of the Select Committee (Home Office, 2007) indicates, is here to stay. The varied quality of current provision is to be expected in a curricular area so recent in its emergence. Indeed, the focus on developing skills and dispositions alongside knowledge – so central to effective Citizenship Education – is something that established 'academic' subjects would have done well to explore in their subject-building days. In putting the *doing* of Citizenship at the core of practice from the start, citizenship educators may be developing an approach, not just to teaching and learning in Citizenship, but to pedagogy in other subject areas too: (functional) English and (functional) Mathematics come to mind. Critically, the citizenship-rich school *does* Citizenship at every opportunity. Thus, it is a very different kind of place in which to teach and learn, one that has five defining characteristics:

1. Citizenship Education is clearly identified in the curriculum model, on the timetable, in assessment frameworks, in Continuing Professional Development (CPD) provision and in the school's improvement and development plans.

2. It enables young people to develop their Citizenship knowledge through a skills-based and learner-centred pedagogy.
3. Citizenship learning, thus, takes place not only within designated timetable space – important as this is – but through a range of opportunities and activities, on and off the school site, that are valued by students, teachers and the wider community.
4. It encourages and facilitates the active and effective participation of all – students, teachers, parents, the wider community – in its day-to-day activities.
5. It models the principles that it teaches about in citizenship in the way that it operates as an institution and a community, and proclaims this outlook in its documentation.

But why should a school seek to become citizenship-rich? Again, there are a number of rationales, but these can be summarised in terms of:

- justice: schools seek to be just communities in which all are equally valued and given voice – a citizenship-rich perspective can help the achievement of this aspiration;
- effectiveness: those schools that involve students, parents and the wider community so as to build a better understanding of the needs of each are better placed to meet these needs – a citizenship-rich perspective places the principles of student participation, community involvement, staff development and family learning at the core of school activity;
- achievement: increasingly, research shows that a strong focus on these citizenship-rich principles brings returns in terms of student performance across the curriculum; and
- inclusion: the same principles deliver practical inclusion – the breadth of citizenship learning is much wider than that of a conventional subject and reaches a broader range of learners including those often thought of as disaffected, disruptive or both.

In two of the most recent reports from the longitudinal study (Kerr *et al.*, 2007; Benton *et al.*, 2008), the authors have replaced the categorisation 'progressing' with the descriptor 'citizenship-rich', an indication perhaps of citizenship's growing stature as both a curriculum subject and a key aspect of school practice, and an indication that the most successful schools are not just making progress but, after much effort, are getting there.

Identity, diversity and community cohesion: a fourth 'strand' or shifting sands?

The most quoted passage in Sir Bernard Crick's first and seminal report (DfEE, 1998) is never far from a presentation or paper in this field and I make no apology for repeating it here:

> We aim at no less than a change in the political culture of this country both nationally and locally: for people to think of themselves as active citizens. Willing, able and equipped to have influence in public life and with the critical capacities to weigh evidence before speaking and acting; to build on and to extend radically to young people the best in existing traditions of community involvement and public service, and to make them individually confident in finding new forms of involvement and action among themselves. (Ibid: pp. 7–8)

Crick and his committee operationalised this aspiration through an approach to citizenship that had three components or strands which were to endure in his subsequent reports:

- social and moral responsibility;
- political literacy; and
- community involvement.

Such an approach clearly articulated a model of citizenship that was about political engagement rather than about right of residence. In the field, as I was to learn in my early days at the Citizenship Foundation, the term was always more contentious. During 2002 and 2003, working with what was then the Learning and Skills Development Agency, the Foundation was evaluating some of the post-16 evaluation projects that had emerged from Crick's second report (DfEE 2000). Resultantly, I found myself observing a HND Banking and Finance block release class at a specialist vocational college on the edge of the City of London. The class was made up of 17- and 18-year-old students from Tower Hamlets and all but one of the 18 or so students were drawn from minority ethnic groups. My task was to probe them about the quality and value of their experience and what they thought of the experimental Citizenship module. The following exchange is one that has stayed with me since:

69

Interviewer (myself):

So what do you think of this new citizenship stuff that you're doing then?

Student (the solitary white member of the group):

Well (rather forcefully), I didn't like the sound of it at first.

(Pause) ... I thought it was goin' be about whether my mates were goin' to be allowed to stay in the country or not.

Nobody before or since has, in my view, articulated the ambiguities and tensions that sit at the heart of citizenship as a term, especially in how it plays out in diverse communities, than this post-16 student – ambiguities and tensions between compliance and empowerment, between national identity and civic engagement and between status and process. For practitioners working in PACE and informal educational environments – where curricular and procedural forms are necessarily looser and 'light touch'[4] – these ambiguities are likely to prove harder to 'correct' than they are in the classroom.

Perhaps because of these ambiguities, citizenship educators (including the author) had tended to stay away from questions of status, identity and residence for fear that these issues smacked of exclusion rather than inclusion. As noted in the opening discussion, increased migration flows (especially from the new EU countries), concerns about the success or failure of long-standing policies somewhat lazily and generically cluster-titled as 'multiculturalism' and the London bombings of July 2005 brought the questions of identity, diversity and community cohesion crashing to the top of the policy agenda.

Sir Keith Ajegbo's report (DfES, 2007a) into the treatment of issues of diversity both within Citizenship Education and across the curriculum arose directly in response to the London bombings, as did the

---

[4] Crick famously used the term in making his proposals for Citizenship Education in schools because he believed that teachers needed the freedom, largely missing in their existing and broader experience of implementing the National Curriculum, to mould provision to local need and emerging events. Some schools, arguably, took this as a message that rigour was of less importance in Citizenship than in other 'real' subjects - 'soft touch' rather than 'light touch' – but Ofsted has sought to correct this perception.

report from the concurrent Commission on Integration and Cohesion (CLG, 2007). Ajegbo proposed, and the subsequently revised National Curriculum Programmes of Study for Citizenship reflect, the emergence of a fourth strand to add to Crick's original threesome (although these had never formally appeared in the original Curriculum Order), somewhat clumsily worded 'identity and diversity: living together in the UK'.

For some critical commentators, the fourth strand represents, not so much an enrichment of Crick's earlier conceptual framework, but a worrying shift in the focus and purpose of Citizenship Education – from promoting political empowerment to engineering integration, an unwelcome shift along the continuum from process to status. This may be a risk but equally, the drawing of complex questions around identity, diversity and commonality into the safer, teacher-informed and mediated space of the citizenship classroom brings a series of offline discussions, concerns and insecurities into a more open public domain. Questions, in particular, around 'Britishness' may remain contentious, especially if the aim is to impose a particular version of Britishness from a bygone, allegedly golden age. But the idea that young people might explore within the classroom what it means (and what it takes) to be an effective citizen[5] in twenty-first century Britain is surely a good thing. Indeed, it is not unreasonable to suggest that while *recovering* an agreed sense of Britishness (or Englishness) may be a lost cause (Denham, 2005; Breslin, 2006; Johnson, 2006), *discovering* or *developing* a new and shared citizenship (Interfaith Network–Citizenship Foundation, 2006) and sense of common identity might be a worthwhile project.

Moreover, whatever the reservations that some in the Citizenship Education community might reasonably hold about the broader focus on integration and cohesion, the new duty on schools with regard to Community Cohesion (DfES, 2007b), introduced from September 2007 and inspected from September 2008, provides a powerful political lever to drive the citizenship agenda, ten years on from Crick's original report. Indeed, emergent guidance on this duty – which it is expected will

---

[5] At the Citizenship Foundation – and somewhat at odds with the title of this collection – we have long preferred the concept of *effective* rather than merely *active* citizenship – the former suggesting a focus on participation and social action that drives political and community change; the latter suggesting the busy doing of good but perhaps, on some occasions, little more.

feature on a revised School Self Evaluation Form (SEF)[6] – is likely to give the Citizenship curriculum a pre-eminent role. Equally, it is likely to under-line the value of one of Crick's original strands – community involvement – as a cohesion-enhancing strategy. If schools can free themselves from some of the shackles of our risk-averse, safety-first culture and venture further out into their communities, the learning benefits are likely to be tangible, whatever the cohesive impact – but they might need some legislative help from elsewhere on the statute book to do so. Informal education providers and those working in PACE settings – although no comparable cohesion duty is currently in place – might have less shackles with which to contend and might have some of the community relationships already in place that citizenship-rich schools are embarked on building.

Education for citizenship: part of a broader inclusion-first framework?

It is paradox of education strategies that are focused (laudably) on raising educational attainment that they serve to reinforce the exclusion of the hardest to reach. Quite literally, to draw on an analysis that I have devel-oped extensively elsewhere (Breslin, 2008), the more successful we are with the 60, 70, 80 per cent, the more excluded the 40, 30, 20 per cent become. The political outcome is a pervasive concern with those 'not in employment, education or training' (or NEET), media headlines about the 'hoodies' of the so-called 'ASBO generation' and the proliferation of gated communities and alarmed homes. Of course, it is precisely for these young people and their families that PACE practitioners and those in the youth, community and informal education sectors do much of their most valuable (but, perversely, least publicly valued) work.

Here, school practitioners might have much to learn from the broader audience for this book, especially the latter's expertise in what might be termed inclusion-first strategies. Such strategies build achievement *from* inclusion (rather than seeking to eradicate the latter through the former). This might be a route to a better and more socially sustainable society. Inclusive schools *are* achieving schools and their achievement is likely to

---

[6] The SEF form is completed and regularly updated by schools and used as the starting point for visiting Ofsted teams who test the conclusions that the school makes about its practice during the inspection, of which schools receive between 48 and 72 hours' notice.

offer a sustainability that reaches beyond the booster class or the targeting of those on the C–D grade borderline. When there is manifest underperformance across the education system, an all-out focus on levels of measured attainment is the right one. However, where low attainment is consistently located among certain social groups and at certain schools (regardless of the frequency of inspections or changes to the leadership team), we have the educational version of market failure. In such a setting new approaches are required. These approaches must be inclusion-first. Any new educational initiative should be appraised, not simply on how effectively it can build the achievement of some, but on how effectively it will deliver inclusion (and thence achievement) for all.

In this context, there is a critical battle that Citizenship Education in schools has yet to win: it is that Citizenship Education is not the 'soft' stuff that schools do after literacy and numeracy have been 'sorted', but a key tool in raising achievement, especially the achievement of the so-called 'hard to reach'. Perhaps the wind is blowing in the right direction. In some respects, the education policy agenda is shifting towards a position that supports citizenship-rich and inclusion-first approaches. On the one hand, the emergence of so-called 'full-service' and 'extended' schools, coupled with the impact of workforce remodelling (processes that are serving to recast schools as multi-professional sites) and the increasing importance placed on school councils, are laying a set of institutional foundations in which the citizenship-rich school should thrive. On the other, the introduction of citizenship to the National Curriculum in secondary schools sits alongside a range of other changes that might be deemed inclusion-first: the evolution of the Every Child Matters agenda into the organising template for various areas of educational practice (including the school inspection regime); the emerging focus on family learning and parental support (embodied in the new title of the department responsible for schooling, the Department for Children, Schools and Families); and the growing realisation that the emotional well-being of children is central to their success in the classroom.

This change of emphasis, if it is that, is long overdue. The important drive to raise achievement – especially when characterised by league tables, inter-school competition and the appearance of parental choice – has, in some settings, added to the very exclusion that we wish to challenge. Once any school or college is achieving the best it can with a given student intake, the requirement is for organisational transformation rather than simply a harder foot on the examination pedal – trying to achieve the latter without the former only results in teacher burn-out and learner disillusion. Here, the application of inclusion-first principles and citizenship-rich strategies begins to offer a way forward. The focus of this collection – active learning as a route to, and preparation for, active citizenship – is an expression of such strategies in practice and an indication that those of us involved in school-based education have much to learn from our colleagues in the professional, adult and community education sector and those working in youth and community settings.

This chapter draws on two recent papers that I have published (Breslin, 2007a; Breslin 2007b) referenced below. I am grateful to Ted Huddleston at the Citizenship Foundation for his comments on an earlier draft.

References

Alexander, T. (2007) *Learning Power*. London: Campaign for Learning-Scarman Trust

Benton, T. *et al.* (2008) *Citizenship Education Longitudinal Study (CELS): Sixth Annual Report. Young People's Civic Participation In and Beyond School: Attitudes, Intentions and Influences (DCSF Research Report 052)*. London: DCSF

Breslin, T. (2004) 'New Subject: New Type of Subject' in *Teaching Citizenship,* (Vol. 4, No. 2), Association for Citizenship Teaching

Breslin, T. (2006) *Citizenship Education and Identity Formation*, in Johnson, N. (ed.), *Britishness: Towards a progressive citizenship.* The Smith Institute-Commission for Racial Equality

Breslin, T. and Dufour, B. (eds) (2006) *Developing Citizens: A comprehensive introduction to effective citizenship education in the secondary school.* London: Hodder Murray

Breslin, T. (2007a) *Developing Citizens: Developing citizenship-rich schools* in *secondary headship,* July 2007. Cambridge: Optimus Publishing

Breslin, T. (2007b) 'Inclusion-first and citizenship-rich: A glimpse of the future of schooling' in *Transformation*, Issue 7, Autumn 2007, Capgemini – National School of Government

Breslin, T. (2008) *Teachers, Schools and Change*, unpublished doctoral thesis, Institute of Education, University of London

Citizenship Foundation (2006) *Submission to the Education and Skills Select Committee Investigation into Citizenship Education.* London: Citizenship Foundation

Citizenship Foundation (2007) *The Citizens' Day Framework: Building cohesive, active and engaged communities.* London: Citizenship Foundation-CLG

Citizenship Foundation (2008) *Why Citizenship Education should be Statutory in Primary Schools: Submission to the Primary Curriculum (Rose) Review.* London: Citizenship Foundation

CLG (2007) *Our Shared Future: Report of the Commission on Integration and Cohesion.* London: CLG

Davies, L., and Yamashita, H. (2007) *School Councils-School Improvement.* Birmingham: University of Birmingham, with the support of the Esmee Fairbairn Foundation and Deutsche Bank

DCA (2007) *Report of the Public Legal Education and Advisory Support Task Force.* London: Department for Constitutional Affairs

DCSF (2007) *National Curriculum in Citizenship.* London: QCA

Denham, J. (2005) 'Who do we want to be?' in *Fabian Review*, Winter 2005. London: Fabian Society

DfEE (1998) *Education for Citizenship and the Teaching of Democracy in Schools: Final report of the Advisory Group on Citizenship.* London: QCA

DfEE (2001) *Citizenship for 16–19 Year Olds in Education and Training.* Coventry: FEFC

DfES (2003) *Every Child Matters.* London: Department for Education and Skills (DfES)

DfES (2007a) *Diversity and Citizenship: A curriculum review.* London: DfES

DfES (2007b) *Draft Guidance on Community Cohesion.* London: DfES

DfES (2003) *Advice on Pupil Involvement in Governing Bodies.* London: DfES

GMG (2006), 'Schools poor at teaching citizenship, says Ofsted', in *The Guardian*, 28 September, 2006. London: Guardian Media Group

GMG (2008) 'Editorial' in *The Guardian, 12 March 2008.* London: Guardian Media Group

Goldsmith, P. (2008) *Citizenship: Our Common Bond: Report of Lord Goldsmith's Citizenship Review.* London: Ministry of Justice

Hannam, D. (2006) 'Education for Democracy and as a Democratic Process', in *Developing Citizens: A comprehensive guide to effective citizenship in the secondary school.* London: Hodder Murray

Home Office (2007) *Report of the Education and Skills Select Committee Investigation into Citizenship Education.* London: The Stationery Office (TSO)

Home Office (2008) *The Path to Citizenship: Next steps in reforming the immigration system* (Green Paper). London: TSO

Huddleston, T. and Kerr, D. (eds) (2005) *Making Sense of Citizenship.* London: Hodder Murray

Institute of Education–DCSF (2007) *Real Decision-making? School councils in action.* London: Institute of Education

Interfaith Network-Citizenship Foundation (2006) 'Faith, Identity and Belonging: Educating for Shared Citizenship', report on a seminar held on 7 February 2006. The Interfaith Network

Johnson, N., ed. (2006) *Britishness: Towards a progressive citizenship.* London: The Smith Institute

Joseph Rowntree Charitable Trust (2006) *Power to the People: The report of Power – an independent inquiry into Britain's democracy.* York: York Publishing Distribution

Kelly, R. and Byrne, L. (2007) *A Common Place.* London: Fabian Society

Kerr, D. *et al.* (2007). *VISION versus PRAGMATISM: Citizenship in the Secondary School Curriculum in England. Citizenship Education Longitudinal Study: Fifth Annual Report (DfES Research Report 845).* London: DfES

Ministry of Justice (2007) *Governance of Britain.* London: TSO

National Foundation for Educational Research (NFER) (2002–08) *Citizenship Education Longitudinal Study (Annual Reports).* Slough: NFER

Ofsted (2006) *Towards Consensus: Citizenship in secondary schools.* Ofsted

Pattisson, P. and Barnett, A. (2005*) A School for Citizenship* in *Teaching Citizenship* (Issue 10). London: Association for Citizenship Teaching

QCA (2007) *Assessment and Reporting Arrangements and Curriculum 2008.* London: QCA

Rose, J. (2009), *Independent Review of the Primary Curriculum: Final report.* Nottingham: DCSF Publications

Whitty, G., Rowe, G. and Aggleton P. (1994) 'Subjects and Themes in the Secondary School Curriculum' in *Research Papers in Education*, Pre-publication draft copy. London: Institute of Education, University of London.

CHAPTER FIVE

Education for citizenship: joining the dots

John Potter

Opportunity

Joined-up thinking

We now have a unique opportunity to make coherent sense of education for citizenship across schools, colleges and adult learning in local communities.

Education for citizenship has for some years been embedded in the school and post-16 curriculums. Now, however, the government has committed itself to encourage 'Active Learning for Active Citizenship' among adults in their local and wider communities[1] through the *Take Part Network* and related programmes, including the Take Part local pathfinder programme. This is great news for those who have laboured long to make the important connection between education for citizenship in school and community. However, though the ideas and the frameworks are in place, we have some way to go before we have forged a robust and effective partnership between schools, colleges and their local communities as far as citizenship and community development is concerned. In this chapter, I explore some of the critical issues that must be addressed on our road to success.

---

[1] Take Part: Active Learning for Active Citizenship, see www.takepart.org. See also the recently published CLG Action Plan for Community Empowerment at www.communities.gov.uk/civilrenewal – and related links.

Local Government White Paper

The Department for Communities and Local Government (CLG) is taking the lead on civic engagement and social inclusion. In October 2006, CLG published the Local Government White Paper, *Strong and prosperous Communities*.[2] Its aim is to promote grass roots approaches to participation, civic engagement and social inclusion through a series of partnerships between local government and local people. Related departmental initiatives have created a platform for systemic change across and beyond government. *Together We Can* set out to unite stakeholders in local government and communities around a cluster of programmes to promote community empowerment.[3] *The Take Part Network* is one element in the programme that was sponsored initially by the Home Office and subsequently by CLG.

Take Part

The aim of Take Part is to 'provide programmes of active learning that enable people to gain the skills, knowledge and confidence to become empowered citizens – citizens who are able: (i) to make an active contribution in their communities and (ii) to influence public policies and services.' Take Part has built up a coherent body of principles and practice that are now published in the *Take Part Framework* (see www.takepart.org). Take Part is recognised by the LSC. Melanie Hunt, the Council's National Director of Learning, warmly welcomed the publication of the Framework:

> *It will be an invaluable touchstone to guide improved collaboration between local agencies to deliver learning opportunities. In this way people can develop the knowledge, skills and confidence to become more active as citizens, to influence their communities and to improve their chances of rewarding economic participation. We are pleased to be working with NIACE and the Take Part National Network to support active learning for active citizenship within our wider priorities and commitments.*

---

[2] The Local Government White Paper, *Strong and Prosperous Communities*. Presented to Parliament by The Secretary of State for Communities and Local Government by Command of Her Majesty, October 2006. Cm 6939.

[3] *Together We Can!* is available online at www.togetherwecan.direct.gov.uk, or you can contact CLG at: Community Empowerment Division, Local Democracy Directorate, Department for Communities and Local Government, 4/5 Eland House, Bressenden Place, London, SW1E 5DU.

National Empowerment Partnership

The organisational infrastructure for developing and disseminating the projects that come under the umbrella of *Together We Can* is the newly minted National Empowerment Partnership (NEP.) This NEP is designed to play a leading role in implementing the *Action Plan for Community Empowerment: Building on Success*[4] by working through local coalitions in each of the nine Government Office regions. The overarching aim of this ambitious programme is to harness the energy of local people to the community empowerment goals that have been set for local government.

Figure 2 shows a much-simplified illustration of the place of the National Empowerment Partnership (NEP).

Figure 2 The National Empowerment Partnership

Schools, colleges and communities

Within this larger strategy we have – for the first time – the opportunity to harness the combined energies of citizenship education across the school, college and community sectors. Building dynamic links between sector initiatives is important for three reasons:

- it helps to create a citizenship culture;
- it is mutually beneficial to all involved; and
- it can offer strong growth points for further work.

---

[4] CLG Action Plan for Community Empowerment – www.communities.gov.uk/civilrenewal – and related links.

Creating a citizenship culture

The original reason for introducing citizenship education in schools was the desire to create a citizenship culture across and beyond education. The intention was to equip a generation of young people with the knowledge, skills and attitudes to make a positive difference to their communities. Citizenship education was seen as an essential element in a healthy, participating democracy. However, unless education for citizenship is extended beyond the school gates, it is unlikely to be taken seriously by the rest of society. The subsequent introduction of active learning for active citizenship into further education and community learning is a sign that active citizenship is for everyone, not just school children. It is, therefore, a step towards building a coherent and inclusive citizenship culture.

Such a culture amounts to more than the chance for people to engage in local concerns. It is about changing our way of looking at the world. Reflection is a key element in citizenship education.[5] There is little point in action for its own sake. Action needs purpose, and our purpose grows from paying due attention to the values, relationships and meaning that should sustain community life at every level. This simple truth is the heartbeat of lifelong learning. We need always to be listening out for it.

Mutual benefit

Secondly, close links between the sectors is important because of the practical benefits that they confer on everyone involved. Educators need help with creating opportunities for their students to learn through active engagement in their local communities. This engagement requires well-structured opportunities to link community action with active learning and reflection. Communities can offer such opportunities to schools and colleges, provided they understand the curriculum requirements involved. In their turn, communities can benefit from the contribution of young people and the professional experience of educators. Both sides can benefit from the more effective use of shared community resources, including premises, and shared facilitation and support.

One of the most practical and imaginative proposals to emerge from the citizenship movement over the past year or two is the creation of

---

[5] See *The Reflective Practitioner: How Professionals Think in Action* (Arena, paperback) by Donald A Schon. The book offers a powerful account of how reflection is an essential element in vocational education.

Citizens' Days. In the words of the Citizenship Foundation writer,[6] a 'Citizens Day' is an event or series of activities involving local individuals, groups, communities and public bodies. It can be held either on a single day or over a longer period of time, typically a week or weekend. Co-ordinated by the local authority, and envisioned as an annual event, it provides an opportunity to celebrate local achievements, to build and renew community cohesion, and to develop greater local engagement. It might also mark the anniversary of an important local event, a specific change in the community or, more pro-actively, the launch of a change programme in the community. Furthermore, it may be decided at a Citizens' Day that a community audit on a specific issue is needed in a particular locality. Young people, trained in the relevant techniques, can be in a good position to undertake such an audit, and so develop their own knowledge and skills while contributing important information to the wider community.

A growth point

Strong partnerships between the sectors can offer growth points for further work. When education institutions are effectively harnessed to their local and wider communities, they can become change-agents capable not only of sustaining but also of developing the people and institutions they serve. At its best education is both an evolutionary and revolutionary activity. It helps us grow and develop to meet the ever-changing challenges that life throws at us. It can also help us see things in new ways by harnessing the energy of students, staff and local communities to creating new solutions to fresh and sometimes daunting challenges.

Challenges

Strategic connections are imperative

Joined-up thought and action in the education and the community sectors, however, remain tentative. Like so many good ideas in politics, this one remains vulnerable to being set aside in the face of the more clamorous claims of security, financial crisis and the destabilising impact of short-term political opportunism.

---

[6] See the Citizenship Foundation website www.citizenshipfoundation.org.uk and go to *Citizens' Day Framework*.

A sober assessment of our current situation, however, points to the fact that the key challenges of our time demand that we give priority to the quality and cohesion of our political and community life. In short, it is imperative — not merely desirable — that we set about making strategic connections between the three limbs of education for citizenship: our work in schools, colleges and communities.

The key challenges

The key challenges we face concern our need to foster and maintain sustainable communities, contexts and cultures.

- **Communities** need to be understood and supported at the *local, national* and *global levels.* The growing emphasis on diversity and inclusion is both timely and important, particularly where community tensions run high.
- The **contexts** for these communities include their *economic, social* and *environmental* circumstances. The global community is already exhibiting dangerous signs of strain over resources — notably oil and water.
- **Culture** significantly, of course, includes *values* and *beliefs* as well as custom and convention. Religious extremism among militant minorities — Christian as well as Islamic — is a growing cause for concern.

If we fail effectively to tackle these challenges we are likely to face major, ongoing and probably growing conflicts over *rights, resources* and *religion.*

These challenges are radically interconnected across and beyond the domains that they immediately occupy. Community relations are about more than neighbourliness and good communications; they involve issues of economic and social equity as well as the political institutions to address them. This connectedness, however, is immensely hard to achieve and flies in the face of most of our attitudes, practices and institutions.

The cultural shift

The characteristics of modernist culture are centralised, top-down, and harnessed to narrowly financial indicators. Sustainable communities, while recognising the power of modernist economics, are shaped by a wider range of influences and styles. They are holistic, diverse and interactive. We now live in a world where emotional and spiritual needs are increasingly visible and important. This is evident in the drive towards an international recognition of human rights. It is also seen in the slowly dawning realisation that the resources (and sustainability) of planet earth are finite, not unlimited. Politically, the twentieth century forged a bipolar world centred on Washington and Moscow. The twenty-first century is generating a multi-polar world in which the relative power of Russia and America is increasingly challenged by the burgeoning Asian economies of China and India. These changes are not incidental to our efforts to promote active citizenship and 'empowered communities'. Such developments call urgently for fresh approaches to politics, economics and the way we relate to each other and the world we inhabit. Above all, these challenges require us to work on the values that underpin our personal and public relationships across competing global communities.

The principles of pedagogy and practice

Our approaches to citizenship, learning and our political and economic priorities will be played out against the backdrop of this cultural shift. Our work must address the implications of the key challenges to shape a sustainable world; and these challenges must apply to:

- everyone;
- all aspects of community life – business, government, civil society and culture. This means that our active citizenship needs to address the need for:
  - ★ sustainable businesses – agencies that provide goods and services;
  - ★ sustainable governance – political institutions, civic culture and values;
  - ★ sustainable communities – civil society, institutions, culture and values;
  - ★ sustainable learning – educational institutions, culture and values; and
- every kind of institution, whether in the private, public or community sectors.

This confronts us with a considerable intellectual task, as well as a major organisational challenge.

The scale of the task

There is no doubt about the scale of the task. It is relatively easy to pay lip-service to holistic and coherent approaches to problem-solving, but it is quite another thing to change the habits of thought and practice that we wrap around ourselves like a comfort blanket. When the Home Office first promoted *Together We Can* as the banner under which we might make the shift from modernism to post-modernism (my description, not theirs), a very distinguished educator muttered to me: 'Together we can; but together we shan't.' He was speaking more in sorrow than cynicism.

The obstacles to making these changes are enormous. The government machine is predicated on departmentalising issues. Ministers seek fame and political fortune through making a mark in, and through, their departments. Civil servants are committed to executing departmental programmes. There is little kudos or reward for those who seek to assemble and execute cross-governmental initiatives.

My experience is that it is hard enough to foster co-operation within a department, never mind brokering work between departments. Things are now changing, and CLG plans to invest overall £35 million in bringing people and projects together to generate 'empowered' communities that are sustainable, diverse and inclusive. There was no doubt about the energy, enthusiasm and commitment of Hazel Blears, the Labour Member of Parliament for Salford and Former Secretary of State for CLG. Nor is there doubt about the sincerity and talent of those members of her department who are working round the clock to implement the Department's Action Plan for Community Empowerment. In the CLG's own words:[7]

> This is a joint action plan for Communities and Local Government and the LGA to take forward a shared community empowerment agenda. It forms an important strand of the Government's overall strategy for constitutional renewal, as set out in the Governance of Britain Green Paper. The cross-government strategy has a number of objectives. It aims to:
>
> 1. give citizens the means of participating in decision-making at every level;
> 2. clarify the role of Government, both at central and local level; and
> 3. rebalance power between Parliament and government and give British people a stronger sense of what it means to be British.

---

[7] Extract from the Executive Summary on page 5 of the *Action Plan for Community Empowerment*.

84

The CLG Action Plan sets out their work towards three key outcomes:

- greater participation, collective action and engagement in democracy;
- changes in attitudes towards community empowerment; and
- improved performance of public services and quality of life.

All this is encouraging and deserves to be taken seriously. There remain, however, tough questions to be faced about the capacity of government, community organisations and business partners to tackle the challenges ahead effectively.

Tackling the five obstacles to progress

Five obstacles in particular stand in the way of our making progress towards the ambitious goals of the Community Empowerment Agenda.

Clarity

At present there is no single, clear and coherent understanding – even among community workers – about what community empowerment means. A useful starting point, however, has been offered by CLG.[8]

There are three key ingredients to community empowerment:

- **active citizens:** people with the motivation, skills and confidence to speak up for their communities and say what improvements are needed;
- **strengthened communities:** community groups with the capability and resources to bring people together to work out shared solutions; and
- **partnership with public bodies:** public bodies willing and able to work as partners with local people.

This definition sets out the goals of community empowerment but tells us nothing about the process by which these goals are achieved. At a

[8] CLG website: www.communities.gov.uk – search for 'community empowerment'. The vision for empowering communities was set out by the then Home Secretary, David Blunkett MP, in two key speeches: the Scarman Trust Forum Lecture on 11 December 2004 and the CSV Edith Kahn Memorial Lecture on 11 June 2003 (available on the CLG website).

recent discussion[9] of community workers in the South East, participants agreed that the *process of community empowerment* should be understood in the context of an agreed set of empowerment values such as those listed by Take Part. These values are:

- social justice;
- participation;
- equality and diversity, and
- co-operation.

The empowerment process comprises:

- **developing awareness of community issues and needs:** this might involve a community audit, discussion group or other forms of formal and informal inquiry. In many cases this awareness can become the trigger for effective action;
- **identifying a key issue to tackle:** this involves various forms of debate and democratic decision-making;
- **tackling the issue:** this will mean identifying sources of support (including possible partners), action-planning, identifying and acquiring resources, and practical action; and
- **evaluating progress:** *monitoring* offers a check on whether participants followed their action plan. *Evaluation* offers the chance to make judgements on how effective the action was and what, if anything, still needs to be achieved. This stage may require reports to sponsors, supporters, or funders.

When empowerment is seen as a process, its wider applications become obvious. This is because community empowerment is a subset of a broader concern that affects every sector. It is clearly essential that government members and officers understand the process and recognise the implications that it has for their own practice. ALAC is already on the curriculum in schools, colleges and youth organisations and, again, the implications of this for community empowerment are central to the thrust of this chapter.

---

[9] A group of community workers were called together by the South East Coalition for National Empowerment Partnerships at Community Action Hampshire in December 2007.

Empowerment, however, is not confined to communities and local government; it is increasingly an issue for the corporate sector. Effective, dynamic organisations that invest in their people are already aware of the importance of working with staff at every level to improve the quality and effectiveness of the working environment and the impact of the organisation on its wider communities. 'Empowerment' is a salient issue for management as well as unions.

Commitment

There is no doubt about CLG's commitment to community empowerment, but it is not yet evident that other departments fully share Hazel Blear's serious intent. 'Empowerment' for many is a relatively new concept and not always a popular one. There is an in-built tendency among those who already hold power – officers, members and ministers alike – to be sceptical, even hostile, in the face of suggestions that they should share their hard-won power with other people. Democracy is, they may argue, about representation, not participation. This mantra is frequently and publicly rehearsed: 'we have been elected to make decisions for people, to do what we know to be right for the country. That is how democracy works.' The pressure for civic republicanism – the approach rooted in the belief that the people are active agents in their own governance – is often strongly (albeit subtly) resisted by those who hold the levers of power. The arguments are brilliantly deployed in almost every episode of that political TV classic, *Yes Minister*.

Three conditions are necessary to convert an executive department from representative to participative approaches to democracy: priority, training and recognition.

(i) Priority

'Empowerment' must be given priority from the top-down, and the opportunity to contribute from the bottom up. This is not a licence for anarchy, the department will hold to its brief from the legislature, but it does mean that senior management will listen to middle and junior managers, who in turn will listen to their staff, and their staff will pay systematic attention to service users and other stakeholders. The same condition holds good in schools and colleges as well as in the community sector itself.

The challenge is to persuade senior managers (particularly in business) that it is in their interest to foster a culture of empowerment.

87

A relatively recent BBC2 programme[10] on hospital reform accompanied Sir Gerry Robinson to Rotherham General Hospital where he had been invited to explore what needed to be done to shorten waiting lists. There were the usual issues about communications, leadership and resources, but his major finding was that if an organisation needs to tackle its problems, it should actively engage with the staff who are dealing with them at the sharp end. In this example it soon became clear that 'empowerment' is a necessary tool in achieving effective business practice.

Similarly in schools, a study by Derry Hannam showed that schools where students demonstrate a high level of participation in the life of the school and its communities are also the schools that do well academically. His study[11] compared like schools with like to ensure a common baseline for the inquiry.

(ii) Training

The second condition for effective empowerment is that leaders, whether in business, government or the community, need to be trained in the basic techniques of empowerment. In schools and colleges 'active learning for active citizenship' is part of the wider citizenship curriculum. In local authorities and community organisations there are still many people who, though sympathetic to the process of empowerment, have little or no idea how to go about it. Active citizenship requires active learning. The *Take Part Framework* offers a basis for such understanding, and there are many Take Part and community development facilitators available with the necessary skills and experience to familiarise managers and staff with the necessary insight and skills.

It follows from this, however, that the mainstream training of managers and service providers in all sectors should – where *empowerment* is an issue – include the *empowerment process* as part of induction and professional development. There is a message here for business schools and local government training, as well as for education and training institutions at every level.

---

[10] See www.open2.net/nhs.

[11] Hannam, 2001. A pilot study to evaluate the impact of the student participation aspects of the Citizenship Order on standards of education in secondary schools, Report to the DfEE.

(iii) Recognition

The third factor affecting commitment to empowerment is that everyone involved, including participants, supporting stakeholders and, where relevant, community and local government leaders should be recognised and valued for this commitment. The recent proposal that local communities – along with their schools and colleges – should establish and support Citizens' Days[12] offers an ideal platform for such mutual recognition and celebration.

Complexity

The third obstacle to achieving an effective programme for empowerment is the sheer **complexity** of pulling it off. It means cementing co-operation between local and national government in partnership with local quangos, community activists, development workers, educators and citizens of all ages, interests and backgrounds. The ambition and complexity of the initiative is breathtaking.

Local

At the local level, it is relatively easy – especially if there is funding for transport and refreshments – to organise talking-shop meetings. It is considerably more difficult to ensure that the process of empowerment leads to solid outcomes and the determination to learn from experience.

National

At the level of national government there are a number of distinct but related initiatives competing for resources and attention. Civic empowerment is a priority in Communities and Local Government. At the Cabinet Office there is the Office of the Third Sector (OTS) whose laudable aims appear to overlap with those of CLG.[13] Now, attached to the OTS, there is the newly formed Council on Social Action. The Department for Children, Schools and Families (DfES, as was) is responsible for education for citizenship in schools and colleges. The

---

[12] Citizenship Foundation (2007). *The Citizens' Day Framework: Building Cohesive and Engaged Communities.* London: CLG.

[13] The OTS aims to: (i) enable campaigning and empowerment, particularly for those at risk of social exclusion; (ii) strengthen communities, drawing together people from different sections of society; (iii) transform public services, through delivery, design, innovation and campaigning.

Department of Justice is promoting Lord Goldsmith's Review of Citizenship[14] (5 October 2007), which sets out to 'articulate more clearly the significance of citizenship, and develop recommendations to ensure that our approach to citizenship is appropriate for modern issues of migration, identity and civic participation'.

'One of the abiding questions I am left with relates to how agencies begin to collaborate when their locus of application is so different,' comments Andy Thornton, Director, Participation and Social Action at the Citizenship Foundation, for instance – education works on the individual and their understanding, and then the Local Government Association/CLG might come in on a 'civic' agenda seeing the local authority as having a lead role on promoting population-wide initiative to build bridges and take responsibility, and then the OTS is strengthening the Third Sector such that grass-roots organisations affect change in local communities. Each agent is working on the same people but from a different perspective, measuring differing elements of success and exploiting slightly differing motivations.

CLG is conscious of the challenge, and the department's Action Plan highlights areas where they intend to work closely with colleagues from across government, and where there will be more opportunities for consultation and dialogue. The proof of this will, however, be in the performance.

Robust frameworks

For this reason, robust and organisational frameworks are needed within which participants at all levels can co-operate around agreed objectives and through shared approaches. Evaluation and review will be essential if further progress is then to be made. Robust frameworks of this kind present major challenges to the way in which government departments, community organisations and service providers tackle the work. At the national level, we need greater clarity about how government departments and community organisations intend to co-ordinate their efforts to promote active citizenship across sectors.

Locally, the current proposals for regional Empowerment Partnerships along with local Community Anchor organisations could be very useful. CLG has promised to fund and support such initiatives:

---

[14] Launched 5 October 2007.

Therefore, over the next three years we will invest, with the Office of the Third Sector, in supporting community anchors to develop their role at a neighbourhood level to help build strong and sustainable communities through providing spaces to meet, supporting the community sector, providing services, providing advocacy and voice and stimulating community involvement and activity.[15]

This solid suggestion would be greatly strengthened if it leads to partnerships with the local schools, colleges and community organisations who are already involved in active learning for active citizenship.

Competition

The fourth obstacle to achieving community empowerment arises from the fierce competition between organisations in the community sector. The 'empowerment agenda' assumes significant levels of co-operation between participating organisations and agencies. The blunt fact, however, is that our market-driven culture drives community organisations in the voluntary, private and public sectors to compete for limited resources and to behave in significant respects like commercial organisations. Some characteristics of business practice, including good budgeting, planning and management are clearly important in any organisation. But the near-commercial culture in which community sector work has increasingly to operate is problematic.

Meeting need

The reason that government funds health, social and community services is precisely because such provision, if left to survive in the market, would follow wealth rather than need. The challenge, therefore, is to provide quality services that can be sustained in the medium and longer term. This leads to further questions that cannot be answered in terms of market economics alone.

Consistency

The most commonly heard complaint from service providers is that contracts are often short term, or unrealistically priced. There are too many stories of community providers who, rather than let their clients down, struggle to use charitable donations to maintain their services in the face of unexpected cuts imposed by the purchasers. If the ambitious

---

[15] Action Plan for Community Empowerment – action point 18.

government plans for empowerment are to be realised, key providers of support services need some consistent funding over periods of at least five years.

Innovation

Pump priming money is often offered on the whim of a new minister or administration with the proviso that as soon as the innovation has proved itself, the project managers must glean resources from other 'mainstream' sources. The problem is that mainstream budgets are rarely in a position to meet the escalating demand for funds to support these innovative programmes, however good they are.

Choice

Market choice approach does not always serve the interests of the client group, who may not be able to make sophisticated choices that depend on processing a lot of sometimes-complex information. Choice is not always the best road to quality. More evidence is needed about how choice, particularly market-style choices, can serve the 'empowerment' agenda.

Competition

The number of community organisations interested in bidding for resources to promote aspects of community empowerment is likely to be huge. Let us hope that the ensuing frustration (among funders as well as applicants) will trigger some more innovative approaches to partnership funding where long-term sustainability – not just innovation – is taken seriously.

Perhaps the *National Empowerment Partnership* could be 'empowered' (and funded) to propose some strategies to overcome this long-standing unresolved challenge. Conditions for funding could be set out that stimulate co-operation rather than competition. A possible solution might be to insist that small charities have to find a larger partner with whom they can work effectively without losing their own name and identity. By the same token the larger charities would be eligible to bid for certain funds *only* if they could show that they were working with a team of appropriate smaller partners. At a stroke this would: (i) reduce the number of charities with whom government and major funders have to deal and (ii) support smaller charities offering quality service.

There are arguably too many major charities competing to achieve comparable objectives. The money wasted on overheads and replication must be considerable. The proposal is unlikely to be popular. Few CEOs wish to be remembered for the demise of the organisation over which they preside. It is, however, possible to conceive of institutional models that would allow major organisations to retain their identity, while at the same time entering into long-term, mutually advantageous partnerships with other agencies. Partnership projects, research, financial, legal and IT services and strategic fund-raising might all be shared.

The government ambition for an empowered community sector offers an opportunity to further strengthen the compact between government and NGOs to work effectively in partnership. In return for the community sector reshaping itself to be more accessible and efficient, the government should undertake to provide longer-term funding contracts focused on agreed and stable objectives. We need to move away from the remorseless pursuit of innovation for its own sake.

Culture

The empowerment agenda runs against the grain of the modernist world of centralised command and control. Since Margaret Thatcher's reign there have been major and significant changes in our political culture. Government and business have moved steadily in the direction of 'big is beautiful'. Central government has systematically reduced the relative powers of local government. The business model of consumer choice – rather than of grass-roots participation – has come to dominate political thinking in both Conservative and Labour administrations. It is no accident that during this period the mutual building societies have been turned into banks with shareholders. Schools, too, have been corralled into a market economy of parental choice driven by the price tag of league table scores. Parents have even moved home to place themselves among the golden postcodes of successful schools. The market has thus become the driver of social priorities.

There are three reasons why the simplistic application of this economic business model to goods and services in civil society is seriously flawed.

1. **Economic wealth** is not necessarily an indicator of personal or social well-being. Economists (and many politicians) used to assume that wealth equals happiness. The phrase 'better off' says it all.

Increasingly the evidence suggests that while unhappiness is often a consequence of relative or absolute poverty, the converse does not necessarily hold true. The current burgeoning of 'happiness studies' suggests that the issue is coming to the fore as we make the shift from modernism to post-modernism. There is more to life than shopping. Efforts to promote active learning for active citizenship must be judged by criteria that indicate (as far as it is possible) well-being rather than wealth.

2. **Performance indicators** encourage us to value what we can measure rather than measure what we value. The sorry tale of the Standard Assessment Targets is a parable for our time. What was designed as a tool for learning was re-engineered as an instrument for social and political control. The flaws in the assessment system have been painstakingly exposed.[16] The single most important performance indicator is the one that enables us to learn from our mistakes. There may be occasions when assessment of learning is valuable, there will always be occasions when assessment *for* learning is essential. In promoting active learning for active citizenship we must acquire and use the tools that promote our capacity to learn from our shared experience.

3. **The economic business model** ignores the world beyond its narrow focus. A reductionist economic model is concerned with nothing but the (economic) bottom line. Financial profit is all. In modernist thinking 'the business of business is business'. In post-modern thinking (or, indeed, medieval thinking) the business of business is not wealth but sustainable well-being. Firms like Shell Oil and Body Shop recognised this when they embraced the 'triple bottom line (TBL)' to promote sustainable development. The TBL measures the *social* and *environmental* impact of their work alongside their financial performance. There is international interest in this approach among local government and business[17] and it is important that the TBL becomes the standard against which we measure our

---

[16] See report from the Assessment Reform Group (2002) *Testing Motivation and Learning*. Cambridge: University of Cambridge Faculty of Education.

[17] ICLEI – Local Governments for Sustainability is an international association of local governments and national and regional local government organisations that have made a commitment to sustainable development. More than 550 cities, towns, counties and their associations in 68 countries comprise ICLEI's growing membership. ICLEI works with these and hundreds of other governments through international performance-based, results-oriented campaigns and programmes. (*Source: Wikipedia*)

performance in promoting active learning for active citizenship. It is also important that we recognise the pioneering role of those businesses that are learning to adopt the TBL, as they have much to teach us.

The government-backed empowerment agenda is a serious sign that we are moving away from the strait-jacket of top-down, short-term modernist thinking towards a culture where we are concerned more with long-term outcomes, participation and global justice. Our efforts will be inevitably patchy and flawed, but there is hope if we develop the capacity to learn continuously and intelligently from our mistakes. We need now to look for potential solutions.

Solutions

We are not starting from scratch. The difference between the situation now and the position a few years ago is that we now have a framework of government policy and organisational experience on which to build. The National Empowerment Partnership offers a network for progress the *Take Part Framework* provides a thought-through platform for developing active learning for active citizenship across sectors; and the work of organisations such as the Association for Citizenship Teaching (ACT) and its members provides the basis for building partnerships across and beyond the education sector. Above all, there is the imaginative and vigorous work of organisations such as CSV Education, the Citizenship Foundation, Changemakers and the Scarman Trust who have already achieved so much. The Post-16 Support Programme promoted by the Quality Improvement Agency (QIA)[18] has already pioneered creative approaches to citizenship education in its sector. The Teacher Development Agency (TDA) through Citized[19] contributes to the development of citizenship teachers. Professional development in citizenship education, however, should no longer be confined to educators, but should be readily available for professionals in the health and social services, as well as educators in schools and colleges.

Policy initiatives such as *Every Child Matters* and *Youth Matters* sit well alongside the empowerment agenda enshrined in the government

---

[18] www.excellencegateway.org.uk/citizenship

[19] www.citized.info

White Paper, *Strong and Prosperous Communities.* There are already networks of professionals engaged in promoting participation,[20] and there are student-led initiatives such as Student Voice (ESSA)[21] and Changemakers. Finally, there has been a systematic move towards intergenerational work.[22]

To move forward we need to do three things to promote active learning for active citizenship across the phases of education and the sectors of community life. We must: (i) Consult, (ii) Act and (iii) Evaluate.

Consult

First, there needs to be a wider and more systematic dialogue between those actively concerned with the potential benefits of active learning for active citizenship as a tool for community development. This should include government, particularly CLG, the Local Government Association and the DCSF[23] whose work includes ensuring that children and young people 'make a positive contribution to society and the economy'. Over recent years, a mass of relevant resources, learning tools and practical experience has been generated. The challenge now is to apply these resources to ensuring that active citizenship becomes a reality across and between sectors.

It should also involve key players in the Third Sector, including those concerned with citizenship education, community development and umbrella organisations such as Councils for Voluntary Service. It is important that the initiative is not wholly owned by any one sector; it must be a partnership between communities and government at local, regional and national levels. This chapter is designed to be a stimulus to such consultation.

A sharp focus for the work is critical. The aim of the initiative is to develop and disseminate a practical commitment to active learning for active citizenship based on identifiable skills that can be learned across sectors. The outputs of the programme will be the shared tools that make this possible.

---

[20] The Participation Workers Network: www.participationworks.org.uk

[21] www.studentvoice.co.uk

[22] www.qca.org.uk/libraryAssets/media/qca-06-2944_aylward_school.pdf. See also *Overcoming Barriers to Intergenerational Engagement:*
www.iahsa.net/malta/programme/21C/Fish_%20Addicott%20_%20Payne_21C.pdf

[23] http://www.dcsf.gov.uk/

Act

The next step is to pilot intergenerational initiatives that bring together schools, colleges and community organisations around the principles of active learning for active citizenship in the context of the government's Action Plan for Community Empowerment. Full account should be taken of the work that has already been achieved in this field. Following the pilot period, effective approaches need to be shared and supported across the regions. The immediate challenge is for the *Take Part Network* to work out with the NEP the most effective way of stimulating and supporting this action in association with local government, schools and colleges and their neighbouring community organisations.

Review

The work needs to be evaluated not just for itself, essential though that is, but against the backdrop of tackling the obstacles described earlier (*Tackling the five obstacles to progress* above). The implications for effective partnerships between government, education and the community sector need to be spelt out and assessed. There will, almost certainly, be consequences for professional training and development, the education curriculum and governance in community sector and local government.

SECTION TWO

ACTIVE LEARNING FOR ACTIVE CITIZENSHIP: REFLECTIONS FROM PRACTICE

CHAPTER SIX

Active Learning for Active Citizenship (ALAC): origins and approaches

VAL WOODWARD

This chapter is a personal narrative by the co-ordinator of the Active Learning for Active Citizenship (ALAC) project and author of the original report (Woodward, 2004), that laid the ground work for its development. This was carried out while seconded to the Civil Renewal Unit at the Home Office, the publishers of the *Active Learning for Active Citizenship* report. That secondment was a part-time one with the author simultaneously continuing to teach, research and provide consultancy services on community work and was extended to allow the policy recommendations in the original report to be put into action through practice. The author should therefore be able to provide considerable insight into ideas embraced within the report and how they were built into the development of the ALAC project.

The starting point was the author's own strong commitment to promoting praxis, linking theoretical discussions to lived experiences and useful research. Concepts underpinning the ALAC report mirrored the personal and professional passions of the author, informed by well-established ideas and current practice. Such a value-laden methodological approach is, of course, contentious yet strongly advocated by many researchers (Truman *et al.*, 2000). While participants in ALAC did engage in discussion about the contested nature of these ideas, with hindsight, there was insufficient opportunity for in-depth reflection and debate during the project's life.

Discussion on drafts of the ALAC report

A draft of the report that was to underpin the subsequent development of ALAC was discussed at a cross-sector planning conference held in Birmingham during October 2003. At this event there was overwhelming support for the underlying value-based approach that was adopted; an empowering community-based approach in an anti-discriminatory framework.

This scene-setting report was subsequently launched at an ALAC conference held on 11 June 2004 in Sheffield. Further conferences were held periodically to facilitate discussion between the hubs, steering group and all other stakeholders. These were held across England, to counter perceptions of government as London-centric.

As stated in the original ALAC report (Woodward, 2004, p.6):

> *Local groups will network in 'learning partnerships', or hubs, and therefore dialogue between all the different scales of operation will be crucial. This is specifically recognising a central theme of this report that local expertise, knowledge and experience should be valued and recognised at all times.*

While the dialogue could have been further strengthened, and more strongly supported through resource and time allocation, participants welcomed even these relatively limited opportunities in principle. For example, as recorded in the ALAC report: (ibid., p.5) the day in Birmingham in 2003:

> *Enabled constructive networking and the subsequent sharing of experience, enthusiasm, commitment and learning.*

A framework for action

The original ALAC report formed the key document framing the ALAC project, as this was then operationalised in practice. As explained in the summary of that report it was commissioned after a large voluntary and community sector organisation, Community Service Volunteers, completed a mapping exercise of relevant government initiatives. Arising from this a cross-government group developed a 'core curriculum'. That cross-government group consisted of those involved in neighbourhood renewal, democratic and constitutional reforms, educational programmes, and 'civil renewal' – (the title of the host unit in the Home Office). The core curriculum that they developed was subsequently adapted and included as an appendix to the original ALAC report, once commissioned and written. However, it was agreed at the first conference held in Birmingham, then consolidated at all subsequent consultation events, that the curriculum should provide a 'light touch' approach so as to reflect the spirit of the ALAC report, allowing for local control and design of programmes of action.

At the same time it was agreed that a national learning framework or set of guidelines would support, inform and influence the development of good practice. In the ALAC report this task was allocated to the steering group but it soon became apparent that a clear lead needed to be taken by practitioners directly involved in the ALAC project. Their conclusions have subsequently been published as the Learning Framework.

A new or different approach?

As stated in the ALAC report (ibid., p.4):

> *Active learning for active citizenship as a concept has been 'stolen' from various sources already embracing such ideas. The phrase is meant to convey a move away from either learning or citizenship being something participants do passively.*

The ideas that a healthy democracy depends on active citizenship and that adult education should encourage this are not new and can be found in government reports at least as far back as 1919 in Britain. Indeed, the mission of the Workers' Educational Association, one of the partners in the ALAC project, has included citizenship as a core principle since 1903, developing ideas advocated by, among others, John Stuart Mill during the nineteenth century.

More recent work by Sir Bernard Crick and David Blunkett (the then Home Secretary) had a strong influence on the development of the ALAC project. In 1998 Sir Bernard Crick claimed that Citizenship Education aimed:

> *... At no less than a change in the political culture of this country. (DfEE, 1998, p.8)*

Sir Bernard Crick, an invaluable member of the ALAC steering group, and David Blunkett, MP, participated in ALAC events. Sir Bernard further claimed that active citizens are those who 'will obey the law, but will seek to change it by legal means if they think it bad, or even if they think it could be better.' (Crick, 2000, p.6) Recognising that ALAC had the potential to neutralise rather than strengthen political dynamics and opposition (Cheney, 1994), the project was designed as part of 'civil' activity rather than civic activities, encouraging participation in a broad sphere of exciting political activity, not just learning how to participate in existing structures. Through ALAC it was hoped that participative processes would be deepened and democratic processes strengthened, building on existing democratic processes, facilitating political literacy and political as well as civic action.

ALAC focuses on active individuals, living in, and contributing to, vibrant communities, building a healthy democracy through learning and reflecting on those activities, and as stated in the ALAC report (Woodward, 2004, p.10):

> *Following on from the work of Sir Bernard Crick and David Blunkett the focus was on citizenship as a capacity within people rather than as citizenship as something people do or do not possess at any one time, in any one place.*

Further, learning for active citizenship should be about people's capacity to be members of a healthy democratic country rather than simply being born with rights conferred through place of birth. Thus being a citizen in Britain rather than just a British citizen (ibid., p.10) reflecting the concerns of Lord Parekh (2000) and others that there was a deep and urgent need to discuss Britishness.

Together We Can

As a people-centred policy and programme of action, ALAC followed a government recognition that:

> *There has been too much emphasis on regenerating the physical environment (rather) than on changing the prospects of people who live there. (SEU, 1998, p.39)*

Despite being an educational initiative ALAC was located at the Civil Renewal Unit, emphasising that the project was about 'people power'.

The vision of the Civil Renewal Unit of the Home Office was 'that of a society in which citizens are inspired to make a positive difference to their communities, and are able to influence the policies and services that affect their lives'. ALAC formed a central part of the emerging Civil Renewal Unit-led *Together We Can* initiative, emphasising that partnership between sectors is essential for sustainable people-centred action. The time seemed right for community groups to really exert influence from the bottom-up.

ALAC was designed on behalf of the government as a joint project between the government and the voluntary and community sectors. The national project's location as part of government created potential tensions, however, relating to long-term debates within the voluntary and community sectors around being 'in and against' the state. This was discussed at consultation events and resulted in strong support for 'positive partnership working strategies' (Woodward, 2004, p.5). As stated later in the ALAC report (2004, p.11):

> *While partnership working can be very difficult, especially if power inequalities between different participants are ignored, it can facilitate positive ways forward.*

As David Blunkett reflected:

> *Democracy is not just an association of individuals determined to protect the private sphere, but a realm of active freedom in which citizens come together to shape the world around them. (Blunkett, 2003)*

Indeed, through ALAC, the British government proved a willingness to experiment with exciting ideas. Too often government is seen as a single block of power, rather than a conglomeration of differing interests with constantly shifting power relationships. As Gary Craig has said, 'the distinction between 'insider' and 'outsider' strategies is in reality rather more complex and dynamic than at first appears' (Craig *et al.*, 2004, p.223).

The design of ALAC embodied an awareness of these complexities, recognising that the state is likely to incorporate such projects primarily to legitimise its actions. Hence the emphasis on grass roots control and attempts to alter power relationships in favour of the less powerful.

Three recommendations for the implementation of ALAC in practice

ALAC was designed to show how an empowering educational approach to active citizenship could contribute to building a stronger democracy and therefore to propose positive ways forward. Evaluation was consequently crucial and formed one of the three recommendations made in the ALAC report.

The first recommendation of the report was:

- That lessons learnt during this first phase be evaluated and fed into a more sustainable and widespread programme of action.

The second recommendation of the report was:

- That voluntary and community sector groups interested and committed to developing active learning for active citizenship be resourced to work within a number of sub-regional 'learning hubs'.

Through this second recommendation participants were to be invited to join in this short-term opportunity to contribute to reflections about longer-term good policy and practice developments, although there was also recognition of Sir Bernard Crick's view that the work of ALAC needed more committed and stable funding. As stated in the ALAC report (Woodward, 2004, p.6):

> *Those who suffer the greatest from short-term funding are already the most vulnerable to social exclusion.*

The third recommendation was:

- That a framework steering group be established, led by the voluntary and community sector, and supported by the Home Office's Civil Renewal Unit, to take these proposals forward.

Too ambitious?

Members of the steering group were chosen for their direct interest and expertise in both active learning and active citizenship. The steering group brought differing government departments together with differing sectors across the voluntary and community domains. The members from government departments reported to politicians via departmental mechanisms, but also through the Civil Renewal Unit *Together We Can* initiative. And senior politicians attended consultation events. Other members of the steering group included leading thinkers and academics in this field.

The project was a complex one, tapping into the diversity and diffusive natures of the voluntary and community sectors, attempting to stimulate joined-up governance and to develop exemplary policy, while also engaging in critical dialogue with everyone concerned. This all relied on the optimism and enthusiasm of every stakeholder.

The ALAC report was overly optimistic about how the steering group could constructively manage the process, specifically claiming that 'members need to be excited, rather than daunted, by the challenges this involves' (ibid., p.6). Each member inevitably brought their own agenda with them to varying extents, further adding to the complexities of designing a coherent project. While this was positive in terms of continual reflection, it exacerbated tensions between action and ideas as these were being implemented in practice.

Everyone involved, including members of the steering group, gave a massive amount in relation to whatever recognition they received for their work, with a large amount being done in participants' own time. Such willingness to enthusiastically develop good programmes of action, despite very limited resources, is typical of the way the grassroots of the voluntary and community sector work. Some of the best examples of good practice and a great deal of policy innovation has come from the voluntary and community sector probably precisely because of the passion, enthusiasm and energy invested. At the same time, community projects are too often saddled with grand objectives and ambitions dooming participants and funding agencies to disappointment, leading to some groups renaming the government initiative 'together we can't'.

Resources

As reported in the *New Statesman*, 'the Home Office has pitted tiny resources, under the co-ordination of one part-time employee, against huge problems including voter apathy, racism and the rebuilding of shattered communities' (Bartlett, 2004, p.31). Because the ALAC project grew out of the ALAC report, rather than being a straightforward political initiative, resource allocation was rather complicated. The steering group agreed to accept the three recommendations in the ALAC report. However, each component of the project then had to apply for funding. Reflecting the reality of habitually working on shoestring budgets across the voluntary and community sector, too little money was applied for to fully realise the component imperatives for action, including insufficient funding to facilitate good networking and full discussions between the various groups and groupings involved. The diversity of the programmes, while central to the project, also raised some inevitable rivalries about differential funding allocations.

Aspirations among participants were very high, with involvement in ALAC tied to hopes for wider changes. This was not a value-free bureaucratic exercise; it was a project infused with high hopes based on strong passions across the voluntary and community sector. The government also invested high hopes in the project despite the relatively small-scale funding and the bureaucratic inertia that made new ways of working extremely difficult to validate and operationalise. It was therefore a difficult project to manage. But it bubbled over with eagerness to explore what worked, what didn't work, why, and what this might mean for the future.

The evaluation process

An external team was appointed with a remit to:

- facilitate self-assessment within each pilot learning hub;
- facilitate the sharing of learning between the hubs; and
- consolidate the lessons learnt from the programme as a whole, so as to facilitate agreement on the terms for a framework for expansion at the end of the programme.

Participants were expected to gain individually and collectively as well as contributing their experiences and expertise to future policy and practice. The ALAC project was therefore designed as an empowering one for participants, developing strong, articulate, independent and informed community activists and community groups, exploiting the potential educational and personal/group developmental opportunities in each and every situation.

Empowerment is a highly contested and problematic concept, yet it is widely used as if its meaning is fixed. Generally an empowering education should aim to build the social capital of citizens so as to strengthen their capacity to influence the worlds they live in, including the consideration of different ways of doing things at both grass-roots level and in partnership with government agencies (Lowndes and Wilson, 2001, p.633). In practice, however, this can include approaches that actually focus upon countering supposed deficits among participants, accepting and not challenging existing power relationships. In contrast, ALAC was premised on the view that participants are not deficient in ability, knowledge and understanding; rather they are positioned in unequal power relationships that block their potential for taking positive actions for change. Empowerment, according to this latter approach, is about actively participating in shifting those blocks rather than being taught how to join in the world as it currently exists. Communities cannot, and should not, be expected to simply 'pull up their socks' and solve all the problems that they experience by themselves. The community and voluntary sectors have consistently promoted the view that changes in power relationships must be included in policy developments. Through ALAC, and particularly through the evaluation of practice at the ALAC hubs, it was hoped that this message might be heard by more powerful individuals and groups.

In practice, however, such messages became rather obscured by the heated debates this caused, mostly because of cynicism that the government could effectively associate itself with such ideas and demands. Ironically, government rhetoric actually did focus on power and inequalities of power within the Civil Renewal Unit, but this was frequently overshadowed by less empowering stances and policies adopted by other sections of government.

The hubs

The second recommendation in the ALAC report was the setting up of seedbeds of empowering educational practice. These localised projects were encouraged to adopt an empowering educational methodology, embracing empowerment as a collective force for change, fighting inequalities and improving democracy.

As outlined in the ALAC report (Woodward, 2004, p.6), 'the first hubs' were:

'Trailblazers' to allow the voluntary and community sector to firm up on what they can do and wish to do, but also for the Government to ascertain the best form of sustained support and involvement.

The word 'hub' was chosen to illustrate concepts of small, localised programmes coming together and relating to a central core through radiating spokes. The hubs were therefore envisaged as active and dynamic structures with the spokes facilitating two-way dialogues.

A national mapping exercise was carried out to help identify existing activities and potential sites for the hubs, although this was limited by time and resources. Also, there was such a breadth and variety of activities happening across the voluntary and community sectors that it would have been impossible to identify everything. The ALAC hubs were therefore initiated at sites of existing good practice where those involved were eager to creatively build and learn from new work related to active learning for active citizenship (ibid., p.6). Other groups were approached but did not secure collective agreement to engage despite individual enthusiasm. Finding the right person or people, at the right time, with the right amount of enthusiasm, energy and influence/power is often very difficult. As stated in the ALAC report:

Different groups are able and willing to participate in practice and policy development at differing times and speeds, and the sheer volume of voluntary and community organisations makes it impossible to involve everyone at all times. (Ibid., p.6)

The structure of each hub was somewhat amorphous. Indeed there was considerable debate about how far the 'spokes' envisaged in the title 'hub' should reach out. Some of the hubs associated themselves with far broader geographical areas than others. Some were based in areas where the population was scattered, while others were based in urban conglomerations of dense habitation.

Likewise, some hubs attempted to create spokes reaching out to a variety of community and voluntary sector groups, while others chose to focus on a few. For example, although they made valiant efforts, it was very difficult for the central core in Exeter to encourage management by a consortium of groups from across the sub region that the hub related to, as those groups were so widely scattered geographically. Moreover, it was also difficult to bring together groups closely associated with small territorial areas, despite the vastly smaller geographical area of the Black Country.

Some hubs were based centrally in a building. Others worked wherever community groups met. The concepts of locality, community and space have been hotly contested within academic literatures (Frazer, 2000) and ALAC allowed such concepts to be used as those leading each hub saw as suitable for their particular locality. It was hoped that the variety of approaches would add to the richness of the lessons gained through the evaluation. As stated in the ALAC report:

> The ways in which community based activities are designed and carried out can be both a strength and a weakness. (Woodward, 2004, p.4)

And:

> Such networks are characterised by diversity, autonomy, voluntary choices and risk. (Ibid., p.6)

Each hub was 'owned' by local stakeholders rather than the government or the national ALAC project. Maximising autonomy reflects an empowering approach. The groups worked together:

> On issues of concern to themselves, their friends, families and communities they identify with. (Ibid., p.4)

Community development involves people doing rather than being done to. As stated in the report this allowed participants to:

> Tap into the creative space between the personal and political dimensions of their lives. (Ibid., p.4)

Improving democracy

According to a research report on political engagement in Britain, it was clear:

> That many of those who say they are uninterested in politics do so because of how they interpret the concept. (Electoral Commission and Hansard, 2005, p.20)

Only a minority link 'politics' with their own personal involvement; it tends to be seen as something done by, and for, others or as a system with which they are not particularly enamoured. (Ibid., p.21)

More than half the public, 54 per cent, feel they know either 'not very much' or 'nothing at all' about politics while barely a majority, 53 per cent, find it of interest and only a minority are politically active (16 per cent). (Electoral Commission and Hansard, 2005, pp.7 and 17)

However:

Twice as many people are very interested in national issues as in politics and even more are very interested in local issues. (Electoral Commission and Hansard, 2005, p.20)

In Britain there is a support for democracy as a principle but not democracy as perceived in everyday lives (Clarke, 2004). 'Contrary to claims of political "apathy", people are interested in the issues that affect them, their families and the world around them' and while most have a strong aspiration to have a say in how the country is run, few feel they have any opportunities for influence (Electoral Commission and Hansard, 2005, pp.23 and 24).

Through the educational processes instigated via ALAC hubs it was hoped to create a greater awareness of how everyday life is indeed political and how political processes can be constructively entered into and improved. Following on from this, it was hoped to increase 'critical literacy', encouraging motivation and interest in deliberation, debate, argument, challenge, evaluation and political action. This was to include political action to change structures and processes of government to make these more inclusive and more responsive. Participants at consultation events strongly reiterated the statement in the ALAC report (Woodward, 2004, p.10):

That there needs to be a more general reconsideration of government structures and practices in order to accommodate a healthier democracy.

As highlighted by the European Commission 'democracies have to create the conditions for an active exercise of citizenship' (European Commission, 2001, p.7).

To do this democracy needs to be an attractive arena of participation. A healthy democracy creates frameworks for citizens to engage with as thinkers, conversationalists and activists. Such a healthy democracy is a politically contested moving ground of ideas and action. A healthy, strong, deep democracy acknowledges power inequalities but encourages citizens individually and collectively to realise what power they have and actively strive to improve their world, according to their values. Participants may well disagree about the nature of a common good and how their worlds need improving, but if they are to live together they need to constantly question and challenge existing taken-for-granted power inequalities and accepted values. The complexities of power and approaches to empowerment underpinned ALAC and this was discussed and accepted by some in government as well as by participants from the community and voluntary sector.

As the major problems we face become more evidently global in nature, democratic processes need to become global. There is therefore an increasing need to nurture and develop active global citizenship and ALAC worked in partnership with agencies such as the Development Education Association on international issues. Work with new citizens to Britain, and on relationships between those new citizens and longer-term residents, formed part of the work at several ALAC hubs. ALAC participants were to be facilitated to reflect on their everyday lives and how these mesh with the everyday lives of others, individually and collectively, locally, regionally, nationally and internationally. Opening up possibilities for changes in one set of power relationships can shed light on ways in which other potential challenges to seemingly insurmountable boundaries can be developed. Democracy demands time, thought and deliberation.

Empowering education

Empowering education seeks to encourage deeper understandings about ways that everyday power relationships can be challenged through individual and collective agency. ALAC was designed so that participants would enter an empowering process that did not stop with their personal educational gains, contributing to community development more broadly, challenging power inequalities and influencing structural change.

As Margaret Mead powerfully stated:

> *Never doubt that a small group of thoughtful, committed citizens can change the world. Indeed, it's the only thing that ever does.*

ALAC owed much to the influence of Paolo Freire (cited in Shor, 1993, p.25):

> *You must be convinced that the fundamental effort of education is to help with the liberation of people, never their domestication. You must be convinced that when people reflect on their domination, they begin a first step in changing their relationship with the world.*

Action and reflection on that action together enhance critical thinking and this affects the ways that people perceive their lives, moving from the helpless recipients of oppressive structures to active agents engaged in rewriting the world. Empowerment is not something that is done to participants, by educators, politicians or others. Rather it takes place through more subtle processes whereby people come to recognise their own situation and develop the ability to do something about it as part of an educational process. Professional educational intervention is needed to open up ways for people to reflect on and develop their agency, but education does not only happen in the formal educational sector. As outlined above, the ALAC project was located at the Civil Renewal Unit (in the Home Office) emphasising people-power, not just education. As part of 'working together', ALAC linked with informal educational groups through a community-based consultancy firm, a local council for voluntary services and a civic forum, but also with the DfES, Higher Education Institutions, the LSC and the Workers' Educational Association.

Support for community education is highly contentious and is unevenly provided across Britain, with a stronger commitment in Scotland than England. In England provision is mostly through non-statutory bodies and has generally been poorly funded. Professional community educators enter into dialogue in an active relationship with learners contributing their own invaluable understandings. Learners are not passive recipients of abstract wisdom – rather they link their every-day life experiences to broader events in the worlds they live in, validating their reality and allowing new insights to be meaningful. Participants link everyday issues to national and global issues at their

114

own pace, reflecting on the political nature of the situations that they wish to change. ALAC was firmly located within a community development tradition of informal empowering education seeking alterations in power relationships.

Community educators have long advocated that people learn most effectively from their peers and through involvement in action, rather than through abstraction in the classroom, developing critical situations for them to enact, and thus providing a lived experience of the problem under discussion. The ALAC report therefore emphasised that:

> 'Learning and teaching styles' should be 'very different from traditional approaches. The emphasis should be 'on learning being flexible, useful and fun.' (Woodward, 2004, p. 7)

Such an approach was also adopted at ALAC events, creating some tensions for those used to a more staid government style. Some found it difficult to accept that a lively participative dance, where, for example, some even took their shoes off, was a legitimate activity for a government sponsored project. Others there from various sections of government embraced such activities with eager alacrity, however.

Similar tensions were created by the design of workshops. Most participants wished to focus on conversation and dialogue and to engage in active learning. They therefore expected workshops to involve the sharing of everyone's ideas rather than relying on expert input. The mainstream-accepted way of running workshops, however, is to expect participants to listen to, and then question, an expert.

Such differing expectations are so embedded in the practice of the different sectors that neither expected controversy. This highlights a form of hidden power prioritising accepted ways of thinking and doing. The community sector generally lost out, reflecting power imbalances. For the mainstream to experiment with different ways to do things, a hidden and powerful set of beliefs have to be challenged. Individual participants in ALAC from the mainstream educational sectors and other parts of the government generally displayed a willingness to do this. Despite a widespread cynicism about those who are 'in' the state, many are there because they wish to create improvements and change, questioning dominant mainstream ways of doing things rather than always accepting whatever is dominant in the mainstream at any one specific time.

The ALAC hubs worked with communities, or groups of people who came together because members identified collective interests. As the ALAC report agreed:

> *Learning for citizenship is dependent on a feeling of belonging and collective experience. (Ibid., p.11)*

While it is far easier for policy development and practice intervention to work with communities as if they exist as fixed entities, Lord Parekh (2000) and others have emphasised the need to understand that citizens in Britain form multiple identities. Citizens themselves define the multiple and fluid communities they engage with, linking into complex and dynamic networks of interaction and identity, which is one reason why the communities engaging with each of the ALAC hubs were so varied, sometimes relating to small geographical locations, at other times to much broader shared histories, experiences or identities. As Alison Gilchrist, a member of the ALAC steering group has written (2004, p.6):

> *These change; they overlap and embody sometimes contradictory loyalties. Communities reflect local circumstances and are shaped by events at home and abroad. We fashion our personal identity from a kaleidoscope of our own and other people's behaviour. We explore similarities and differences through our relationship with others, setting up broad, but shifting ideas of who we are.*

Community Education across Britain embraces a wide variety of community groups but empowering community education involves such groups in learning about the world around them. Social, political and intellectual capital needs to be built so as to empower local citizens to analyse their current situation and develop plans of action. The ALAC report stated that:

> *Learning about active citizenship will therefore focus on the hidden inequalities in power surrounding everyone and affecting their life chances. (Woodward, 2004, p.11)*

Acquiring skills is therefore not enough to promote Active Learning for Active Citizenship and:

> *Indeed, may even obscure and exacerbate issues of inequality. (Ibid., p.11)*

Fighting inequalities

Inequalities are so well hidden within the common-sense rationality of our society that they can be, and frequently are, dismissed and ignored, thus perpetuating power inequalities. Neutrality therefore leads to complicity with the powerful. ALAC resisted neutrality; instead, it was hoped initiatives making up the ALAC project would expose hidden inequalities and that such a process would be validated as essential within the dynamics of a vigorous democratic society. While inequalities are difficult to shift, citizens have agency that can make a contribution to change in our worlds from the local to the global levels. We simultaneously experience numerous interrelated but diverse power relationships throughout every aspect of our lives. While empowerment processes cannot eliminate unequal power relations, they can make their exercise more visible and therefore open to democratic processes of change.

As stated in the ALAC report (ibid., p.12):

> Inequalities in society create barriers for most people that community education and development workers are experienced and skilled in enabling those joining in community-based activities to overcome.

Informal learning is especially valuable among groups who do not unproblematically fit with the mainstream and who face barriers through tangible inequalities, such as caring responsibilities or language, or less tangible, often hidden inequalities, such as feelings of marginalisation and powerlessness. Instead, ALAC was designed around transformative empowerment. By understanding better the inequalities that exist and how they are held in place, social, intellectual and political capital can be built encouraging groups of people to enter democratic processes of change.

> The learning we engage in cannot be isolated from relations of power; it is integral to those relations. It would be wrong to conclude that learning can be classified unequivocally as either emancipatory or oppressive. The privileging of some forms of knowledge, attitudes and practices over others has been identified as central to the means by which the dominance of some interests in society over others is consented to, rather than forcibly imposed. (Gramsci, 1971)

117

ALAC's educational programme was designed to encourage citizens to understand inequalities better so that they could more positively act to change them if they chose. As stated in the ALAC report (Woodward, 2004, p.11): 'citizens need to understand power'.

Also included in the ALAC report is the statement that:

> *Providing education for and encouraging active citizenship needs to actively challenge exclusionary attitudes and practices, not just guard against excluding groups of people. Reflection and critical consciousness must be encouraged at all times to instigate challenges to the unacceptable nature of some political activity associated with extremist groups such as the British National Party. (Ibid., p. 13)*

As the Reiffers Report (Commission of the European Communities, 1997) suggests, citizenship is closely related to the kind of society and polity we want to live in. Fighting inequalities underpinned the whole ALAC enterprise, in contrast to the claim by Lord Parekh and others that inequalities are generally ignored within mainstream literatures on citizenship (Barnes and Shaw, 2000; Parekh, 2000; Sayce, 2001).

As already stated, several hubs worked with groups of citizens new to Britain and challenged any tensions with their longer established neighbours, one focused on working with people with learning disabilities and another with women. Such work was designed to strengthen the active citizenship of such groups. Empowerment can only complement top-down policy initiatives to lessen more material inequalities. Empowering active citizenship among such groups recognises power inequalities but also the wealth of existing political activity that is too frequently under-recognised because a narrow definition of politics is used. This is strongly influenced by the way active citizenship is defined and therefore how sectors of society are perceived 'as citizens' (Gaventa *et al.*, 2002, p.5). ALAC embraced a broad definition of politics that tied active citizenship into the broad sphere of civil politics and everyday action.

Conclusion

The Active Learning for Active Citizenship project therefore aimed to lessen inequalities through long-term change rather than instant solutions. ALAC created spaces within the mainstream for alternative ways of seeing and doing to thrive. Participants and other stakeholders were to enter an educational process that created benefits for themselves at the same time as challenging taken-for-granted aspects of their lives and subsequently working to alter inequalities in power. Active citizens were actively learning, utilising collective spaces to create a healthier civil society, change unhealthy governance practices and further strengthen democratic society.

Participants claimed positive learning outcomes for themselves, their families and their communities. At a policy level ALAC was held up as an example of good practice from which others could learn. The ideas underpinning the ALAC project could therefore certainly be seen to be both useful and powerful.

However, the tensions created by bringing together a crowd of highly charged workers who depended so strongly on a commitment to what they were doing, were not addressed sufficiently. This made designing a truly cohesive set of plans for the government to work with, once the project was finished, fairly impossible, despite so much excellent work being carried out at the hubs, highlighted in the Evaluation and captured in the templates forming the Learning Framework. The government therefore failed to fully take on board the stated aim in the ALAC report 'to ascertain the best form of sustained support and involvement' (Woodward, 2004, p.10).

Encouraging local autonomy inevitably creates tensions for overall paths of development and does not easily mesh with central policy development. Processes of praxis, bringing together research, policy and practice are extremely complex and this small-scale project probably lacked the capacity to fully develop the ideas underpinning it. The synergy and tensions between policy development, radical thinking and concrete action proved difficult. ALAC has perhaps not had the strong and clear long-term influence hoped for, but it was a very good try and has had impact.

As Paulo Freire said (1974, p.41):

> The insistence that the oppressed engage in reflection on their concrete situation is not a call to armchair revolution. On the contrary, reflection – true reflection – leads to action. On the other hand, when the situation calls for action, that action will constitute an authentic praxis only if its consequences become the object of critical reflection ... otherwise action is pure activism.

The ALAC report contained three underlying principles and three recommendations:

- That lessons learnt during this first phase be evaluated and fed into a more sustainable and widespread programme of action.
- That voluntary and community sector groups interested and committed to developing active learning for active citizenship be resourced to work within a number of sub-regional 'learning hubs'.
- That a framework steering group be established, led by the voluntary and community sector, and supported by the Home Office's Civil Renewal Unit.

These were met and ALAC succeeded in showcasing very positive ways to go forward in terms of improving democracy, empowering education and fighting inequalities, revitalising the public life of communities as an arena of deliberation, learning and action, unleashing the potential for everyone to participate in the promotion of social justice from the bottom-up. Also ALAC contributed, albeit to a small extent, to a redesign of the state's ways of doing things, strengthening the Civil Renewal Unit's ability to recognise the value of non-mainstream thinking and action. It is not really surprising that such a small-scale project failed to immediately change the worlds in which it operated. Although it is sad that the lessons do not seem to have had an immediate and obvious overall impact or to be widely accepted or implemented, a small dent has been made in the powerful contemporary mainstream. Cynicism too often prevents people from constructively grabbing opportunities or believing in the possible cumulative effects of small-scale movements. Change from the bottom-up is intrinsically small scale, although this can be cumulative for the long term. ALAC might be seen as a powerful community development project, exploiting contemporary spaces in government and civil sectors of society to promote just such incremental change for the longer-term.

References

Barnes, M. and Shaw, S. (2000) 'Older People, Citizenship and Collective Action' in Warnes, T., Warren, L. and Nolan, M. (eds), *Care Services in Later Life*. London: Jessica Kingsley

Bartlett, K. (2004) 'A Good Citizen Is No Longer Good Enough.' *New Statesman,* 7 June, 30–31

Blunkett, D. (2003) *Civil Renewal – A new agenda* (Edith Kahn Memorial Lecture), CSV. London: Home Office

Cheney, P. (1994) 'Decentralisation and local control' in *Concept: Journal of Contemporary Community Education Practice Theory,* Vol. 4, No. 2

Clarke, J. (2004) Dissolving the public realm? *Journal of Social Policy,* Vol. 33, No. 1, pp. 27–45

Commission of the European Communities (1997) *Accomplishing Europe through Education and Training: Report of the study group on education and training (Reiffers Report).* Luxembourg Office for Official Publications of the EC

Craig, G. Taylor, M. and Parkes, T. (2004) 'Protest or Partnership? The Voluntary and Community Sectors in the Policy Process', *Social Policy and Administration,* Vol. 38, No. 3, June

Crick, B. (2000) *Essays on Citizenship.* London: Continuum

DfEE (1998) *Education for Citizenship and the Teaching of Democracy in Schools: Final report of the Advisory Group on Citizenship.* London: QCA

Electoral Commission and Hansard (2005) *An Audit of Political Engagement 2.* London: Electoral Commission and Hansard

European Commission (2001) *Report of the Working Group on Broadening and Enriching the Public Debate on European Matters* (Rapporteurs: B. Caremier and J. Wyles). Brussels: EC

Frazer, E. (2000) 'Citizenship education: anti-political culture and political education in Britain,' *Political Studies* Vol. 88, No. 1, pp. 88–103

Freire, P. (1974) *Education for Critical Consciousness.* Lanham, MD: Sheed and Ward

Gaventa, J., Howard, J. Sharkland, A. (2002) 'Making Rights Real: Exploring citizenship, participation and accountability', *IDS Bulletin,* Vol. 33, No. 2

Gilchrist, A. (2004) *The Well Connected Community.* Bristol: Policy Press

Gramsci, A. (1971) *Selections from the Prison Notebooks.* London: Lawrence and Wishart

Lowndes, V. and Wilson, D. (2001) 'Social Capital and Local Governance', in *Political Studies,* Vol. 49, No. 4, pp. 629–646

Parekh, B. (2000) *The Future of Multi-Ethnic Britain.* London: Runnymeade Trust

Sayce, L. (2001) *From Psychiatric Patient to Citizen.* London: Macmillan

SEU (1998) *Bringing Britain Together: A national strategy for neighbourhood renewal.* London: HMSO

Shor, I. (1993) 'Education is Politics: Paolo Freire's Critical Pedagogy.' In McLaren, T. and Leonard, P. (eds), *Paolo Freire: A Critical Encounter.* London: Routledge

Truman, C., Mertens, D. and Humphries, B. (2000) *Research and Inequality.* London: UCL Press

Woodward, V. (2004) *Active Learning for Active Citizenship in the Voluntary and Community Sector.* London: Civil Renewal Unit/Home Office

CHAPTER SEVEN

Learning from the ALAC hubs

ALISON ROOKE

As the previous chapter has illustrated, the ALAC programme was initiated following a literature review and mapping exercise to identify relevant learning programmes in the voluntary and community sector, recognising and valuing the knowledge, expertise and understanding of those directly involved in work at local levels (Woodward, 2004). While this mapping exercise provided no more than a snapshot in a dynamic and constantly changing scene, this was sufficient to identify a wealth of approaches, working with a range of groups and communities. The mapping exercise enabled the sub-regional learning networks or 'hubs' to be identified, to build upon previous learning. These hubs were proposed 'where it is known that community-based groups in partnership with others are able and willing to initiate new work on active learning for active citizenship once resources are made available' (ibid., p.6).

These hubs were selected to reflect the experiences and approaches adopted in different regions, within different social and economic contexts, to facilitate comparisons and contrasts. They were also selected to encompass diversity in terms of the learners and learning priorities. There was a particular emphasis upon facilitating the participation of marginalised, disadvantaged and oppressed minority communities, including: black and ethnic minority communities as well as white British communities; women from disadvantaged groups; people with disabilities including people with learning disabilities; migrant workers, refugees and asylum seekers. There was early recognition too that learning for active citizenship needs to be envisaged as wider by far. ALAC was not based upon a deficit model of citizenship education – pouring knowledge into a minority of supposedly inadequate individuals and communities. Professionals and policy-makers, in common with the rest of the population, stand to benefit from ALAC, including learning how to develop strategies to promote social solidarity and social justice, challenging inequalities as well as learning how to listen to those whose voices have been less heard.

This chapter describes the hubs' work in detail, setting out their approaches to learning, the hubs' partners and the diverse groups of learners. It will then summarise the outcomes from the ALAC hubs and the overall learning that has been shared between them. It has been on the basis of these lessons that the Take Part programme has been developed, encompassing the learning developed by each of these ALAC hubs, as the building blocks for the Take Part local pathfinders.

The ALAC hubs

The first hubs that were identified and funded in 2004 were the South Yorkshire Hub based in Sheffield, the West Midlands hub based in Wolverhampton, and the Greater Manchester Hub. Each of these had different approaches to learning, that included teach-ins, accredited training, short courses tailor-made in response to local groups' requests, residentials, international study visits, and university accredited modules, together with the development of networks providing support for those involved in participation and leadership, offering opportunities for ongoing peer-to-peer learning.

The South Yorkshire Hub

Based in Sheffield, this was a partnership between the Workers' Educational Association (WEA) and Northern College, an adult residential college near Barnsley. Both of these organisations are well-established providers of adult community education, and have worked together over many years. Much of this work has had an international perspective, with courses focusing on local economic regeneration and Europe, migration and racism. The South Yorkshire Hub maintained this tradition, providing a wide range of learning opportunities, often at short notice, to local groups and organisations. The South Yorkshire Hub has sponsored weekly teach-ins at the College on 'Issues that Matter': Palestine, Aids, Asylum, Liberia and Roma in Europe. Attended mainly by college students as an 'extra' to their programmes, the meetings have also been a way of intro-ducing non-college learners to an adult residential college environment, giving them an opportunity to both present their case to a wider audi-ence (Africans have talked for instance about living in Sheffield) and consider taking up the wider programme offered by the College. Other College learning events have been directly supported by the hub includ-ing residentials on 'Combating Racism', 'Living in the UK' and 'Black Britons'; workshops on 'Why vote?', and international adult education seminars for practitioners and activists. Working together, the College and the WEA ran a six-month programme on Migration and Europe, with evening sessions in Sheffield, a two-night residential at the College and a study visit to Glokala, a people's high school in Malmo, Sweden.

The College has long had links with the European people's high school movement, but it was the hub that made this programme possible. Participants came from refugee organisations, the local racial equality council, school support workers, and officers from a primary care trust and housing provider. The programme – 'Home is Where the Heart is' – looked at contemporary EU issues, including the impact of the 'No' vote in the French and Dutch EU referendums, the implications of Turkey's application for membership, and the rise of right-wing sentiment across the continent. While in Malmo, the group met refugee and asylum seekers, and visited adult education and community projects that encour-aged community cohesion. The group went on to write a report to be circulated to relevant organisations in order to influence local policy and practice.

As part of its continuing commitment to internationalism, the College, again supported by the hub, has been working with gypsy and traveller groups, researching EU and specifically Hungarian policies towards Roma communities. This included a study visit to Hungary in mid-March 2006, hosted by the Civil College in Kunbabony, to gather information useful to citizenship, education, employment and cultural programmes in the UK. In common with the other hubs, the work of this hub is being taken forward in the Take Part programme.

The West Midlands Hub

Based in Wolverhampton, this is a community-based hub linking Wolverhampton Asian Women and Diabetes Group, Working for Change and Fircroft College. This hub worked with diverse women, exploring innovative and creative ways of encouraging them to get involved in communities and public life. The hub's work was initially delivered through the IMPACT programme which offered accredited training and support around power, participation and leadership, together with a network that offered encouragement, skill sharing, information and mutual support. One of the important messages to emerge from this hub has been that many women have a thirst for the increased confidence, skills and knowledge needed to equip them to make a difference, be involved and be taken seriously. A key feature of this hub's work has been the flexibility of delivery which has been developed with full considera-tion of the barriers and responsibilities facing women, who most often shoulder the burden of domestic life.

IMPACT has a community-based approach working with a diverse group of women from across the Black Country, exploring innovative and creative ways of encouraging women to get active in their commu-nities and public life. The course works by supporting women to value and develop their skills, knowledge and experience, identify shared experiences and common issues and understand more about how power relationships work, and how politics and structures affect everyday life. The hub has concentrated upon providing citizenship courses for women, especially but not exclusively women from black and ethnic minority communities, thereby creating safe spaces where women can explore issues around diversity and difference, looking at ways of working together to influence decisions that affect them. The course itself consisted of a sequence of learning sessions, two residential weekends at Fircroft College, a trip to Parliament in London and a visit to the European Parliament. It was complemented with the provision of individual advice and guidance on educational pathways by Fircroft College.

Women from the courses found the experience invaluable, both in terms of challenging barriers and power structures and changing their views of the world around them. Additionally, paying for caring and travel costs and providing courses that are delivered flexibly has been critical, given that women typically shoulder the burden of domestic life in the country – no matter what their culture might be. The IMPACT course recognised that consideration of fairly straightforward matters such as transport can make a huge difference to women's experience and learning as the following participant describes here: 'Taxis were arranged for me – I hadn't gone out of the house by myself for 10 years – I got back to (me) as a person – it was a big, big confidence boost.' The work of the

West Midlands hub continues, including participating in the Take Part local pathfinder programme.

The Greater Manchester Hub

This was initially based around the delivery of a Manchester Metropolitan University (MMU) module in community audit and evaluation. This hub offers opportunities to work towards professional qualifications in youth and community work at various levels. Partners included regeneration partnerships, Community Pride, Groundwork and residents groups. The hub's offerings include teaching research, evaluation and audit skills to enable community members as individuals and as part of a community group to do these for themselves. This has included: identifying the requirements for effective volunteering; evaluating a Healthy Living Network; exploring who is involved in different types and levels of decision-making; and looking at the appropriateness of NHS services for women experiencing domestic violence. Three new university modules have been developed and are being delivered both within the university and in community settings as a result of the work of the hub. Recruitment of participants has been through existing organisations such as Women's Aid, the Third Sector Coalition and Community Forums. The training has been delivered in a variety of community venues alongside participatory research and evaluation.

The Manchester hub's work has included the Gender and Community Engagement (GEM) project which carries out research and makes recommendations for gender balanced community engagements, as well as developing and delivering gender awareness training. So, for example, Asian women carried out research into barriers to Asian women's participation in local formal community engagement structures. The hub's work has also included a School for Participation and a Healthy Living Network which has brought together local people to address health inequalities and promote healthy living. Recently a conflict resolution forum has developed. This has been working with parents who identify and research local community conflicts and practice conflict resolution skills in these local contexts. As this participant stated:

> *We have all dealt with certain issues within the community and learning mediation skills has helped us to resolve issues in the community, violence between people. We are now able to take a step back from a situation and look at things from different perspectives.*

127

Following on from this, new university modules have been written based on ALAC's work. Furthermore, a team of trainers has requested more training in ALAC work facilitation, and this has resulted in the development of a 'Training the Trainers' module. Trainers have run seminars at the university for community group members and academics on conflict resolution.

There are valuable lessons being learnt here about the benefits of participatory planning, learning, and evaluation. One of the key features of this hub's work has been the ways in which participants have often been engaged in a cycle of action and reflection. In this way analysis of practice is as much a part of the learning process as in formal workshop and teaching sessions. Furthermore lessons have been learnt about increasing the capacity for both individuals and groups to engage with local participative structures at neighbourhood, regeneration and local policy levels.

In addition to continuing work via the Take Part local pathfinder programme, from 2008 Manchester Metropolitan University has been participating in a cluster, led by the University of Lincoln, along with Goldsmiths, University of London – to promote research capacity building in the Third Sector. This is part of a five year national programme of research capacity building, supported by the Economic and Social Research Council, the Office of the Third Sector and the Barrow Cadbury Trust. There are significant opportunities here for building upon the learning from the ALAC programme, strengthening research in relation to learning for active citizenship.

The South West Hub

Based in Exeter, this was led by Exeter Council for Voluntary Service in partnership with local carers' groups, mental health advocacy groups and the Devon Learning Disability Team. The South West hub has a particular focus on promoting civil renewal by empowering some of the most excluded people to speak up for themselves and their issues, in order to influence the planning and delivery of services in their communities and to take an active role in community development. Exeter Council of Voluntary Service has developed particular expertise in providing 'Speaking Up' courses to enable people with learning disabilities, physical disabilities and mental health issues to make their voices heard effectively. This has led to the provision of courses for carers, as well as providing inputs to training programmes for professionals, including the police, thereby enabling them to listen more effectively. This hub has also included Cornwall Neighbourhoods for Change, the Plymouth Community Partnership, Plymouth Guild, and Students and Refugees Together supporting the integration and social inclusion of asylum seekers, refugees and black and minority ethnic groups through mentoring and cultural activity. Plymouth-based initiatives include training opportunities for social workers, placed with community organisations and groups. The work continues to be developed via the Take Part programme.

The London Hub

This has been based in the Civic Forum, the organisation that facilitates participation London-wide, engaging with the Greater London Authority and related bodies. In partnership with Birkbeck College, University of London, the hub has been providing courses for representatives and activists from a wide range of community organisations and groups including black and ethnic minority groups, people belonging to faith communities, suburban residents, members of lesbian, gay, bisexual and transgender communities, and older people, as well as for professionals and volunteers who work with them. Like Greater Manchester, this hub has also been offering accreditation and opportunities to learners to access higher education programmes. Accredited cross-community learning and dialogue has been taking place at Birkbeck College in community leadership sessions jointly led by participants, Birkbeck academics and London Civic Forum staff. London Civic Forum hosts complementary active learning sessions at locations around the capital, for participants and governance officials (including elected representatives) to engage with each other. The emphasis was on drawing on participants' existing knowledge and experience of community work to create a learning programme, while highlighting the wider governance structures in which this work is situated. Networks, skills and contacts gained by participants have been used to benefit their wider communities, and to increase levels of engagement with local, regional and national governance. Cross-community partnerships have also been established and several former participants have subsequently been elected to London's Civic Forum council (the organisation's policy-making body). Here too, the work continues to be developed via the Take Part programme.

The East Midlands Hub

Based in the Lincolnshire Citizenship Network and led by the University of Lincoln, this hub works in partnership with a diversity of voluntary sector project managers, Integration Lincolnshire, the local Crime Reduction and Disorder Partnership, Local Education Authorities, Boston College and the Church of England. The hub has involved organisations from the entire county. There have been contacts with representatives from more than 50 local organisations, including voluntary sector organisations, statutory sector managers, community workers and volunteers. Core partners have included a range of networks, agencies and organisations such as Voluntary Organisation Community Action Lincolnshire (VOCAL), the Crime, and Disorder Reduction Partnership, local educational authorities, Integration Lincolnshire, Boston College, Lincolnshire Development, COMPAC, Lincoln Dioceses and Community Development Lincolnshire.

The Lincolnshire ALAC Hub has been working from the principle that while citizens have the potential competence and capacity to identify issues and injustices in their communities and to work collectively to help resolve these, a process of learning and inquiry may help support and extend them. Within ALAC's principles and values the Lincolnshire hub developed a framework that recognised the need for catalysts to support self-organising and self-constructed communities.

Individuals and groups of learners were engaged as catalysts. Different collective learning experiences (workshops, seminars, conferences) permitted the gradual evolution of a network of learners. This process had the additional intention of increasing community connectivity, enabling learners to create their own networks and capabilities for observation, reflection and action. The Lincolnshire project sought to develop two strands simultaneously through this process; firstly individual learning that constituted the public domain and civil society, and secondly the improvement of community structures (that is, the networks, capabilities and responsiveness of collective provision).

The project made use of, and extended, an existing network – 'The Lincolnshire Citizenship Network' – and the services of tutors from the university who facilitated this network. The network consisted of approximately 30 people from many community organisations who had met at annual events over a couple of years to explore citizenship themes. These themes have included work in schools on citizenship and organisational citizenship. Several 'activators' from this network emerged as key champions for the ALAC project and invested much time and effort to collaboratively shape the form that the ALAC Project took in Lincolnshire.

In addition to citizenship capacity building through workshops and seminars and supporting learning related to crime prevention by bringing generations together, this hub has developed expertise in working with migrant agricultural workers in this region, an extremely vulnerable group, with particular barriers due to language issues and shift working. The work of this hub has facilitated the enrolment of migrants at the Boston College and also supported their retention. Community workshops have been held at the University of Lincoln, with a focus on new learners not currently engaged with the university. A new language provision course for ALAC participants was provided in Boston while the Faculty of Business and Law at the University of Lincoln designed a post-graduate programme in Community Learning and Organisational Development (focused on the voluntary sector). Through this process several distinct themes have developed over time. Each has been supported by the ALAC facilitators to build up internal 'conversations' about citizenship in these spheres and encourage participants' self-reflection and analysis of activity. The themes explored in these learning processes included: Citizens and their relationship to the National Health Service; the inter-relations between citizens of different generations, what citizenship means for migrant workers and host communities; and building a stronger active citizenry within the voluntary and community sector.

In addition to playing a key role in the Take Part programme, the University of Lincoln is leading the research capacity building cluster to strengthen research in the Third Sector, focusing upon active learning for active citizenship.

The Tees Valley Hub

This has been led by SkillShare, a well-established community-based training organisation in Hartlepool, alongside the Tees Valley LSC, Adult Education, the five boroughs of the Tees Valley (Darlington, Hartlepool, Middlesbrough, Stockton, and Redcar), and a number of other voluntary and community organisations in the area including organisations that represent carers. In Tees Valley, the hub has worked with or had contact with 410 local organisations. This hub has had a particular focus upon promoting citizenship skills and learning opportunities at neighbourhood level and expanding learning opportunities aimed specifically at carers. Five local citizenship partnerships have been established, one in each borough. Each is now tailoring their work to local priorities. For example, Hartlepool provided residents with the opportunity to find out how the local authority works, in order to promote more effective participation and Darlington has focused upon equality and diversity issues. This hub has been developing innovative ways of using information technology to support and enable young and isolated carers to be more active in decision-making. Here too, the work of the hub is being taken forward via the Take Part programme.

Active learning in the hubs

At the heart of the ALAC process has been a spirit of openness which has aimed to offer opportunities for active citizenship learning to all. This has meant that significant numbers of participants from 'hard to reach' groups have benefited from ALAC, including: significant numbers of people with mental and physical health conditions that affect people's ability to attend; people with care responsibilities; people with learning difficulties; people with physical disabilities; and those facing the challenges associated with being refugees and migrant workers. At the end of the government-sponsored programme in March 2006, over a thousand learners had participated in ALAC programmes. Of these, 270 participants had gained accreditation and gone on to further and higher education, 292 participants had attained accreditation, 22 participants were on the way to achieving this and 161 participants had significantly improved their employment prospects. These figures were expected to increase as the impact of participation in ALAC spread outwards.

While these statistics give some idea of the impact of ALAC on the participants' lives they are less adequate in more qualitative terms, however. The ongoing progression of ALAC participants has been considerable and diverse, particularly when considering the variety of participants' starting points. Examples of formal progression have included participants training as trainers, registering for graduate teaching programmes and undertaking foundation degrees in community and voluntary sector management. Individuals have reconsidered the relevance of their previous study and qualifications.

This impact has also multiplied out as family, friends and colleagues have been encouraged to study. One of the hidden impacts of the hubs has been the way that professional and stable learning processes have been established for participants, some of whom have been away from learning for considerable periods of time. In several hubs, participants from early cohorts have progressed into shaping or helping to facilitate the later cohorts of the ALAC programme. For example, participants in the West Midlands have gone on to establish 'Impact Plus', an organisation where women can reflect on their active citizenship in their communities and continue the hub's work. This has included training as trainers and delivering citizenship themed courses and workshops to women and black and minority ethnic communities in the West Midlands. The following paragraphs sketch out some of the more qualitative accounts that illustrate the impact of the ALAC hub's work. The longer term impact of all of the hubs was still being realised as the effects of active citizenship were multiplying out from the individual, to family and friends, to groups, to communities and to neighbourhoods.

One of the central features of ALAC has been the numerous ways in which participants have become more involved in civic life. This has encompassed becoming involved in volunteering for the first time and becoming more involved in volunteering with an emphasis on citizenship, becoming activists, getting involved in community groups and systems of governance and influencing service delivery. Many participants went on to take up positions in community groups/organisations and became more involved in public decision-making. In this process they have developed influence and leadership skills while developing a greater understanding of governance structures and policy. So, for example, in London many participants were active already, but 56 per cent of participants reported greater contact with local or central government, or greater contributions to public decision-making, while 46 per cent reported increased involvement in networks. In Lincolnshire, through participation in ALAC, three participants who were migrant workers became informal community leaders, supporting others facing similar poor work and living conditions. Due to this activity the experiences of subsequent migrants have been improving. As one participant stated, 'new immigrants recognise that life has been easier for them'. Three of the participants recruited friends in the factories where they work. As another reflected, 'I think the project has been good for me; it has given me opportunities and I want the same for my friends.'

133

In the West Midlands, through Impact Plus, participants have used their own language skills to initiate voluntary work with refugee children. This included developing work with girls around self confidence. They also used the knowledge gained through ALAC to support women not born in this country to understand British citizenship and governance systems. Through more formal volunteering, participants have become more active in civil and civic society, for example, working with a voluntary organisation planning a research project to talk to women's groups about health issues, encouraging asylum seekers with medical qualifications to enrol on appropriate courses to enable them to work within the NHS and thus fill gaps in NHS services, helping young people and starting a new project for 13–17 year olds, and for 18–35 year olds with help from church members and local people. Other participants have gone on to contribute to obtaining funding for a drugs awareness programme, organising exchange visits between groups of Asian women with diabetes, and getting involved in organising action around sex trafficking.

One of the overarching themes has been the ways in which participants have become engaged as individuals, and in addition have become more organised, knowledgeable and effective as members of groups and organisations when engaged in community activities. A small sample of the many examples here include participants becoming volunteers in their own neighbourhood to identify local issues around the environment, for example neighbourhood action to save trees, becoming involved around supporting young people who are representatives on committees in understanding their role, and organising estate-based activities such as neighbourhood watch and family fun days.

Many of the ALAC participants went on to gain employment, too. And, through participation in ALAC, participants' relationships to existing work also changed. After recognising their own skills and capabilities, many of the participants' employment aspirations were raised and employment prospects were significantly improved. So, for example, one participant left university with a degree but thought she had no recognisable skills. Participation in the ALAC training course helped her to recognise her skills and direct her to a new job in community work. Another participant had worked in clerical work before being out of work and living on disability benefits for ten years. After being involved in ALAC she went on to be employed in a management role. Other examples include participants becoming sessional staff at a local community hospital signposting people to appropriate services, and referring patients to the Patient Advisory Liaison service. The following quotation illustrates the experience of a participant who went on to become a school governor:

> I am going to different meetings and becoming more involved – now a School Governor – had been asked before but always steered away from it in the past – but now I feel as if I know a bit more about governance – what it is and what it is supposed to be, knowing the system a bit more. I have been doing it for two months now and feel very comfortable. I am a Community Governor and had to go through the nomination and election process. I now do performance management with the Head and another Governor.

One of the notable outcomes of the ALAC programme has been the way in which participants as individuals and as part of community groups have used the skills and knowledge that they have gained to volunteer as trainers, thereby passing on their knowledge and skills.

Others have become involved in improving service developments. By taking part in ALAC courses participants have been able to contribute to improved service delivery and development. As the following quote by a user involvement co-ordinator in the South West explains:

> The Speaking Up course has been instrumental in equipping users with the motivation, self-confidence and skills to participate in meetings, and to make a positive contribution. Most of these events, such as meetings with professionals or interview panels, can be very intimidating. Entering a room full of professionals and sitting at the same table with them can be very daunting for all parties involved, but for users in particular, and create a huge barrier to effective participation. The same goes for jargon and meeting format, and it's only through continued user involvement and support of users that the meetings are gradually becoming more 'user-friendly' and thereby effective.

Participants have volunteered in primary care settings, running fitness classes and stop smoking sessions. Carers have gone on to become peer group representatives in health and social services matters and have contributed to training social workers at a local university. Participants have also gone on to carry out organisational health checks with a drop-in project for homeless young people.

Finally it is also worth noting that participants have learnt about and become more involved in governance structures. This has included learning about the roles and responsibilities of elected officials from a local to European level and about how to communicate with such representatives. Participants have also gone on to hold one or more positions of responsibility and influence within their communities. In London, nine participants on the London hub's programme were subsequently elected to London Civic Forum's Council, which sets organisational policy and is the organisation's forum for engagement with London's governance, including the Greater London Authority. These have included becoming: a bid assessor for a New Deal for Communities area; a representative on a regional and national residents' forum; the chair of a local women's development agency; the chair of a parent and teachers' association; a member of a youth education forum; a school governor and special educational needs governor; the chair of a women's voluntary organisation; a board member of a diabetes group (in the role of company secretary); the vice-chair of a patients' forum; and a community forum committee member (subsequently instrumental in getting a local learning centre built).

The learning and achievements of participants in civic and civil life is a testament to the wealth of approaches, knowledge, expertise and understanding of those directly involved in ALAC work across the hubs, at the local level. The ALAC programme has clearly led to a wide range of outcomes which have included both outcomes that have been planned and the unanticipated multiplier effects of these, as active learning has been impacting not only upon individuals but also upon their friends, their families and their communities. Many of the participants who were mothers have been reassessing their position within their own family, recognising they are 'more than just mothers – and there have been children recognising this too'. Partners have been appreciating the benefits of ALAC too, respecting the time and space that participants have needed to do their coursework. In some cases, this has led to changes in family relationships, with partners more active in domestic responsibilities. As the following participant has explained:

> *The first residential was a big concern for me. (It was) the first time I had ever left my family overnight and in a strange place on my own. I had to do a lot of preparation – a lot of practical organising; food, school clothes, washing, etc. I then threw myself into it and thought 'if the worst comes to the worst I can always leave and go home!' But it was great – and it changed our family relationships in ways I didn't think about (before)– my husband spent time with the kids on his own, took them out for a meal – never done that before –*

changed his relationship [with] the kids – closer. They can't wait for me to go on the next one and go to Brussels for two nights. They keep reminding me to sort out the passport and all that.

It is worth noting that a number of working class mothers have raised their children's expectations of education and employment possibilities and encouraged them not to just accept but to change the actors that affect their lives. For instance, a mother's participation in ALAC provided a powerful role model for her daughter who subsequently decided to continue with her education rather than dropping out. Her daughter has since received a prize for excellence in vocational studies at school.

The learning that characterised ALAC, and the impact of this learning, within and between communities, has taken place through facilitated workshops. But at other times it has been the result of activities that have cascaded out from ALAC. Communities have come together around common concerns, identifying their issues and training needs, sharing information between groups and communities, increasing dialogue between communities and raising community awareness about local services and how to access them. And groups and communities have been taking a more strategic approach in addressing the issues that affect them. Participation in ALAC has enabled participants to address the barriers that specific communities face. These have included breaking down barriers of generation, locality and culture as the following illustrates:

Meeting different people on the course was really useful. For me as a Ghanaian, I think we should get more involved in events by other communities. For instance I saw notices about a party for Eid. Anyone could go [participant was not Muslim] but I wasn't sure about going. But after going on the course I thought I would try it, and I went and had a great time, even though there weren't many people there. I think it's something that more Africans should join in with – there's a lot of singing and dancing, which we enjoy.

The work of the ALAC hubs has also led to beneficial ripple effects on services/service provision and the development of more effective forums and partnerships. It is worth noting that as well as individuals and communities, the various organisations and partners that made up the hubs have learnt through their participation in ALAC. This has led to more effective and appropriate services and new partnerships. By building active citizenship and by empowering effective representatives the hubs have made a significant impact on services in many areas. As a result, groups and communities have been taking a more strategic approach on issues affecting communities. The hubs' impact on service delivery has been directly relevant for a wide range of government initiatives, including neighbourhood regeneration, New Deal for Communities, Sure Start services, the NHS, transport authorities, education authorities, housing departments and children's services. ALAC has also had an impact at the level of strategic planning and development. So, for example, the GEM project, part of the Greater Manchester hub, has made a significant contribution to Manchester's Local Development Framework. Members of the GEM project, (who were trained as a team in participatory community auditing) undertook an evaluation of the composition of who was involved in decision-making from community to Local Strategic Partnership (LSP) levels, and followed this up with focus groups, exploring what could be done to facilitate fuller representation and more active participation. The findings of their work have been instrumental in the development of good practice guidelines including the local authority Statement of Community Involvement 2005, and in getting decision-making bodies to reflect on and improve their representativeness.

In the South West ALAC has enabled the Speaking Up course to be developed for other learner groups. This has been done jointly with community organisations engaged with the groups concerned. Many of their staff have been trained through joint delivery so that they can now teach the course. The activities of ALAC South West have led to the development of a Joint Agency/Service User Involvement Project. In support of this initiative local Primary Care Trusts and Devon County Council went on to fund two posts, including one at Exeter Council for Voluntary Services.

New initiatives/policy/political impact

The ALAC hubs have had an impact on policy and the development of initiatives at both national and local level. This impact has been through the active participation of individuals, but most importantly through the active and effective participation of groups. The London hub held a round-table discussion as part of their contribution to the Power Inquiry (Joseph Rowntree Charitable Trust, 2006). The discussion was facilitated by staff from the Inquiry and involved people from communities that have sometimes been described as marginalised, but who were actively engaged as citizens on a local or neighbourhood level, or as part of a community of interest. While active in their communities these participants had been disengaged from formal politics and felt under-represented by formal governmental structures. The discussion explored the reasons behind this.

As part of their activities, the London Civic Forum also held participatory consultation sessions around the Commission on London Governance (re-assessing the powers of the Mayor and the Boroughs) and the Office of the Deputy Prime Minister's consultation on the same subject. The outcomes of these sessions fed into the regional and national government consultations. In Manchester the Refugee and Asylum Seeker Network group chose as their focus for ALAC learning to draw up a refugee charter, working with the Community Pride Initiative and Manchester Refugee Support Network. The charter was written by refugees and asylum seekers with the aim of raising awareness of the issues that they face, showing the positive contribution that they make and opening channels of participation for refugees and asylum seekers in the city. This was launched at a major function in January 2006. This was expected to have a major impact on the delivery of services for refugees and asylum seekers in Greater Manchester and has already led to other areas undertaking similar work.

The impact of ALAC as a national network

Participation in the ALAC network has been a positive experience for the hubs. The formation of regional ALAC networks has increased awareness of Active Learning for Active Citizenship within individual organisations, and across communities and groups in the regions. Similarly it has raised the profile of the work of organisations and groups within the individual hubs. The ALAC network has also provided an opportunity for the voluntary and statutory sectors to work together in more effective ways. This has been a valuable opportunity to network, sharing and exchanging information, gaining awareness and insight into good practice, improving motivation and increasing the profile of the hubs' network, nationally. The participatory evaluation provided on-going support for these processes of reflection and shared learning. As one hub leader reflected:

> It is very useful to be connected to other ALAC projects, some of whose work relates to other aspects of our non-ALAC work. The sharing of ALAC information and approaches, and the discussions about the different facets of

> *ALAC, have all been very inspiring and useful to inform the future development of our active citizenship activities.*

This was why the hubs decided to continue to work together when government funding for the ALAC programme came to an end in 2006, maintaining the basis for their involvement in subsequent initiatives, including the Take Part programme and the Third Sector research capacity building programme, and focusing upon learning and active citizenship.

References

Joseph Rowntree Charitable Trust (2006) *Power to the People. The report of power: An Independent Inquiry into Britain's Democracy (also known as the 'Power Inquiry')*. York: York Publishing Distribution

Woodward, V. (2004) Active Learning for Active Citizenship. CRU, Home Office

Proving a point: effective social, political and citizenship education in South Yorkshire

TED HARTLEY

The ALAC team were Graham Birkin, Amanda Morgan, Kevin Gillan and Dan Olner. This chapter draws on reports and comments from them all.

Background

South Yorkshire WEA was chosen for this civil renewal initiative because of its record and commitment to community-based citizenship work over the past 12 years. Work with the Somali community in Sheffield had been extensive with a full-time member of staff; community activists' training courses had been put on under European Social Fund (ESF) and the WEA had supported the CICERO project with its emphasis on 'go-and-see' EU citizenship.

Underlying approaches to citizenship learning

The opportunity to engage in the ALAC initiative came at a most welcome time for adult educators in the WEA in Sheffield. The need for this type of activity has never been greater nor more urgent, yet the resources necessary to undertake the work have never been scarcer. Money is available for any type of skills training, especially for younger people. Indeed, the current policy has established hegemony in this area, while adult education with *a social purpose*, to quote Tawney from the last century, is regarded as a disposable luxury by the agencies that run post-16 education on behalf of the government.

While dominant in the UK, this emphasis on skills is not the only post-16 approach available to adult educators. Mainstream EU lifelong learning policy, worked out carefully and finding widespread support, advocates a broader approach to this sector's actions. Largely due to the leadership of Jacques Delors, who is reported to have said that skills training might produce good plumbers, but won't produce good citizens, and is set out in the 1996 report to UNESCO, *Learning: The Treasure Within*. The needs are well expressed by Zhou Nan-Zhao in his paper for UNESCO.[1]

> *In an information-intensive age, education is mandated to respond to demands in two directions: on the one hand, it has to transmit an increasing amount of constantly evolving knowledge and know-how adapted to a knowledge-driven civilization; on the other hand, it has to enable learners not to be overwhelmed by the flows of information, while keeping personal and social development as its end in view. Therefore 'education must ... simultaneously provide maps of a complex world in constant turmoil and the compass that will enable people to find their way in it'. (Delors et al., 1996, p.85)*

Four pillars of learning make up this rounded approach:

• **Learning to know.** This type of learning is radically different from 'acquiring itemised codified information or factual knowledge', as often stressed in conventional curriculum and in 'rote learning'. Rather it implies 'the mastering of the instruments of knowledge themselves'. 'Acquiring knowledge is a never-ending process and can be enriched by all forms of experience'. 'Learning to know' includes the development of the faculties of memory, imagination, reasoning, problem-solving and the ability to think in a coherent and critical way. It is 'a process of discovery', which takes time and involves going more deeply into the information/knowledge delivered through subject teaching. 'Learning to know' presupposes 'learning to learn', calling upon the power of concentration, memory and thought, so as to benefit from ongoing educational opportunities continuously arising (formally and non-formally) throughout life. Therefore 'learning

---

[1] Zhou, Nan-Zhao (n.d.) *Four 'Pillars of Learning' for the Reorientation and Reorganisation of the Curriculum: Reflections and Discussions.* This can be found at: www.ibe.unesco.org/cops/Competencies/PillarsLearningZhou.pdf.

to know' can be regarded as both a means and an end in learning itself and in life. As a means, it serves to enable individual learners to understand the very least enough about the nature, about humankind and its history, about his/her environment, and about society at large. As an end, it enables the learner to experience the pleasure of knowing, discovering and understanding as a process.

- **Learning to do.** This pillar of learning implies in the first place for application of what learners have learned or known into practices; it is closely linked to vocational-technical education and work skills training. However, it goes beyond narrowly defined skills development for 'doing' specific things or practical tasks in traditional or industrial economies. The emerging knowledge-based economy is making human work increasingly immaterial. 'Learning to do' calls for new types of skills, more behavioural than intellectual. The material and the technology are becoming secondary to human qualities and interpersonal relationships. 'Learning to do' thus implies a shift from skill to competence, or a mix of higher-order skills specific to each individual. 'The ascendancy of knowledge and information as factors of production systems is making the idea of occupational skills obsolete and is bringing personal competency to the fore.' Thus 'learning to do' means, among other things: ability to communicate effectively with others; aptitude toward team work; social skills in building meaningful interpersonal relations; adaptability to change in the world of work and in social life; competency in transforming knowledge into innovations and job creation; and a readiness to take risks and resolve or manage conflicts.

- **Learning to live together.** In the context of increasing globalisation, the Delors Commission places a special emphasis on this pillar of learning. It implies an education taking two complementary paths: on one level, discovery of others and on another, experience of shared purposes throughout life. Specifically it implies the development of such qualities as: knowledge and understanding of self and others; appreciation of the diversity of the human race and an awareness of the similarities between, and the interdependence of, all humans; empathy and co-operative social behaviour in caring and sharing; respect of other people and their cultures and value systems; capability of encountering others and resolving conflicts through dialogue; and competency in working towards common objectives.

- **Learning to be.** This type of learning was first conceptualised in the Report to UNESCO in 1972, *Learning to Be* (Edgar Faure *et al.*),

143

out of the fear that 'the world would be dehumanized as a result of technical change'. It was based on the principle that:

> *The aim of development is the complete fulfilment of man, in all the richness of his personality, the complexity of his forms of expression and his various commitments — as individual, member of a family and of a community, citizen and producer, inventor of techniques and creative dreamer.*

'Learning to be' may therefore be interpreted in one way as learning to be human, through acquisition of knowledge, skills and values conducive to personality development in its intellectual, moral, cultural and physical dimensions. This implies a curriculum aiming at cultivating qualities of imagination and creativity; acquiring universally shared human values; developing aspects of a person's potential (memory, reasoning, aesthetic sense, physical capacity and communication/social skills); developing critical thinking and exercising independent judgement; and developing personal commitment and responsibility.[2]

These four approaches seek a balanced approach to lifelong learning, to a way of combating social tension, to securing the economy, to feeding imagination and creativity.

This approach, coupled with a fundamental belief in participation, social justice and democracy, provided the team with its platform upon which to mount the pilot activities

So there is an alternative, and a better way, but this will need to be won from a government that has fallen for the skills option at the expense of the rest. A high risk strategy indeed when faced with unique tensions in communities!

The context

The ALAC invitation to test out approaches and new ways of engaging people appealed in a South Yorkshire context that was changing rapidly after the harsh years of Tory rule. A recent report to the Chief Executive[3] now clarifies the sort of profound movements that people were experiencing prior, during and after the ALAC pilot period.

---

[2] Zhou, Nan-Zhao (as before).

[3] *Community Cohesion: Developing a New Strategy* (report to Cabinet 13 June 2007, available at www.sheffield.gov.uk.

Between 2001 and 2006, Sheffield's black and minority ethnic (BME) population increased from 8 per cent to 30 per cent. Diversity also increased beyond settlers from 'old Commonwealth' countries to embrace people from many African, Middle Eastern and Far Eastern countries experiencing turmoil. Equally work migration, especially from the A8 EU countries, sharply increased from Poland, Slovakia, and the Baltic states. All these changes took place without discussion or education, and fuelled by the outbursts from the febrile end of the mass media where xenophobic views were often expressed. Terror attacks in London, undertaken by young men brought up in Yorkshire fuelled anti-Islamic feelings. The arrival in schools of large numbers of non-English speaking children put strain on their services, similarly for housing, health and social services.

Sheffield's response is positive with a clear set of values that reflect Sheffield and its people. The ALAC work and its local reports contributed indirectly to this development.

Look at the broader national context: there is a social crisis which manifests itself in xenophobia, Islamophobia, tough social problems in the poor communities (knife and gun crime, petty crime and drug-based networks). There is the extreme disaffection demonstrated by home-grown terrorism. The process of widespread social and economic atomisation, accelerated under the Tories and continued under New Labour, based on the US free market model, has brought about community and individual crises: shifts and changes in major services, consequent on privatisation, have resulted in widespread confusion: people no longer know who runs their local FE college, their local health service, what their local councillor is doing and how they can interact to improve services and representation. They can also see changes in their own communities that go largely undiscussed or unexplained: the sudden impact of work migration, the equally sudden arrival of refugees and asylum seekers into their communities – all bring new uncertainties and added social strains.

What we did in detail

Courses for women refugees were offered with a voluntary sector organisation in Rotherham. These attracted women from a range of countries to the classes. The group started off modestly with some women from Pakistan, Yemen, Bangladesh and Iran, and attendance was a bit erratic. As the weeks went by attendance gradually grew, as a number of women

145

from different African countries started to attend (for example Nigeria, Angola and the Congo). A crèche was provided which made it possible – as most of the new women had small babies. No charges were made for this or any of the ALAC activities over the trial period.

Similar topics were covered in the second course, but discussions developed in different directions, as is inevitable with different groups of people.

This time we had three visiting speakers. The first came along to give advice and guidance on training and other personal issues. The two women from Community Fire Safety returned. All the women from the last group were very pleased with their free smoke alarms and Risk Assessments that followed the Safety Officers' last visit.

The final speaker was a retired female doctor who talked to the group about women's health issues. This included information about reproduction, contraception and breast examination for lumps. The women found this session really interesting and useful, although more visual aids would have been helpful.

The group was very successful and offered the women and myself the opportunity to mix with people from a variety of cultures and learn about each other.

The courses did stimulate interest in the idea of becoming a UK citizen and some useful orientation work was possible.

At the end of the course there was a certificate presentation and party, which was enjoyed by all.

E-citizenship

As a project, we were very conscious of the digital divide which separates those with easy access to the Internet from those without. This is especially true for the new citizens and migrant workers in the area. One piece of work drew together a group of refugees and asylum seekers from the different African countries and they set about learning the skills involved in creating and managing a website. Using Mambo freeware the group quickly got to grips with the techniques and very soon they were able to network with other groups in Europe and with kinship groups back in Africa. The group became very interested in each other's countries and in globalisation issues. At this time the remarkably successful and popular 'Make Poverty History' initiative developed and the group also became involved in this. The high spot for the group was to go to

Edinburgh and join the camp of campaigners making their points to the G8 summit. People wanted to discuss American foreign policy and the pursuit of oil. These tricky subjects were approached with care and preparation, giving as many sides to the issues as possible so that individuals could form their own views. Coincidentally, a topical book,[4] readable and stimulating, written by a local scholar was published and formed a lively focus for several sessions. In one the writer was able to come along and take the many questions in person.

Another e-based citizenship project was the RACATEL (Raising Civil Awareness Through English Language) project run during the second year of the ALAC pilot.

This Grundvig learning project was designed and developed at a British Council contact seminar held in Stratford-upon-Avon in January 2005. Interested colleagues from over 15 EU member states all got together to find partners, define projects and set about using the Grundtvig programme. One of the initial workshops sparked off the idea of doing something on the citizenship theme based on using this interest. Each interested party did have a fleeting experience of visiting his or her own municipal website and formed a view about its effectiveness. We developed the idea of studying the municipal websites of all the partners at the centre of the project. This was a simple and manageable idea, one with immediate attraction and one which did not seem to involve much initial costs.

Four partners signed up to working together: the WEA (the largest adult education provider in the UK voluntary sector) based in Sheffield, South Yorkshire, the language school in Leon (Spain), the Link School in Malta and Mykolas Romerus University in Vilnius, Lithuania. After some further discussion about methodology and practicalities the application was submitted, approved and work began.

The first meeting, in a snowy Vilnius, developed the methodology still further. An evaluative framework was drawn up which would enable each partner to look at the websites from individual or collective citizens' point of view. This framework would cover aesthetics, informativeness and accessibility. It would take in items such as inclusivity, diversity, content and concerns. Groups in each member state applied this to the

---

[4] Rutledge, I. (2005) *Addicted to Oil: America's relentless drive for energy security.* London: I.B. Tauris.

local site and to the other partners' sites to come to full evaluation. Visits were made to the local town hall to discuss issues with the site workers there and local case studies and issues were explored by the groups.

Central to all this was the use of English. It soon became clear that there was a variety of terminology in use to describe such things as councils, mayoral systems, local authorities etc, so a table of comparative terms in the different languages and their application was devised and circulated. The core group met in each other's location which quickly developed a shared purpose and brought better understanding about the different learning contexts in use.

A final large meeting, with 23 staff and learners, took place in Malta in June 2005. While we were there the immigration crisis erupted and created in Malta a mini fortress-Europe debate which was widely reported across the EU. This brought a new and real interest to the project group, which decided to follow up the large and complicated EU migration question in their own localities.

Year two of RACATEL brought a new focus for the project. Each partner used a common questionnaire to explore the local reasons why citizens are so disengaged from the democratic processes. This is a common and growing problem and the information that people have given displays a common set of attitudes. People are disenchanted with political leaders because of their tendencies to deceive, to make money out of their offices, to ignore people's views and their wishes. People in England felt betrayed when the government joined the Iraq war and still feel this was an undemocratic decision that has damaged the relationship between citizen and government. Respondents in Italy (attending the Malta language school) felt that widespread corruption was the most damaging feature of local and nation political life in Italy. Lithuanians felt that the post-Soviet world is very individualistic and sets people against each other, with the government looking more to economics than to people and communities. A website, built for a very small cost on the Mambo platform, was another group-based project and a great success registering over 150,000 visits in its first 18 months.

Several courses were developed with the local Pakistani community who wished to explore the theme of Muslims in Europe.

After a lot of planning and organising, 24 participants went to Granada and Cordoba, Spain, in mid-March 2006. The trip was the culmination of a series of meetings looking at Islam and Europe, past and present. There was much controversy and only towards the end were we beginning to understand each other and the topics we had focused on.

The meetings were open: there was a group of younger men from a mosque in Darnall, (Sheffield), Muslim and non-Muslim women, some Christians and some non-believers. We held ten meetings in the Pakistani Muslim Centre, starting with what it means to be a Muslim in Darnall today.

This first session led to a discussion between the young and the old, and how the early migrants, Mirpuris from Azad Kashmir, had a different view of life to their children and grandchildren. Recruited to the steel works in the 1950s, the lives of the older generation were dominated by working the shifts that few others wanted. They had little English and less help, but in some ways were more integrated because they were steel men in a steel city, an identity shared with the people around them. Their children and grandchildren, going to the local schools and often to university, no longer had the certainty of a job in steel but looked wider to jobs in computers, housing, the local authority. In spite of high qualifications, many were unemployed or underemployed, driving taxis or working in restaurants. The mosque as a centre for community life was important, perhaps more so than for the older generation.

So from discussion about identity, religion and place we moved to the 'war on terror' and the globalisation of allegiance. The *umma* – the world Muslim community – is an important aspect of Islam, with Muslims everywhere feeling a responsibility for each other. Many in the group believed the wars in Afghanistan, Iraq and the Middle East were fuelled by Islamophobia, and that the 'war on terror' was a war against Islam. For them the British government's response to the London bombings encouraged an atmosphere of generalised suspicion, where all Muslims were seen as 'not one of us' and potential terrorists.

The group wanted to know more about Muslim history, searching back to the Golden Age of the Moors in Spain, almost eight centuries that ended with the Catholic re-conquest of 1492. Most of us knew little of that period of European history, of the architecture, libraries, hospitals, sophisticated irrigation systems and advances in science. The Moors and Islam were the link between the worlds of the Greeks and Romans, keeping scholarship alive in the European Dark Ages, through to the Renaissance and the Enlightenment.

We discussed too the relative tolerance shown to Christians and Jews under the Caliphate, in contrast to the forced conversions, expulsions and

Inquisition practised by the returning Catholics, led by what came to be known as the Catholic monarchs.

So it was this that led to the proposed visit to Andalucia. We intended to spend six days visiting the sites of early European Islam, learning more about a faith currently so misunderstood and misrepresented. There have been plans for further sessions on these topics so that other people in Sheffield can find out more about this period of our common European history.

'Bloody Foreigners' was another short course that investigated the story of immigration into Britain. The course focused on the story of migration to Britain, based on the book *Bloody Foreigners* by Robert Winder. The course looked at the contribution made by people from all over the world to British society, and ended with a study visit to Liverpool where we met representatives from Liverpool's black community and visited the Museum of Slavery.

There were a lot of people interested who also wanted to discuss Jewish, Irish and African immigration, and what happened with the *Windrush* arrivals in the 1940s. Following this we looked at the 1950s when the people from Pakistan and the Near East (notably the Yemen), were often recruited to work the shifts that nobody else wanted in the steel works and public transport.

The courses ended with a discussion on the latest arrivals: migrants from the new Europe, and refugees from civil wars, natural disasters and persecution. Some of the group were from Liberia and the Ivory Coast, providing a live twenty-first century connection to West Africa, the source of Liverpool's wealth in the days of slavery.

One of the unexpected outcomes from the group was the writing of a moving and personal story from one woman who fled the Cameroons to seek safety in Sheffield. She made a lot of friends in Sheffield and took on voluntary work in the local community. Very regrettably, though, she was not allowed to stay here and has since returned to the unstable area from where she fled.

Another very keen interest emerged from the group work and discussions with what might be described as disaffected groups of people: this was the genuine desire to explore the nature and values of the UK democratic system. It is easy to underestimate the knowledge and experience that refugees and other groups have about western democracy. Most of the people in the discussions had been brought up in countries that did not offer the experience of a democracy (Pakistan, for example, has been a military dictatorship; most of the African countries represented were not democracies as we know them; many refugees came from theocracies, and therefore had little understanding of the separation of religion and the state, of the benefits of secularisation). Needless to say, the debates were lively and productive. Visits to the local town hall and discussions with local councillors and MPs fuelled a desire to visit Westminster, so, undeterred by recent terrorist events a small group of ALAC South Yorkshire activists visited London, took in some of the sights and spent time with MPs in the House of Commons.

This took place a week after the joy at the successful Olympic bid and the horror of the London bombings. twelve members of the 'Living in Sheffield' group – a joint project by ALAC and the Northern Refugee Centre – visited Parliament and saw some of the sights of the city. Staying at a Youth Hostel in Euston Road they walked through the cordoned-off streets, stood by the wreaths in Russell Square and saw the pictures of the missing pasted on the hoardings. The group went to the Africa Exhibition at the British Museum, with its impressive 'Tree of Life' sculpture made of welded cartridges and small arms from the wars in Mozambique. They watched the jugglers and street performers in Covent Garden and went to Trafalgar Square and the river. On the final afternoon they took a boat to Greenwich, ending with legs astride the meridian. The highlight of the 36 hours was an introduction to the ways of Parliament, meeting research assistants from the All-Party Africa Group in Portcullis House, and getting contacts for MPs in Liverpool and York. The intention of the All-Party Group is not only to argue for positive UK–Africa links, but also to include the British-based Africa diaspora in their work. At present, most contact is with London-based Africans. The research assistants hoped the Sheffield visit would widen their links with Africans living in the UK. The group left Portcullis House through the Members' tunnel under Bridge Street. In Parliament they were shown the Lobby with its mosaics representing the four UK nations, saw the cracked marble sword damaged by a suffragette in the struggle for the vote, and sat in on *Question Time*. Two of the questions referred to the two-tier labour force in the Mother of Parliaments, with contracted-out cleaners receiving just over the minimum wage, about a third lower than the directly employed staff. Conditions were described as scandalous with workers taking their breaks in locker rooms provided for the chemicals. One of the MPs pointedly contrasted his life as a citizen with those citizens who cleaned up after him. The Leader of the House said the matter was being looked into. On the train back to Sheffield one of the group said how impressed he was with the manner and content of *Question Time*. A key issue for his community was their lack of primary identification documents. He intended to join with others to put pressure on his MP to raise the question in the House.

Community-based action research

The Somali community in the city approached the project for help: they were experiencing acute problems with their school-aged and slightly older children (second-generation immigrants in most cases). Poor performance at school, bad behaviour on the streets and buses and brushes with the law were a mounting feature of life within the community. In order to get to the bottom of the problem, to understand it better and come up with possible solutions they proposed a programme of extensive interviews with parents (largely women) and some of the young people. Meetings took place in the community to shape the process, and links were made between the South Yorkshire Somalis and a similar community in Tower Hamlets. Using the new networks other interested individuals joined in the discussions, so much so, that a weekend was set aside for a residential event at Fircroft College in Birmingham to exchange views. A further visit to Tower Hamlets grew from this and then the research was developed with the group. The research was co-ordinated and conducted by members of the Somali community and the data collected.

The findings were presented at a Town Hall meeting which was well supported by the Council. From this, funding was attracted to a new group, Somali Link Project, and a programme of new link arrangements between school and home were developed; the project got its own worker to keep the programme going. This piece of work was valuable in demonstrating a sound process, in engaging and involving the community around education-centred issues and for showing a positive intervention in problems affecting a home-grown, second-generation ethnic community.

What emerged

One of the main conclusions to be drawn from the pilot is that there is a great need for safe space where people can get together, with a skilled tutor, to discuss the difficult issues of the day. Most people felt that the flow of information they received was often uneven and, with really complex issues, such as the Israeli/Palestine conflict, analysis was limited. It was important to be able to say what was felt without getting into debates about anti-Semitism, or racism and important to work through the issues with people at their own pace and levels of understanding. This opportunity seems to be very rarely available to people. We came to the conclusion that social political and citizenship education (SPACE) was a vital component of a healthy democratic society.

Another conclusion was that discussion, debate and analysis strengthened the social fabric. Discussions about theocracy and secularism in government, drew out a clearer understanding of what a western democracy was about, what it stood for and what its values were. This helped to move the citizenship debate onwards from the generally contentious debate about 'Britishness', about national identity, about being a British citizen to a shared set of objective values generally held by mature democracies that were necessary to be a citizen in Britain. These values and beliefs coalesced through debate as:

- democracy;
- equality – for and between all people;
- toleration – religious, artistic, political;
- freedom of expression;
- social justice;
- fair play; and
- civic duty.

Another important outcome from the pilot activities is the change of attitude by some of the participants towards politics and participation. Many stated that they had been turned off by politics, by the personalities, the combative relationships, the contempt for the public, the shameless self seeking that goes on. There was the feeling that politics is not taught any more (this was a view from former workers who had received a lot of basic political education through their unions, branch meeting discussions and conferences. This civil aspect of the unions has

153

largely been squeezed out of existence). After discussions and quite penetrating exploration of ideas and issues, several learners stated that they felt less disengaged and more prepared to keep connected and involved in the issues of the day. This is a positive sign that might well be turned into something concrete through the implementation of measures sketched out in the Green Paper, *Governance of Britain* (June 2007). Over-all, the ALAC pilot told us that there was the continuing need for political education, not necessarily qualification related, but certainly of the tried and tested liberal tradition. This was generally lacking and hard to find.

The work continues...

In South Yorkshire there is a new Migrant Workers' Support Network which is a partnership between Take Part, Unite (the new union formed by the merger of Unison and TGWU), the Northern Refugee Centre, Sheffield University and other interested organisations. The aim is to campaign with, and for, equal and proper treatment of migrant work-ers in line with employment law and decent terms and conditions. There is a strong educational theme and a determination to ease new migrants and their families into their new communities so that they can take part in the civic and civil life around them, support their families in local schools and enjoy proper access to help and services when needed.

The WEA has continued to make this sort of learning available through a series of courses and mini projects funded through the Academy for Community leadership, using European Social Funding. There are many strings and drawbacks to the funding and this does make it hard for providers to reach out, develop and stimulate new areas of learning.

The ALAC pilots have formed themselves into the Take Part Network, which will be playing a strong part in the new national and regional consortia for community empowerment. The National Learning Framework encapsulates much of the approach, methodology and innovation in the case studies. This is freely available from the Take Part website, www.takepart.org.

Take Part is involved in the newly formed National Strategic Empowerment Partnership (NSEP) at national level and at the regional level in regional consortia. This is a Department of Communities and Local Government initiative which is set to develop community empow-erment over the next few years. Finally, and most importantly, Take Part is developing adult citizenship learning as part of the government's commitment to the implementation of the 2008 Empowerment White Paper, *Communities in Control: Real people, real power.*

As ever, the key issue is political will, both nationally and at the local level, and the making available of resources. The case is proven: let's see what happens next!

CHAPTER NINE

Borders, glass floors and anti-racist popular adult education

JOHN GRAYSON

The context

The South Yorkshire Hub for ALAC in changing times

Adult Education for Active Citizenship is a descriptive term full of contradictions, and therefore full of free spaces and potential for relevant committed adult education. ALAC work at the Northern College in Barnsley, South Yorkshire demonstrated the full range of these contradictions and possibilities for traditions of popular adult education. It was decided that the College would join the Hub to organise a range of new initiatives and to develop a number of new spaces for citizenship education using methods and principles of popular adult education, or a 'critical pedagogy' as some colleagues grandly describe it.

The College, its students and practice had long been at the centre of major economic and political change since its foundation in 1979 (Ball and Hampton, 2004), through the Miners' Strike of 1984, and the devastation wreaked by the destruction of the coal and steel industries on communities in the region. Popular adult education at the College and in towns and villages throughout the coalfields was a major resource for regeneration and the reconstruction of civil society, if not the economy (see Francis, Grayson and Henderson, 2002; Grayson and Jackson, 2004; Horton, 2002).

By 2004 it was clear that South Yorkshire was changing rapidly again: this was not surprising. Europe has rapidly become a test bed for 'business

156

rule' (or neo-Liberalism), and a headlong retreat from the welfare state values of post-war social democracy or reformed communism. This head-long rush to bring back the crude and unregulated market to economic and social life has been led by the Blair/Brown governments in the UK. In South Yorkshire the impacts of privatisation and continued loss of man-ufacturing jobs has created an area with relatively low unemployment but a low wage and growing service economy. This rapid change has created an atmosphere of personal and family, job and economic, insecurities. It has fostered neighbourhood anxieties and fear of 'crime' and 'disorder'. Globalisation of labour markets has rapidly increased flows of migrant workers and 'illegal' migrants. In the UK, particularly in the old industrial areas like South Yorkshire, it is linked to a politics and media more and more proclaiming bigotry and intolerance, and mindless nationalism, typical of a country actually at war – at war with 'terror', and the peoples of Iraq and Afghanistan.

Common sense racism?

Political discourses, within which popular adult education operates, had by 2004 forefronted the manufacture of fear in communities, with the demonising of the migrant, the 'asylum seeker' as the root of social ills. 9/11 and the Iraq War in 2003 heightened tensions. As Sivanandan has put it, we face 'a politics of prejudice and fear to create a culture of xeno-racism and Islamaphobia; the asylum seeker at the gate and the shadowy Muslim within' (Sivanandan, 2006).

The result was the generalising of a 'common sense racism' infecting debates and political practice. Symptomatic of this was the rise of the Fascist Right, the BNP. Modelling themselves on the programmes and tactics of Le Pen in France, Yorkshire had become the fastest-growing region for racist parties, and election of BNP and UKIP councillors. By May 2004, 126,000 people voted for the BNP in European and local elec-tions in Yorkshire and the Humber region. Where candidates stood, they averaged 16 per cent of the vote. In May 2005, the biggest increase in the BNP vote was in Yorkshire where their vote increased from 3,245 in 2001 to 60,990 in 2005, representing 2.8 per cent of the regional total. Indeed, at the local elections of May 2007 Yorkshire alone still accounted for nearly a third of the entire vote for the BNP in the UK. In Barnsley, where Northern College is situated, the BNP were able to field 14 can-didates in 2006 and 18 candidates and garner 8,000 votes in May 2007.

To a large extent this resurgence of a dormant racism in British popular culture and politics – what Paul Gilroy has called 'postcolonial melancholia' (see Gilroy, 2004) – has been fuelled by a moral panic on migration and rapid changes in the ethnic make-up of the population of Britain. In the last ten years, and particularly since 2004, there has been a migration of workers and refugees to the UK on a scale greater than the migration of workforces from the West Indies and the Indian subcontinent, and Africa from the 1950s to the 1970s.

Recent legislation and events in the UK have actually redefined citizens and the very meanings of citizenship. Asylum seekers and refugees, and migrant workers 'without papers' are simply seen as 'illegal'. Being born in a country no longer always gives one citizenship, nor does marriage. Citizenship has to be earned through language tests and history quizzes. These are not people who have committed illegal acts: stripped of their rights, their very person, their identity is illegal. The UK Audit Commission estimated in 2006 that there were 285,000 'failed' asylum seekers who have no legal status or state support, and are being pursued for deportation (Narey, 2006, p. 32). Steve Cohen has memorably described their Orwellian treatment in his book *Deportation is Freedom* (Cohen, 2006).

The emergence of a category called 'illegals' is a fundamentally new twist to state racism. The spectre of a Nazi legal world looms with people without any rights who can be abused and detained without recourse to any legal protection. With failed asylum seekers and migrant workers the current estimate in the UK is anything between one million and two million people. Millions more live in EU countries, 12 million in the USA (Legrain, 2006).

Citizenship in Europe is now about both 'inclusion' and 'exclusion'. Judith Shklar describes:

> *A symbolic glass floor – citizens exist above the floor and can look down on those beneath who are excluded from citizenship and are thus the most deprived in society. (quoted in Lavalette and Ferguson, 2007, p. 118)*

Internal 'borders' are now as important as frontiers (Balibar, 2004). It is interesting that the original funder of ALAC – the Home Office – now has a Border and Immigration Agency, and apparently (at the time of writing in 2007) aims to 'safeguard people's identity and the privileges of citizenship' – presumably, from against those below the 'glass floor'?

Cosmopolitan communities have been conjured up. Rural areas in Yorkshire have a labour force dominated by migrant workers. In what was the steel and coal heartlands of the UK where a few African Caribbean and British Asian people came to work in the 1970s, some of our housing research in 2006 discovered a Slovakian Roma community in Rotherham and Sheffield of around 1,500 people. (Grayson, Horton and Petrie, 2007). Their presence has gone unreported, and they already outnumber 'indigenous' Romany Gypsies in the area.

Sheffield is one of the UK's main centres for Somali settlement contributing nationally to the largest Somali community in the world outside Somalia. The global has certainly become local.

> *A culture that took 200 years to build was torn apart in 20 ... Today, in place of a static local workforce working in the factories and drinking in the pubs their grandfathers worked and drank in, a truly global working class is being created. (Mason, 2007, p.xi)*

These migrant workers and their families are, in the main, here 'legally' as EU citizens, settled citizens or refugees. Nevertheless, many of them are 'trafficked', owing money for transit or access to work, or bonds for housing. It is therefore unsurprising that in October 2006 the Home Office chose to locate its new dedicated Human Trafficking Centre in Sheffield which 'will focus the expertise of many agencies on fighting "modern slavery"'.

Beyond rights to responsibilities

The rapidly changing cosmopolitan face of South Yorkshire acted as a crucial backdrop and promoter of Northern College's contribution to the South Yorkshire Hub of ALAC. The popular adult education programme was developed against an equally important backdrop of new discourses around disputed definitions of active citizenship and civil liberties.

Active citizenship

By 2004 there had been a drift into a world of state social policy dominated by the ideas of the conservative communitarians of the USA. In this world citizens have already gained their rights. What they have to share with governments and political elites are responsibilities. In this world it is not the wealthy who have to develop 'responsibilisation', but the poor and the socially excluded.

Community developers and adult education 'trainers' are told that local communities, particularly poor and working class communities, need capacity building, and more social capital to exercise these responsibilities. They have to take responsibility for their own poverty, for crime and 'community safety'. And now British Asian 'communities' are told they have to take responsibility for ethnic divisions, even 'terror'.

Active citizens in their positive roles according to the New Labour definitions, should restrict their activism and work in partnerships with the local and national state, or follow the middle classes and become volunteers, consumer lobbyists, and givers to charities and media 'appeals'. Community development workers often seem to have bought this definition. In 2003 in a national survey of community development workers in the UK, less than 40 per cent were willing to mention 'campaigning' as part of their work. In a period throughout Europe of widening inequalities and social divisions to retreat to a neutral facilitator role encouraged by the state, abandoning core values is in practice to become the 'sticking plaster', the therapist, the counsellor; not an agent of change, bringing resources for a broad struggle for social change.

The problem of 'order'

Public language about racism, active citizens and community 'engagement' is often combined with an overpowering emphasis on social order and punitive policing at local levels, and a very negative social and political image for young people. This is a serious issue for community development and adult education because, often, the active citizens who emerge in this climate are those demanding a 'law and order' quick fix from government (Thompson, 2000). We already have more surveillance cameras in the UK than anywhere in Europe (4.2 million, one for every 14 citizens) and yet community activists demand even more. Anti-social behaviour has become one of the main issues community activists want to discuss on all training courses. Community activists are invited to join 'the police family' as neighbourhood wardens with some police powers, and volunteers working in police stations. In our anti-racist popular adult education work we attempted to develop a progressive alternative agenda for community active citizenship, by working with anti-racist groups, asylum seeker support groups, and refugee community organisations to offer an alternative to dominant populist and racist agendas.

The UK now has the largest database of DNA in Europe with one third of young black British men represented there. A nation of citizens is becoming a nation of 'suspects'. The results of these trends have to an extent simply reduced local freedoms, particularly those of young people. England and Wales, with a record 80,420 citizens in prison (31 March 2007), probably the largest prison population in the EU, had in 2006 3,350 young people (under 18) in custody, and has prosecuted 210,000 young people for criminal offences. England and Wales lock up 23 children per 100,000 population, France six, Spain two and Finland 0.2 (Campbell, 2007). A nation of citizens is also rapidly becoming a 'custodial democracy'.

We are faced with a very real dilemma in the present social crisis. There have always been two roads to 'community'. Many colleagues have believed in a 'consensual' stance for community development and adult education, working with the system and attempting to increase the power of people and communities within it. Those of us who have always believed in a creative 'conflictual' approach, working 'in', but if needs be 'against', the system see our position vindicated by trends in the politics of community. It was from this position that the anti-racist work for ALAC at Northern College was developed.

Demonstrating praxis, popular adult education practice confronting racism

The anti-racist programme developed with ALAC at the Northern College in a very modest way suggested that it is possible to develop a coherent and relevant popular adult education response to these social, cultural and political challenges which have generated the New Racism.

Theory and popular adult education

Popular adult education work needs to be rigorously theorised and self-reflective to give confidence to practitioners and coherence to the programme. There is also a need for an interrogation of theory which can then be translated into 'really useful knowledge' for the work, and for the information and resources used in the work for developing critical consciousness.

*The tutors who delivered the programme had engaged with the wide-ranging
debate which had begun on multiculturalism, identity, cosmopolitanism 'at the
same time as 'community cohesion' and 'integration' policies signalled the death
of multiculturalism'. (Kundnani, 2007 p. 7)*

The team decided to choose an overtly 'anti-racist' starting point for the
work based around the concept of the UK as a 'Mongrel Nation'
(borrowed from a TV series with Eddie Izzard), and to seek to develop
courses based on solidarity and alliance building around working-class
issues across ethnic divides. Perhaps what we were moving towards, in our
work, is what Paul Gilroy calls 'a reworked and politicised multiculturalism' (Gilroy, 2004). We instinctively felt that multiculturalism and a
pluralistic integration of people and traditions had to recognise conflict
and open debate. We felt, like Tariq Modood, (Modood, 2004) and
Darcus Howe,[1] that social movements, and political struggles around
anti-racism had been, in the past, the creative force for building a
multicultural society.

It seemed to us that to create and to develop adult education initiatives which argued for this through anti-racist materials and content, and
through methods which gave ourselves and students a framework and
process to facilitate and support 'political debate and political contestation',
might be a creative response to the new racism around us.

We set out to work in solidarity with anti-racist community
organisations and social movements of refugees and migrant workers,
organising around local anti-racist campaigning. Our practice was aimed
at developing critical consciousness and providing 'really useful
knowledge', linking to political action in a traditional popular education
way.

Between 2003 and 2006 we organised at the Northern College a
programme of residential short courses of two or three days, called
'Combating Racism' to discuss and develop our approaches with
workers and activists in voluntary and community organisations. We were
not offering 'Diversity Training'; we were recruiting from, and
resourcing, anti-racist organisations in Yorkshire to develop anti-racist
working, solidarity, and strategies. This residential programme included
'Kicking Out Racism in Your Community', 'Challenging Racism for

---

[1] See his regular column in *New Statesman* for a consistent argument on this theme.

Community Trainers' and 'Divided We Fall: Resolving Conflict in Communities'. We confronted media distortions with 'Minorities, Myths and the Media'. Working with asylum seekers and refugees, we developed a residential version of the refugee-led course, 'Living in the UK', and a course for Refugee Community Organisations (RCOs): 'How to Organise RCOs'.

Research and anti-racist popular adult education

Much of our citizenship adult education practice was developed from a research perspective. This seems to us crucial in a world where quantitative research on 'numbers' of 'illegals' or migrants defines issues. Contesting racist data and projections we felt was an important starting point for anti-racist work. In recent years a right-wing immigration research organisation, Migrant Watch, has been able to dominate a public agenda largely uncontested. We actively researched information and relevant reports and summarised them and made them available in handouts as 'really useful knowledge'. There has never been a more important period to make available alternative and academic sources unreported in mainstream media. We used materials developed by campaigning research organisations like 'Searchlight' for their own educational work and campaign training. This approach became important in work that the Northern College team (Louise Mycroft, Jane Weatherby, and myself) did with Kirklees workers and activists in the summer of 2005 after the 7/7 bombs, parallel to the ALAC programme, in communities (Huddersfield and Dewsbury) from which the London bombers originated. (See Mycroft, Weatherby, and Grayson, 2005.)

The ALAC programme also enabled us to demonstrate how important the research work carried out by adult educators is to the quality of citizenship education. Participative, community-based research is often a key starting point for our work. The methodology is important in committed research linked to popular adult education initiatives. A good example would be the work of one of our team, Marion Horton, whose work with Gypsy and Traveller people and organisations has been developed in part from methods of 'close contact qualitative research' (Horton, 2004; Horton, 2007). Here, in research on health, caravan sites and housing, methods were developed emphasising solidarity and equal, respectful, culturally-sensitive and trusting approaches. In research work with Gypsies and Travellers, we find that simply shedding light on a culture almost unknown in society as a whole, and using findings in adult education 'awareness raising' counters the almost universal 'common sense' racism against them (see Acton, 1997; Clark and Greenfields, 2006).

Local research working in our practice is always put into a wider historical and political context beyond the particular group or community. In particular, this provides rich historical material for anti-racist work. Thomas Action, the only Professor of Romany Studies in the UK, argues that research on Romany Gypsies and 'gadjos' (non-Gypsy people) should have this historical context.

> *This means… that historical investigation, study and knowledge are not optional extras, the private indulgence of a few intellectuals and romantics – but vital for any group or individual seeking self determination. They are too important to be left as the playthings of manipulative nationalist politicians. In other words, if political practice, community activism, and policy planning are to change rather than reinforce the deeply embedded structures of Romany–gadjo misunderstanding they have to be grounded in a profound understanding of how Romany–gadjo relations have developed. (Acton, 2006, p.30)*

Using these approaches, and the networks generated by the research, Gypsy and Traveller students were attracted to the anti-racist programme.

Safe spaces working

The descent of state policies to the level of a new racist authoritarianism, and 'nativism' (Kundnani, 2007), when dealing with 'illegals', has produced a backlash from those working on the frontline of state services. Voluntary organisations have emerged to give 'safe houses' and food parcels to destitute asylum seekers. Workers employed by local councils and community organisations who came to the courses had formed a 'poverty forum' in Hull, and had actively supported anti-deportation campaigns. There is almost a 'guerrilla' mentality in these sectors.

Refugees and asylum seekers have also, under crisis pressures, developed their own support and protest organisations. There is even a new acronym, the RCO, the Refugee Community Organisation.

Part of the popular adult education anti-racist work developed around the ALAC work was to develop 'safe' environments and spaces for front-line community workers, paid and unpaid, in the field of anti-racist community development. Thus gatherings of workers with asylum seekers and refugees were organised. In 2004 a regular workshop and support meeting for workers with Gypsy and Traveller groups was created. Allied to these initiatives was the development of 'awareness raising' workshops for workers and voluntary organisations about the actual experience of asylum seekers. The work was linked to work already being developed by RCOs and in a different context Gypsy and Traveller organisations.

Teach-ins and practice workshops

The Northern College contribution to the ALAC Hub included a return to a tradition of popular adult education in a series of directly politically challenging 'Teach-Ins' for the college students, community activists, and community organisations in South Yorkshire. The 'teach-in' format originated in the student movements of the 1970s where researchers and political activists 'outside the Academy' offered an alternative space for developing critical consciousness, challenging official and media views of social and political issues. Local refugee organisations analysed from direct experience Palestine, Somalia and the Rwanda massacres; campaigners offered analyses of AIDS in Africa, child labour and trafficking and trade union murders in Colombia; a Romani Gypsy campaigner and researcher-fronted discussions on racism and Gypsies in the UK and Roma in the new Europe. We offered radical analyses of the Iraq War and the growth of Far Right politics in the region. Mobilising the students attracted to the ALAC programme in general meant that there were Zimbabwean refugee academics, Congolese refugees, and Iraqi Kurd students joining the debates with community activist students and Barnsley and Sheffield community groups. Students were challenged with the reality of the current political situation, and could share their analysis of the roots of racism and international conflicts, and current campaigns and struggles.

Good Practice seminars and workshops were also organised to reflect radical and successful practice and also to reflect the experience of international initiatives in popular adult education. Thus, we created workshops with Keith Russell of the Warren young peoples' centre in Hull, pioneers in 'empowerment' approaches, and workshops which included visiting speakers and Northern College partners from Sweden, Hungary and the USA.

A global approach

We felt that our approach to anti-racism and citizenship needed to have an immediate European and Global dimension. Using established links with Swedish colleagues we worked actively with a brand-new folk high school in Sweden – the Glocal (The Local is Global) folk high school in Malmo. New technologies allow us to build effective networking and work beyond borders, but we are slow in actually involving real people in communities in this process as opposed to the professionals and academics who gather regularly in our international fora. Regular international people-to-people programmes are crucially important, and in 2005–6 we organised from the ALAC programme, study visits for refugees and workers to Sweden, and Gypsies and Travellers and workers to Hungary.

A future for popular adult education citizenship work?

For many years socialists and those on the Left in general who have been involved in popular adult education within the publicly funded sector have been working on developing 'spaces' within the system. I suggested at a Sheffield workshop in 2005 that perhaps we were actually in 'holding pens' waiting for our demise. The ALAC 'pump-priming' funding and hub organisation achieved a great deal on very modest public funds, and should be seen by government as a way of encouraging innovation and co-operation in citizenship education. The central problem of course remains that in a period of 'business rule' rather than a social democracy, government priorities are determined by the needs of the market. Northern College itself has been perhaps terminally injured in this new climate by funding cuts and having to turn to new marketised skills-based and vocational programmes.

Perhaps on the other hand popular adult education, with its directly political and mobilisation agenda to build an egalitarian social democracy, should be realistic about its relationship to the state, educational institutions and governments. There are clearly challenges, contradictions, even spaces, still to be created within these relationships with the state, but there are also possibilities 'beyond state funding' in civil society in general – networks to be built with social movements, trade unions and campaigners, and new radical popular adult education provision to be created.

166

References

Acton T. ed. (1997) *Gypsy Politics and Traveller Identity*. Hatfield: University of Hertfordshire Press

Acton T. (2006) 'Romani Politics, scholarship, and the discourse of nation building', in Marsh, A. and Strand, E. *Gypsies and the problems of identities*. Istanbul: Swedish Research Institute in Istanbul.

Balibar, E. (2004) *We, the People of Europe? Reflections on transnational citizenship*. New Jersey: Princeton University Press

Ball, M. and Hampton, W. (eds) (2004) *The Northern College: Twenty five years of adult learning*. Leicester: NIACE

Campbell, D. (2007) 'Bulger, Blunkett, and the making of a 'prison fetish' '. *The Guardian*, 31 March.

Clark, C. and Greenfields, M. (2006) *Here to Stay: The Gypsies and Travellers of Britain*. Hatfield: University of Hertfordshire Press

Cohen, S. (2006) *Deportation is Freedom: The Orwellian world of immigration controls*. London: Jessica Kingsley

Francis, D., Grayson, J. and Henderson, P. (eds) (2002) *Rich Seam: Community development in the coalfields*. London: CDF

Gilroy, P. (2004) *After Empire: Multiculture or post-colonial melancholia*. London: Routledge

Grayson, J., Horton, M. and Petrie, A. (2007) *The European Roma of South Yorkshire*. Barnsley: AdEd Knowledge Company

Grayson, J. and Jackson, K. (2004) 'Engagement with the Community: Some significant aspects of the short course programme' in Ball, M. and Hampton, W. (eds) *The Northern College: Twenty five years of adult learning* , pp. 112– 30. Leicester: NIACE

Horton, M. (2002) 'From Kiveton to Kunbabony – Change in South Yorkshire', in Francis, D., Grayson, J. and Henderson, P. (eds) *Rich Seam: Community Development in the Coalfields*. London: CDF

Horton, M. (2004) 'The health and site needs of the Transient Gypsies and Travellers of Leeds.' May 2004 to September 2004. Leeds: Leeds Health for All

Horton, M. (2007) 'Health and Home Place: Close contact participatory research with gypsies and travellers in Leeds, England, UK', in Williamson, A. and DeSouza, R. (eds), *Researching with communities*. Auckland, New Zealand: Muddy Creek Press

Kundnani, A. (2007) *The End of Tolerance: Racism in 21st Century Britain*. London: Pluto Press

Lavalette, M. and Ferguson, I. eds (2007) *International Social Work and the Radical Tradition.* Birmingham: Venture Press

Legrain, P. (2006) *Immigrants: Your country needs them.* London: Little, Brown Book Group

Mason, P. (2007) *Live working or die fighting.* London: Harvill Secker

Modood, T. (2004) 'Multiculturalism or Britishness: a false debate' in *Catalyst,* Winter 2004/5

Mycroft, L., Weatherby, J. and Grayson, J. (2005) 'After the Bombs …' in *Adults Learning,* September 2005, Vol. 17, No. 1. Leicester: NIACE

Narey, M. (2006) 'Moral Outrage', *New Statesman,* 13 November, pp. 30–32

Sivanandan, A. (2006) *'Race, Terror and Civil Society'* in *Race and Class,* Vol. 47, No. 3

Thompson, J. (2000) 'When active citizenship becomes 'mob rule'' in *Adults Learning*, September 2000, Vol. 12, No. 1, pp. 23–24. Leicester: NIACE

CHAPTER TEN

Constructed conversation: the Lincolnshire active learning approach

Zoraida Mendiwelso-Bendek and Rebecca Herron

The East Midlands ALAC Hub hosted by the Lincolnshire Citizenship Network is a network of individuals and organisations interested in promoting informal learning processes for community empowerment. From the start (2001) the Lincolnshire Citizenship Network has made the participation of the public sector, civic institutions, the community and voluntary sector in joint deliberations a priority – its aim being to *construct* over time *conversations* that create new spaces and opportunities to address social inequality, enabling communities to create and sustain new forms of interaction and decision-making. The notion of *constructed conversation* is used to highlight conversations in which the participants agree to observe predefined rules of engagement.

The *Take Part: Active Learning for Active Citizenship* programme has given the network the opportunity to develop new spaces to meet and develop structures and processes in relation to a range of issues identified by the community to be of importance to them. These include, among others, issues surrounding effective dialogue between adults and young people, supporting and developing community project leaders working to address social inequalities, and active citizenship learning for immigrants and mental health service users and carers.

Constructed conversations

The topic of constructed conversations has been developed from multiple perspectives, going from the biological and managerial to the political and philosophical. For instance, Winograd and Flores (1986), based on Maturana's proposal that conversation is the braiding of language and emotions (Maturana, 1988) and Searle's speech act theory (Searle, 1969), offer a structure for 'conversations for action'. They claim that these conversations, which lead to the co-ordination of actions, show universal patterns. Thus, participants in the flux of conversations for action make requests/offers to each other, negotiate their conditions of satisfaction, clarify performance criteria and signal the closure of the conversation.

On his part, Beer's protocol for Team Syntegrity (Beer, 1994) offers a structure for non–hierarchical conversations, which gives participants equality of arms in their dialogues.

From the perspective of the basic principle of justice, Rawls (1971, 1993) proposes a kind of constructed conversation, which adopts an original position with a veil of ignorance, as the basic platform to structure conversations.

For transparency, Habermas (1984) proposes the notion of ideal speech as a constructed conversation where the rules and relations of engagement strive for the best rational argument and participants are prepared to satisfy each other for the *validity claims* they reciprocally raise. Participants, in the course of communicative actions, reciprocally exchange sentences that can be accepted or contested as validity claims oriented to reaching understanding to generate a sense of general interest and common good.

The theme of constructed conversation is further developed by Ackerman's designed conversation, in which an authority monitors that the exchanges among participants conform to patterns of political neutrality and 'liberal dialogue' (Ackerman, 1980).

At the level of communitarianism, Walzer (1990) claims that the rules of engagement in designing conversations should be support by universal values to build the public domain.

Conversations are essential to our daily communications and the challenge is to *align them with democratic principles* (Espejo, 2003). It is important to structure these conversations in such a way that all relevant viewpoints to the issues at hand are represented and in numbers that support meaningful interactions – avoiding the dominance of some at the expense of the most. Equally it is important to avoid conflating different levels of meaningful interactions by collapsing global and local issues in one conversation. These are all structural considerations restricting conversations in order to make them more relevant and socially valuable. Also it is important to increase individuals' self-observation and self-reflection to improve the outcomes of their engagement in the community (ibid.).

The ALAC East Midlands project is based on the idea that citizenship is a stable construction that emerges from our moment-to-moment interactions as we build up the public domain (Mendiwelso–Bendek, 2002). To improve these interactions we need to observe them – giving them context – to help us learn *concepts and practices* at the same time. The observer needs to be inside and outside the action, simultaneously observing us as actors and observers, in a circular causality (Von Foerster, 1982). In this relationship between action and observation, observation can improve our action and vice versa (De Zeeuw, 1996).

ALAC East Midlands is using these considerations to support groups to learn *through their conversations*. Conversations that are structurally constrained, avoiding, among others, imbalances of numbers, personalities and experience, can help us to get the best from participants in *their (our)* construction of civil society (Beer, 1994). 'Constraint' in this sense is an enabler of a group's self-organisation, enhancing their autonomy and the opportunities to produce collective outcomes that otherwise would be difficult to achieve. Aspects of ALAC's work have had this structuring. Groups have been provided with spaces to reflect and act collectively. In these spaces these groups have constructed dialogues and exchanged views around decision-making issues, making more visible the collective knowledge and its relevance to improve participants' actions, as well as the monitoring and challenging of their collective participation, with the support of facts, information, experiences, stories and other forms of evidence contributed to (and by) the conversations.

ALAC has offered opportunities for learning by exploring issues; learning how to engage in processes, to identify community actors, to observe ourselves, and to observe and define good practices. It is learning to see the connection between observation and action. It is an informal learning process but has a stable structure, including facilitation and monitoring, with a timetable, with structure, and with stable groups of participants with the commitment to produce visible outcomes for the community as a whole.

Constructed conversations within ALAC work from the principle that while citizens have the potential competence and capacity to identify issues and injustices in their own communities, offering support to these conversations (in terms of discussion topics, structure, monitoring and principles) supports all involved to work collectively and as such has helped to produce expected and unexpected outcomes in alignment with strengthening the public community.

The Lincolnshire Citizenship Network

The idea of constructed conversations has underpinned our work in the ALAC programme. Within ALAC's principles and values, a framework has been developed that recognises the need for catalysts to support self-organising processes which can lead to the creation of self-constructed communities. Accordingly, the Lincolnshire Citizenship Network has engaged individuals and groups of learners as catalysts of community processes. Different collective learning experiences (workshops, seminars, conferences) have permitted the gradual evolution of a *network* of learners. This process had the additional intention of increasing community *connectivity*; enabling learners to create their own networks and capabilities for observation, reflection and action.

The Lincolnshire project sought to develop two strands simultaneously through this process:

- *individual learning* that constituted their engagement in public domain and civil/civic society; and
- the *improvement of community structures* (that is the networks, capabilities and responsiveness of collective provision).

The project made use of, and extended, an existing network – The Lincolnshire Citizenship Network – and the services of tutors from the University of Lincoln who facilitated this network. The network has consisted of approximately 30 people, from many community organisations, who have met at annual events over a number of years (since 2001) to explore citizenship themes. These themes have included work on citizenship in schools and organisational citizenship.

Several 'activators' from this network emerged as key champions for the ALAC project and invested much time and effort to collaboratively shape the form that the ALAC Project took in Lincolnshire.

In 2004, the Lincolnshire Citizenship Network was recognised as one of the hubs in the country to work in the programme Active Learning for Active Citizenship (ALAC). Equally, DEFRA's Rural Social and Community Programme (RSCP), East Midlands Development Agency

(EMDA) and Lincolnshire Enterprise have included ALAC Lincolnshire among their projects. Based on ALAC national and local learning processes, the Lincolnshire Citizenship Network is carrying out a countywide project to produce collective guidance on processes for active learning for active citizenship.

The Lincolnshire ALAC hub works in partnership with a diversity of voluntary sector project managers and organisations; each looking at different voluntary and community sector activities striving to improve civil society. Community issues explored within the hub include issues surrounding effective dialogue between adults and young people, supporting and developing a group of Project Leaders working to address social inequalities, and developing (in a participatory manner) 'active citizenship learning' for new arrival communities and the users of mental health services and their carers.

The work of the Project Leaders Group and the New Arrival Communities group within ALAC has particular synergy as many of the issues of concern to the Project Leaders were directly relevant to the citizenship experiences of the new arrival communities. We wish to present here the process and outcome of some of the activities undertaken by these two groups as part of the ALAC Programme – both to show some of the outcomes of this research process and to offer some insight into the various modes of delivery and making operational the conceptual framework of constructed conversations.

In both cases, the ALAC facilitators became participants in the ongoing process of reflection and action that has aimed at stimulating civil renewal. The hub has contributed to the creation of new resources and activities leading to learning processes such as the creation of radio programmes by migrant workers participating in ALAC workshops and new ESOL and Participatory Evaluation training provision.

The ALAC hub has offered facilitation for a number of activities within each project in the network, including workshops, conferences, celebration events and *constructed conversations* within the projects. It has also facilitated a number of semi-formal classroom activities such as IT sessions, English Language classes and the exploration of citizenship concerns through music composition workshops.

The following two Case Studies are intended to give a flavour of the activities of the East Midlands Hub in two of the largest four activity areas – the learning within 'new arrival' groups and 'project leader' groups aimed at Community Empowerment.

Constructing conversations: Case Study 1 – 'New Arrival' communities

Engaging participants

The **first case study** looks at the evolution of community-based provision for migrant workers ('new arrival communities') in the area of Lincolnshire. This activity involved a large number of participants from the voluntary and community sector, from the public sector and from the migrant worker community. It sought to identify current concerns and engage those involved in processes that could influence and resolve key issues.

Lincolnshire is a largely agricultural area and the south of the county, around Boston, is highly dependent on the availability of a European migrant workforce – predominantly young people from Poland and Portugal, but including a wide range of nationalities and age groups.

Participants from New Arrival communities have several distinct learning needs (shared to varying degrees by other groups of learners in the network) and identified by the hub through their conversations within the programme:

Communication – English is often a second language within this group, so the use of language within the constructed conversations has always to be considered. Developing English language skills is also a key motivator for participation and initial engagement, as for many it is a barrier to active engagement in civil life – including employment.

Knowledge of structures and processes – engagement with civil and civic structures is often hindered for new arrival communities by a lack of knowledge of 'how things operate in the UK'. This analysis of structures and processes is an important element of the Lincolnshire approach. It is linked to a discussion about roles and responsibilities and is created ('constructed') through a process of dialogue that explores with many different community members their experiences and local knowledge.

Identity and membership – the process of learning involves a continual process of reflection and observation of the self and others – a process of observation that takes in reflections about activity and the meanings associated with that activity. In this way our actions (or lack of them) as citizens can be reflected on the consequences and alternatives considered.

Forms of delivery

Bearing in mind the above considerations, several different learning activities have been developed. Each has intended to create spaces for informal learning that supports individual and collective empowerment in different ways:

Music workshops – initial ALAC activity with a group of learners from new arrival communities used music specialists as group tutors. In this way the group was able to overcome fairly severe restrictions in language fluency by working together to make a song about their experiences as European citizens in the UK. In the process of constructing the lyrics they were able to tackle a wide range of citizenship issues and to express these in an intrinsically aesthetic form that overcame differences in language proficiency in a very effective manner.

ESOL with civic engagement – this notion of combining adult informal citizenship learning with other forms of learning and activity is a key element of the Lincolnshire approach. A second example is through the provision of *English as a Second Language* courses coupled with learning about active citizenship. This has proved a stimulating combination for both participants and tutors with citizenship issues providing content for literal 'constructed conversations'.

Community radio production workshops – a third example of combining ALAC with other relevant activities to support active citizenship has been the coupling of the ALAC Programme with the launch of a Community Radio station at the University of Lincoln. Siren FM and the Polish group have had regular meetings and training to produce community radio programmes. Programmes are being produced by them in both Polish and English and focus around discussing citizenship issues of relevance to the communities they engage with.

Mentoring (employment and training opportunities) – an additional example of how the Take Part ALAC hub seeks to support the creation of stronger actors within the community is the role of mentoring individuals. This mentoring covers aspects of structure and process (for example, what opportunities exist, how training is accessed, how to apply to certain jobs or convert qualifications) and communication (how to present your own identity, for example through CVs or interviews and how to think about roles within society, future possibilities and how to organise for them).

Constructing conversations: Case Study 2 – project managers' group

Creating a learning network

Using the ALAC principles and values, the East Midlands Hub initiated and facilitated a range of community interactions designed to create and maintain conversations about social justice and issues surrounding active citizenship and community empowerment.

The **second case study** consists of learners from several different organisations from across Lincolnshire. What links them together is that a key community project worker in each project became an active learner within the ALAC hub. Initially each of these learners engaged with the project on an individual basis, discussing and reflecting how their actions were actively shaping civil society (or not, as the case might be). Then, over a period of time, a network of learners was formed. This network of community project managers met on a regular basis to share their experiences. In doing this they were able to challenge each other on issues related to active citizenship, to share experiences and to share with the hub their views on effective learning processes within their own particular voluntary or community activities. Much of the insight into community-based learning processes has been gained in this way.

The emphasis throughout has been about designing interactions that are appropriate and meaningful for those participating. This has meant a mix of informal and formal provision – ranging from one-to-one conversations to group workshops and conference events.

What is distinct about each learning activity is the participants' commitment to discuss issues surrounding community empowerment, and at the same time to build up their skills and those of others that enable community engagement.

Through this process participants also create their own sense of identity as a community of learners, with a shared sense of exploration into the unknown and an acknowledgement of the unique contributions each might make to better collective decision-making.

These processes can work to overcome the traditional (passive) civil and civic relationships of 'them and us' – *distinctions between organisations and citizens* – to create a more active citizenry (on both sides).

Identifying issues

Constructing conversations as informal education demands a different approach to classic curriculum design. Instead of deciding *a priori* what the 'course content' will include, the facilitators (and participants) have had to be prepared to allow issues and topics *to emerge* through a process of conversation and interaction.

Issues form through many small interactions and through feedback from other participants and as a result may be simultaneously owned by many of the participants. As a way of supporting the development of active decision-making this is an important feature, as are the communities that are formed around the conversations of most interest.

In the initial stages of development, ideas and notions may be vague. Later, while still not necessarily definitive, key concepts may become more easily visible to participants. At this stage learning may be recorded as an outcome of the conversations.

Co-authoring a 'guide to processes'

Such a process was undertaken by the group of community project leaders. Following extended monthly participation in ALAC meetings, a group of Community Research Associates[1] met in a workshop situation to co-author a guide to practice (Mendiwelso-Bendek and Herron, 2006). The following is a summary of their discussions. It serves two purposes here – firstly to give an example of the outputs of this kind of process and secondly as an exploration of the content of community-led discussions around active citizenship.

What is meant by Active Learning for Active Citizenship and how can informal learning processes support community engagement?

One topic to emerge from the conversations was a response to the programme's name and what that meant for participants. The process of constructed conversations lends itself to this type of critical, reflexive activity. While this is not an easy concept to summarise, participants drew up their own list of characteristics for an ALAC programme. Several opinions were highlighted, ranging from the fairly abstract, 'learning opportunities for community engagement' to the concrete 'helping people develop knowledge, skills and confidence to satisfy their own needs.'

- The conversations focused around the capacity of ALAC to provide problem-solving capability, for example: 'creating community learning opportunities that support people in taking charge of their own futures'; 'bringing different members of society together to engage in active learning in order to resolve community issues (for example, individuals, community groups, voluntary and public sector employees and other decision-makers)'; 'identifying possible solutions/new resources/new knowledge (that is 'knowledge is power'), for example, supporting individuals'.

---

[1] A term used to recognise community members who became active researchers within the Lincolnshire Citizenship Network (active rather than passive learners, setting and exploring their own agendas within the broader parameters of the project).

- Some of this capacity for problem-solving was seen to come from improved community networking within the ALAC learning processes: 'making connections (building bridges)'; supporting individuals and groups to identify bridges/links required or desired and enabling people to act on their own, either to make new connections or remove existing barriers'.
- Conversations looked at how ALAC related to individuals having a voice and having rights and responsibilities; 'enabling individuals and groups to have a say in services they receive'; 'exploring people's rights/entitlements/choices and responsibilities'; 'giving groups confidence to set their own agendas and to become interdependent members of their community and more active citizens, and ensuring that local statutory providers make changes where agreed'.
- There was also an emphasis on creating appropriate support structures: 'identifying ways people *fall through the net* of provision and designing ways of preventing/dealing with this'; 'looking for gaps in the support structure: supporting people to identify what they need in order to be able to help themselves to find the right support, to set up their own groups, to access a service, to go to local groups or to find information'; 'recognising that *some things can't be changed* in the short term and coming to terms with what this means; 'lobbying to make changes in the longer term'.

What characterises informal, community-based learning and how should ALAC be delivered?

The Project managers identified that ALAC was predominantly about adult learners, learning in community settings and learning about community contexts and issues. The main purpose of this learning was to influence decision-making:

- They also identified that it is important to work in ways that are learner-centred/learner-led, including focusing on learning based on experiences and on forms of learning that do not require prior qualifications or accreditation to take part in.

- It was felt that most productive learning groups would involve a mix of stakeholders/community learners, including funders, providers, users of services (and, where appropriate, their carers) and others in the community (for example employers, trade unions, regional strategists, national policy-makers, etc). This mix was seen as important as it allowed the natural progression from conversation to action, which was essential if the learning was to lead to action. It was acknowledged that sometimes these interactions would have to be designed carefully to enable all to participate, but that this was precisely the rationale behind '*constructed* conversations'.

- Informal learning is seen as something flexible but stable – starting from individual and group experiences and developing a dialogue about active citizenship issues that arise from these constructed conversations.

- Learning processes should be encouraged that are dynamic and responsive to changes in the environment (that is changes in issues, policy, structure and person) and that support the creation of knowledge about how to 'get things done' and influence policy and decision-making (for example, access people and organisations, identifying sustainable and fair routes that are comfortable and stable).

- Project managers highlighted the importance of using a variety of techniques to encourage participation. These might include, for example, discussion groups, use of expressive art (music, drawing and dance) and different tools or visual stimulation (Lotus Blossom diagrams, problem trees, maps etc).

- Supporting bridge-building – for example, between people with different languages, different national/natural languages or differences in forms of (English) language used between institutions/within communities).

- Language was identified as being very important – making use of language expertise within the community and letting people use their own words. Ways of promoting this include: repeating/reflecting your understanding and interpretations of something you think you have heard; exploring 'difficult' language (for example, jargon busting); facilitating joint drafting of documents and doing things in pairs or small groups to avoid the potential embarrassment of forcing someone to demonstrate their literacy and other communication skills.

- It was also felt important to 'meet people on an individual basis'. There is a need for open-mindedness 'trying to meet people with no preconceived ideas', meeting on people's own territory, being flexible on the time allocated to individuals and moving at people's own speed, remaining committed to individuals.

- The importance of finding safe spaces was also highlighted. This includes ensuring confidentiality when required and providing familiar and relaxed places, safety for all involved and moving locations of meetings to enable access for all to at least some of the events.

- A professional approach was supported. This was seen as one that is non-judgemental, involves 'absolute trust', respect for people and shared power/care for the balance of power.

- Recurrent citizenship themes were expected to underpin provision:
  - social justice;
  - rights and responsibilities;
  - individuals, collectives and the State;
  - the individuals' relationship with others;
  - identity and belonging;
  - civil and civic society;
  - governance and civic engagement; and
  - community engagement and building civil society.

Outreach practice/identifying 'what's in it for participants' and potential barriers to participation

Key elements were identified by the project managers:

- It is important to identify early on what practical things learners want (for example language courses and IT provision) and to build these into more generic learning. This might involve liaison with employers and the consideration of working commitments and restrictions. The result of doing this can be to provide support for citizens in their existing workloads/activities and in new developments and policy formation.
- It is also important to recognise and try to overcome practical barriers to learning. These might include for instance: transport, provision and costs, location of events, care provision (for example childcare), the time of day of events and the working patterns of participants.
- The importance of confidence building and establishing trust and freedom for discussion was recognised.

Organisational issues/sustainability and planning

Finally, the project managers considered organisational aspects to designing Active Learning for Active Citizenship activity:

- The importance of maintaining a good relationship with funders and organisational flexibility was highlighted. It was felt that a sustained engagement was needed with funders to build trust that the voluntary and community sector organisations are doing the best job possible (built on experience and an understanding of daily realities). Building policy and other relationships with funders as part of the design and implementation of ALAC programmes helps to ensure equal relationships between funders and communities.

- Building sustained relationships between civic bodies and active citizens was also seen as important for identifying *holes in the net* of current provision/policy and for maintaining a sense of what the ALAC activity is about if and when external environment changes or outside priorities alter. This is important in order to maintain the internal integrity of a project (for example if the environment changes).
- It was felt that this conversation is constructed through creating clear channels of communication. These include:

  - ★ lobbying, listening and learning from discussions;
  - ★ following up decision-making processes to ensure changes are implemented and effective;
  - ★ telling funders when there is a problem/disagreement; and
  - ★ maintaining integrity.

- It was felt that ALAC programmes need to remember the importance of investing time working with funders to build a positive shared culture in relation to funding and auditing processes and that this should involve a focus on *outcomes and impacts* rather than simply *outputs*. This involves avoiding the temptation to overly pre-specifying numbers within contracts (except in cases with a clear reason for inclusion) and of creating for ourselves unrealistic targets which create undue stress and are frequently counter-productive. The emphasis in programme specification should be on quality not quantity and this helps to enable flexibility to meet individual needs in different contexts.
- It was felt desirable to develop a strategy for community learning and engagement that supported individuals, while at the same time worked within groups to achieve aims. Thus learning is a mixture of individual and collective extension and development. Community-led exploration of learning needs should include issues of concern and priorities for change and practical issues (such as venue, accessibility: how, what, when). Consideration of whether *individual* or *group* learning will involve the identification of different requirements for support and provision.

Conclusion

The East Midlands Hub introduced the notion of constructed conversation to move interactions from the conversations in ordinary life to the conversation in the public domain. This shift required exploring the effects of offering interactive spaces that effectively imposed restrictive structures to conversations but not, at any stage, to their content. On the contrary, the purpose of introducing constraint has been reducing the domination of the most powerful in dialogues. Our intention has been to demonstrate that constructing the rules of engagement in conversations can produce significant learning improvements in engaging participants in the public domain, and consequently, that constructed conversation can empower individuals, groups and organisations. However, the case studies illustrate the need for pragmatism in supporting interactions in the public domain. The ideals of constructed conversations need a gentle introduction to the realities of individuals and communities. At this stage of our work we believe that we have achieved significant results engaging people; however there is much more to learn regarding improving dialogues and conversations and this paper is only an account of early experiences driven by the ideas of constructed conversations.

References

Ackerman, B. (1980) *Social Justice in the Liberal State*. New Haven: Yale University Press

Beer, S. (1994) *Beyond Dispute: The invention of team syntegrity*. New York: John Wiley and Sons

DfEE (1998) *Education for Citizenship and the Teaching of Democracy in Schools: Final report of the Advisory Group on Citizenship*. London: QCA

Espejo, R. (2003) 'Social Systems and the Embodiment of Organizational Learning' in *Complex Systems and Evolutionary Perspectives on Organizations: The application of complexity theory to organizations*, edited by Eve Mittleton-Kelly. Pergamon–Elsevier Science, pp. 53–70

Habermas, J. (1984) *Theory of Communicative Action: Reason and the rationalization of society, V. 1*. Cambridge: Polity Press (translated by Tomas MacCarthy)

Maturana, H. (1988) 'The Search for Objectivity, or the Quest for a Compelling Argument', in *Irish Journal of Psychology*. Vol. 9, No. 1, pp. 25–82

Mendiwelso-Bendek, Z. (2002) 'Citizens of the Future: Beyond normative conditions through the emergence of desirable collective properties', *Journal of Business Ethics*, Vol. 39, pp. 189–195

Mendiwelso-Bendek , Z. and Herron, R. (2006) *Take Part – East Midlands – Active Citizenship in Practice.* Lincoln: Lincolnshire Citizenship Network

Rawls, J. (1971) *A Theory of Justice.* Oxford: Oxford University Press

Rawls, J. (1993) *Political Liberalism.* New York: Columbia University Press

Searle, J. (1969) *Speech Acts: An essay in the philosophy of language.* Cambridge: Cambridge University Press

Von Foerster, H. (1982) *Observing Systems.* Salinas, CA: Intersystems Publications

Walzer, M. (1990) A Critique of Philosophical Conversation, in *The Philosophical Forum*, Vol. XXI, No. 1–2, pp. 182–203

Winograd, T. and Flores, F. (1986) *Understanding Computers and Cognition: A new foundation for design.* Reading, MA: Addison-Wesley

Woodward, V. (2004) *Active Learning for Active Citizenship.* CRU. London: Home Office

Zeeuw, G. de (1996) 'Interaction of Actors Theory', in *Kybernetes*, Vol. 30, No. 7/8, pp. 971–983.

CHAPTER ELEVEN

The five Cs: Confident, Challenging, Co-operative, Constructive and Critical women IMPACT: women active in community and public life

JILL BEDFORD, SUE GORBING AND SAL HAMPSON

It opened my life to new opportunities and encouraged me to take risks that I would never have done had I not enrolled on the course.

It has made me feel alive again, it has opened up arenas that I quite possibly never thought I'd be able to sit in – let alone speak in.

Introduction and background

IMPACT grew out of a women's health project when the focus moved from running workshops on 'dealing with the menopause' and 'how to be mother and stay sane' to working out how we, as women, can influence the decisions that affect our lives. It evolved from a series of workshops around women and leadership which by 1998 had expanded to include a programme of training, practical support and mentoring. The first accredited 'course' of this type began in January 2000 and it focused on women's own experiences and opinions while setting out to explore local, national and European decision-making structures.

Another strand of work, funded through the Barrow Cadbury Trust in 2002, led to critical reflections on the political, social and economic contexts affecting women's development agendas, leadership and women's organisations.

We felt that vision, excitement and commitment were needed more than ever to encourage and motivate ourselves and other women to make a difference around 'women' and gender and to cut across the fragmentation, competition and individualism we saw operating in many women's organisations and initiatives at the time. We gained funding from a variety of sources – Health Action Zones, National Lottery, Barrow Cadbury Trust – to develop our ideas around women becoming more active in community and public life – through using a community development approach which counters the notion of elevating a few women as community leaders to talk on behalf of others and engage with civic structures as a token voice for women.

The success of the pilot courses led to further developments around the main topics of citizenship, democracy, leadership and participation and to an invitation by the Home Office ALAC programme to showcase the IMPACT approach as a creative learning initiative (2004–6).

ALAC provided opportunities and resources for those involved in this work to take it one stage further and bring together a local partnership comprising:

- Fircroft College: an independent residential further education college in Birmingham.
- Wolverhampton Asian Women and Diabetes Group: a support and lobbying group with an interest in Asian women's health – working across cultures to achieve change for women – involved at the start of this work.
- GATE: an adult educational advice and guidance service.
- Black Country Women's Development Network: a voluntary organisation with staff working to develop women's fora in the Black Country.
- Working for Change: an independent group of trainers and facilitators who had originally conceived the idea and worked to develop it over the years.

There were two co-existing agendas within the IMPACT programme; the public agenda around encouraging and supporting women to become more active in engagement/governance and in communities – and a more subtle agenda around women having more power in their lives and more power and influence in the world.

Consistency, continuity and sustainability

The consistent work done over the past ten years is due to a passion for women's development and, at times, felt like 'swimming against the tide'; funding for this type of work is hard to attract as it is long term and this resulted in using a patchwork of different funding opportunities which were generally short term and target driven – with different grants requiring different reporting mechanisms. The Barrow Cadbury Trust was an exception as they gave a three-year grant which was very flexible and was used to develop the work on an ongoing and progressive basis. This was crucial. (See *'Women, Leadership, Participation and Involvement Report'* at www.bct.org.uk.)

One of the original trainers, living back in her homeland of Zimbabwe for the last three years, has taken this approach and methodology with her. She is working with pastors' wives in a theological college and has long-term funding and support from the college to develop training and mentoring for women to become active in community and public life in their hometowns and villages. The college has training and has developed a team of facilitators and trainers to extend the work across the regions – in a very uncertain and unsafe political context.

Having continuity of funding and support opens up what is possible. So far, here in England we have patchy, fragmented and uncertain funding which immediately limits how we can start to structure and sustain initiatives. Women we have worked with in this initiative expressed interest in receiving training for themselves to do this work and carry on promoting the empowerment of women in different areas and communities, but we have been reluctant to progress this without some clarity around how to support them financially in the medium to longer term.

There is a need to develop trainers, facilitators and materials/resources so that similar opportunities can be offered to a wider range of women.

Why women?

Some startling facts and figures…

It is predicted that it will take:

- 20 years to achieve equality in civil service top management;
- 40 years to achieve an equal number of senior women in the judiciary;
- up to 200 years – another 40 elections – to achieve an equal number of women in Parliament. (Equal Opportunities Commission, 2006, survey of women's representation in positions of power.);
- more women than men live in poverty on deprived estates and women in general have lower incomes than men; and
- while women are the majority in community groups, they are under-represented when it comes to being in decision-making positions.

Challenging assumptions: gender issues in urban regeneration (1997 Oxfam, UK Poverty Programme)

One of the IMPACT courses included a simple audit as project work; participants were asked to select a decision-making committee or forum in their town and then to ask questions such as:

- How many men on your board/group/forum?
- How many women on your board/group/forum?
- How many people with disabilities?
- How many black and/or ethnic minority members?
- Who is the Chair?
- How does one get on the Board?

Information gathered was very patchy as there was very little systematic recording of such information and by the end it still was not clear how to become a member of many of these committees and boards. Many of the civic governance structures felt impenetrable and most of the participants felt that it had been a bruising experience as they had been treated with indifference and sometimes outright hostility and suspicion. The experience reinforced feelings of cynicism for some participants, but others wanted to get 'out there' and change things.

Over the past ten or so years, women we have worked with have expressed disappointment with accountability in systems of policy and decision-making. The majority of people active within these systems are men and generally represent a male interest which is viewed as 'the norm' and is perceived as gender neutral. However, people generally articulate their views, plans and policies based upon their experience of the world – and a male experience is significantly different from the experience of women. For example, 'safety' is perceived differently by men and women and how people perceive threats and danger will affect how they construct strategies and policies to minimise them. Consequently the notion of gender-neutral policies needs to be critiqued. It is our experience that the small numbers of women who are active within these systems often find it hard to be accepted and seen as legitimate unless they adopt the 'normal'/male mode of working and adhere to the existing structures, processes and culture.

Some of the IMPACT courses have featured a Round Table event where women who are actively involved in decision-making and policy planning at a senior level share their experiences with an audience of women. Invariably their stories include the challenges and difficulties of working within a culture which does not take account of women's lives and contributions. The following is a sample of comments from one such event.

What has got in the way?

- Not having gone to university.
- Choosing to go against the grain – being difficult at times.
- Surviving – the energy it takes.
- Lack of self confidence.
- Feeling muddled.
- The world outside – a shifting world that affects us.
- Thinking that others knew the masterplan – 'if only I too knew what was going on, then I would know what to do and how to do it': a myth.
- My short attention span.
- Fear of flying – fear of trying it out.
- Family expectations – not to get above yourself.
- Not knowing when it was appropriate to say some things and not others.

Which strategies have you found useful?

- Joining in the debate and finding my voice.
- Working across the boundaries.
- Avoiding cliques.
- Developing a full range of interpersonal skills and styles.
- Being straight and direct with people.
- Being explicit about personal values.
- Knowing that as women we can be very powerful.
- Always saying something in a meeting.
- Sharing things like childcare with other women.
- If asked to do something, saying yes and then worrying about how to do it later.
- Never, never saying 'just' or 'only' when talking about yourself.
- Not taking it all too seriously – having a sense of humour.
- Preparing the ground and not waiting to be asked.
- Networking – friends and family.
- Keeping going back to the source for sustenance and comfort.
- Wanting my children to stand tall and comfortable with their place in the world.

In spite of the existence of a variety of 'women's initiatives', ranging from specific projects to women's training programmes, there seemed to be little in the way of positive networking, with many women and women's organisations still feeling marginalised and excluded from mainstream political activity. This was reflected in the results of several research studies, including Oxfam's *Challenging Assumptions: gender issues in urban regeneration* and *The Gender Report – Women and Regional Regeneration in the Midlands* (CURS, University of Birmingham). Both reports found that women are less often found in influential positions within urban regeneration programmes. In terms of public policy, it appears that there is 'persistent lack of attention to women's inequality' (CURS) and 'no systematic way of ensuring women's needs and concerns are built into planning' (Oxfam).

Clearly the Gender Equality Duty is a timely legislative tool to help change the ways that civic structures and public policies affect women and men differentially. It will be interesting to see how this pans out in the next few years. However, we still need to work with women in the here and now, to ensure that they have the potential to access the places where decisions are made, priorities set and resources distributed. While personal development work and confidence building is a key component, it is not enough to create real and lasting change. It is not enough for women merely to access existing services and resources. They need to be equally involved in decision-making on issues that affect them, their families and their communities.

In summary then, we would argue that whatever system of policy making/decision-making we choose to examine, women are not really represented and find it hard to call those who make decisions on their behalf to account. Ideas about gender go to the very heart of our society and consequently are highly contentious.

Women and difference

Women came to IMPACT from all walks of life, sharing experiences and challenging each others' assumptions. Some women had not been out of their home for years because of illness, disability or a lack of personal confidence. Others had just left college or university, had retired from paid employment, were local councillors, volunteers and carers.

> *As a group of women we were able to share the richness of our lives irrespective of socio-economic status, faith, sexual orientation, age, ethnicity, disability, colour, creed, profession, etc.*

> *Irrelevant of our backgrounds – every single woman had some sort of inspiration in life – some sort of goal.*

> *We discovered that all the women on the course had suffered the same sort of inequalities and barriers.*

Some of the shared barriers are:

- lack of self-confidence – lack of qualification;
- doing things for everyone else and not for myself;
- not being able to articulate ideas and concerns clearly;
- depression and isolation;

- lack of knowledge and opportunity;
- childcare issues and other caring responsibilities;
- not being listened to and not being taken seriously;
- lack of transport and inaccessibility of venues;
- people making assumptions about women because of their culture;
- lack of support from employers;
- costs involved;
- financial dependence on others; and
- male-dominated meetings.

> *We have the same kind of issues no matter what our background or culture.*
> *We are seen as home-makers and have doubts about ourselves achieving any*
> *bigger ambitions.*

The IMPACT programme and the years of work preceding it acknowledged the differences between women and worked across 'difference' within a symmetry of similarity; responding to the community cohesion agenda before this particular terminology and associated policy drivers surfaced. If we focus solely on what separates women from each other then we lose the power that comes from the recognition of shared experiences around 'gender'; as Lister states, we run a risk:

> *... If 'woman' is simply deconstructed and left in fragments, there is no woman*
> *left to be a citizen. The fact that the category 'woman' is not unitary does not*
> *render it meaningless (Maynard, 1994). Black feminists, such as bell hooks*
> *(1984), Audre Lorde (1984) and Patricia Hill Collins (1991) have argued*
> *that, provided the differences between women are fully acknowledged, they do*
> *not preclude solidarity on the basis of those interests still shared as women.*
> *Central to these interests is women's exclusion from full citizenship, as the pat-*
> *terns of entry to the gateways to the various sectors of the public sphere remain*
> *profoundly gendered. Thus, the project of engendering citizenship is not inval-*
> *idated, but it has to be conceived of as part of a wider project of differentiating*
> *citizenship. (Lister, 1997, p.39)*

While we appreciate the many differences between women and recognise that some women have less power than others, we reject the term 'disadvantage' as a 'cover-all' label. Women are discriminated against and negative stereotypes exist and persist within, and between, communities and population groups.

We have worked in different ways to create *safe spaces* where we encourage a 'respectful discourse'; where we can get beyond assumptions around education, work, marriage, sex, tradition, faith, class, age, culture, housework, children, politics and power; where we can 'hear the hurt'. These are spaces for difficult discussions and joint celebrations; spaces to explore what shapes and shaped us and what we want to do about this.

The organisation accountable for IMPACT in the ALAC programme was the Wolverhampton Asian Women and Diabetes Group – a small community-based charitable company with a commitment to working across cultures to achieve better healthcare for Asian women around living with diabetes. It was important for a black women's organisation to take a lead and to be visible as this led to many Asian women taking part in the Impact programme. But unfortunately this could have had a part to play in the small numbers of African Caribbean women taking part. It could be said that the colonialist legacy of complex relations between Asian and African Caribbean communities is still being played out in an English context.

In the IMPACT programme, assumptions that race and culture would be the significant differential factor for participants were challenged when the evaluation revealed age as the most significant difference. This was a space where, coincidentally, young Asian women met and shared ideas and experiences with older white women. They learned about the similarities of their lives, the broader experiences of older women and the 'modern' interpretations of younger women. All the participants recognised that this would not have happened in ordinary life as people generally live within their comfort zones – work, friends and family – and often have little opportunity to meet and talk with people outside of their everyday silos. In discussions around the impact of the course, the overarching themes were of respect and enduring friendship between very different women.

A framework for change

> It has made me feel alive again, it has opened up arenas that I quite possibly never thought I'd be able to sit in – let alone speak in.

From 1996 through to about 1998 we worked with women around assertiveness and personal change, focusing upon women taking increasing responsibility for their own health and welfare.[1] This was all well and good – but something was missing and our emphasis changed to encourage women to challenge existing service and approaches. While personal development work and confidence building is a key component for individual change, it is not enough to create real and lasting changes to how services are planned and delivered to women as a whole, taking gender into account. As well as being able to access appropriate and relevant services and resources, women need to be equally involved in decision-making on issues that affect them, their families and their communities.

At this point we started to explore 'leadership' in relation to women and change – change for self and family, change for the community and change in the wider society. We were clear that women are active in different spheres at different times:

- active in their own lives;
- active in the community; and
- active in the wider world.

Women are generally not active in the wider world until they are active in their own life and so we can liken this to a journey to influence, starting with becoming influential in your own life and then moving on to becoming influential in other spheres.

IMPACT is grounded in feminist approaches to citizenship, power and influence. In particular we would like to draw attention to the following theoretical points. As Lister argued:

> *A rounded and fruitful theorization of citizenship, which can be of potential value to women, has to embrace both individual rights (and, in particular, social and reproductive rights) and political participation and also has to analyse the relationship between the two. (Sarvasy and Siim, 1994)*
>
> *(Lister, 1997, p.35)*

IMPACT explored these two notions in terms of women's own understanding of themselves as citizens and their potential for being 'active in

---

[1] Individual development funded within the neo-liberal political context of the period – however the surface neo-liberal values were in fact subverted within a community development approach: 'subversive space', common within feminist approaches.

community and public life'. This relates directly to what Lister terms 'to be a citizen and to act as a citizen' (Lister, 1997, p.35).

IMPACT explicitly recognised that political and civic structures and processes are gendered:

> *Reflecting the fact that women's long-standing expulsion from the theory and practice of citizenship, in both its liberal and republican clothes, is far from accidental and only partially rectified by their formal incorporation in virtually all societies in the twentieth century. Gendered patterns of exclusion interact with other axes of social division such as class, 'race', disability, sexuality and age in ways which can be either multiplicative or contradictory, and which shift over time. (Brewer, 1993; Brah, 1996) (Lister, 1997, p.38)*

Four essential ingredients

Our model evolved from reflective practice, during which time was taken to consider the ways in which we had been working with women and to tease out the key components to successful work. In order to provide opportunities for women to start to recognise their potential for leadership and participation, the model proposes that there are four essential ingredients. Each suggests specific learning outcomes, which combine to create the conditions for women to be confident and active in the public domain.

1. Value your own skills

Here the focus is on work with individuals, whether in terms of confidence building, validating life experiences or practical skills development, for example, presentation skills, public speaking, chairing meetings, budgeting, planning, dealing with difficult situations, being more assertive. In general, these can be the building blocks towards increased self-esteem and an acceptance of one's own value and experiences.

2. Know yourself through and with others

At this stage we can reflect upon our own situation in relation to the wider context of women's experiences. It provides the opportunity to make sense of the factors that shape our lives, for example, education, religion, family, motherhood, sexuality, class, race and economic depend-ence. It is at this point that we realise that while we have many experiences in common, we are all products of our particular and diverse cultures, and backgrounds and traditions. If we can learn how to value ourselves and communicate with others in a genuine way, we are in a better position to develop a network of support and deal with the inevitable conflicts and work together to make positive changes.

3. Know how the external world operates and choosing where you want to be

To be able to make changes and get our voices heard we need to know how the system operates: how decision-making structures are set up, how these structures work, who is involved, how accountable they are, and who holds power in any given situation. This means knowing about the local, national and international structures that impact upon our lives. If we are clear about our place within the system; as a voter, a constituent, a consumer, a citizen, we start to have a clearer understanding about our rights and responsibilities. Once we have this knowledge we can make choices about where we want to be and the roles we want to play, for example, an elected member, a school governor, an MP, a magistrate, or on a Citizen's Panel.

4. Know where to go to get what you want

In order to make changes we have to make our voice heard, ask people for information and know how to get what we want from individuals and organisations. This can involve negotiating, campaigning, lobbying – or simply being more assertive!

IMPACT used a community development approach to planning and evaluating the work. As we were very familiar with the ABCD frame-work, we adapted this to our purpose. Indeed we used this to help to construct the citizen and wider citizenship outcomes in the National Framework for Active Citizenship Learning. (See www.takepart.org)

At the heart of the ABCD approach is the idea of community empowerment. It is important to recognise that 'community empower-ment' is both a process and a product – not just what you do, but also how you do it. It is the means by which wider changes of benefit to communities are realised.

Figure 3 A model: Working towards leadership, participation and involvement

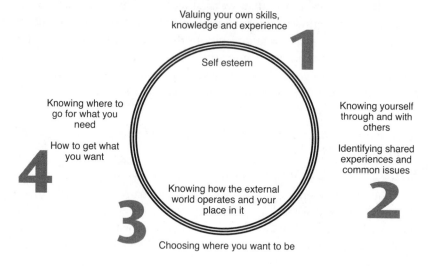

A community development approach is about working with communities, in ways which:

- consider the needs of the individual in terms of their knowledge, confidence and skills;
- promote and includes the experiences of different communities;
- recognise the strengths and benefits of collective working and wider networks; and
- encourage and enables people to take part and to influence what is happening – to be 'engaged'.

During the IMPACT programme some of us from IMPACT had the chance to take part in a Grundvig course on European citizenship learning where we were introduced to a citizenship typology with three differing understandings of 'citizenship' and 'active citizenship':

- the citizen as a 'voter, and 'volunteer';
- the citizen as an individual within a group(s), actively participating in existing structures, taking up opportunities for participation including participation in the planning and delivery of services;

- the citizen as an individual who also participates within group(s) actively; and
- challenging unequal relations of power, promoting social solidarity and social justice, both locally and beyond, taking account of the global context.

This really helped us to think through and identify the citizenship outcomes we wanted from the IMPACT programme. Table 1 summarises some of the main points.

Table 1 Citizenship outcomes from the IMPACT programme

	Individual citizenship	Active citizenship	Critical citizenship
Core assumptions	To solve social problems and improve society, citizens must have good character, be honest, responsible and law abiding members of the community.	To solve social problems and improve society, citizens must actively participate and take leadership positions with established systems' community structures.	To solve social problems and improve society, citizens must question, debate and change established systems and structures that reproduce patterns of injustice over time.
Aims	Acts responsibly in own community.	Is active member of community, organisations and/ or political parties.	Critically assesses social, political and economic structures which leads to social injustice.
Attitude	Is a loyal citizen to the government.	Gives critical support to the government.	Has a critical distance from the government.
Knowledge	Knows about the political system.	Knows how government agencies work. Knows how to organise collective tasks.	Knows how government agencies work. Knows about social democratic movements and how to effect systemic change.

Table 1 Citizenship outcomes from the IMPACT programme (*continued*)

	Individual citizenship	**Active citizenship**	**Critical citizenship**
Activities	Works and pays taxes. Obeys the law. Recycles. Gives blood. Votes.	Organises community projects and collective initiatives. Lobbying and campaigning for changes.	Seeks out and works on issues of social justice. Direct action.
Educational theory	Positivism.	Humanism/ pragmatism.	Critical pedagogy/critical theory.
Didactical approaches	Adaptation: People are taught a particular set of notional values and norms – e.g. that the current system is the best.	Integration: People are taught how to participate and become active citizens.	Critical thinking: People are encouraged to ask questions and critically analyse the current system and power structures.
Methodological approaches	Learning by doing. Individual learning. Supported individual social action.	Learning by doing. Collective learning. Engagement in civic projects.	Learning through examples. Change oriented. Political social action outside mainstream structures.
Aims of learning	Instrumental.	Participative.	Transformative.
Values concerning citizenship	Citizenship is based upon universal national identity.	National citizenship plus recognition of diverse cultural identities.	Diverse citizenship is accepted and sought after in principle.
Results of courses	Awareness of individual responsibilities. Low level of knowledge of participatory rights.	Awareness of individual responsibility within a social context. High knowledge level of micro politics – participatory rights. Low knowledge level of macro politics – political, social and economic interdependence.	Awareness of collective and global responsibilities. Lower level of knowledge of participatory rights and interference.

Adapted from J. Westheimer and J. Kahne, 'What kind of citizen? The politics of educating for democracy', *American Educational Research Journal*, Vol. 41 (2004/2)

We were very clear that we wanted women to challenge the way that things are currently happening – to become 'awkward citizens'. It helped us to realise where our agenda sat and it also helped the women we were working with to recognise where they were situated at different times in different ways – and that people move between these 'types'. When we introduced Impact participants to this, they found it really helpful in tracking their own citizenship activities over the years. 'Citizenship' can be seen as a continuum rather than an all-or-nothing affair, often reflecting the demands of caring and other obligations which could also be interpreted as the exercise of 'citizenship' obligations.

It is a useful tool to get to grips with the tensions and contradictions involved in working around 'citizenship' and gender – where we explicitly recognise the inequalities in the structures, processes and cultures of governance. If we want to change these, then we have to challenge ourselves and others to become active critical citizens.

> *To solve social problems and improve society, citizens must question, debate and change established systems and structures that reproduce patterns of injustice over time.* (Taken from Table 1)

Consequently, it would be fair to say that IMPACT was vision led as opposed to needs led; the delivery and methods were rooted in a learner centred, participative and informal educational pedagogy within an explicit vision in relation to gender, equality and social justice.

The IMPACT programme

IMPACT was a participative training course nested within a network offering encouragement, skill-sharing, information and support. It was a place and a space for women to meet, share, learn, grow, get involved and, hopefully, to encourage other women to get involved. It was 'women only' as the dynamics and interaction within a 'women only' space are very different from the dynamics when there are men present. This 'women only' space offered an opportunity to move beyond the usual gender dynamics.

> *People wanted to share and it was just women – you can't be that open, especially in front of men that you don't know. It was a bit of a risk to be that open but people did take risks.*

IMPACT challenged the notions of individualism and competition by bringing women together in association, to collectively reflect upon and analyse the barriers to, and opportunities for, creating change for themselves and others. We suggest that once women make these connections, and see their own concerns and limitations reflected in the struggles of others, they can collectively develop strategies around how to overcome the barriers and make positive changes.

> *That outer strength to come in – the group was initially outside of me – I've opened up and let in what they have to offer and then I've made my own decisions.*

Our approach to creating a safe space for learning requires that we always start with and from the experiences and knowledge of the individual learner, thereby involving the learner as a participant in the learning process. We then share this in the group context, creating a collective pool of knowledge and experiences. At this point it is often useful to provide further information and concepts/theories to aid further reflection, understanding and analysis.

For example, an exploration of 'power' and 'power relations'.
- Individuals explore situations in which they have felt both 'powerful' and 'powerless'.
- This is shared confidentially in small groups and key themes are reflected back to the main group.
- A concept of power is shared and explored with the group in relation to their own experiences.
- This concept is used to critically explore notions of being powerful and being powerless in the external world.
- Different types of power are explored in different contexts.

The trainer role here is more of a facilitator role, creating and maintaining healthy group dynamics to enable people to validate their own knowledge, skills and experiences, as well as to provide relevant information and theory to allow deeper understanding and critical reflection.

> *Everyone boosted each other's confidence by telling their own experiences and listening to each other. There was lots of group work, lots of discussion.*

You were constantly asked for your input – being given that allowance of time and choice to participate and not make a fool of myself. It was about consideration of what people needed – the time, where they were sat, who they were sat with ... Where we shared as a group, (the trainers) shared with us – it was about equality.

Equality issues were central to the programme and so childcare expenses and respite care expenses were offered alongside travel costs when they were needed.

Taxis were arranged for me – I hadn't gone out of the house by myself for 10 years – I got back to (me) as a person – it was a big, big confidence boost.

Co-training

There was a clear policy around co-training and, where possible, team training as this models the values of participation, equality and co-operation. It takes more time to plan and costs more, but the learner generally gets a better experience and more personalised attention.

... The trainers made a real point of respecting each other and each other's opinions – even if you didn't agree with them. They developed ground rules which were crucial so people know to respect and the ground rules were owned by the group.

The IMPACT courses were delivered using a team training approach where two experienced trainers worked with two learner trainers who had each been involved in some of the previous work with women prior to the IMPACT programme. Planning sessions then became teaching sessions with critical reflection and learning structured into them. One learner trainer, who herself had been a participant on an earlier version of the course (women and influence), offered her thoughts on the process as follows.

What made you decide to do this?

I wanted to continue being involved in this type of women's work after the 'women and influence' course finished – to keep me in the loop and so I didn't go back to just doing what I had been doing,

(I wanted) to be part of a bigger picture around a shared vision. I needed space to discuss and share what was going on as I became a representative on the local LSP – to try to make sense of what was happening. I/we paid a price for challenging how things got done at the CEN and the LSP, although what we suggested is now normal practice and everyone has ended up benefiting, although it was awful for us at the time.

I wanted a space to talk and discuss these issues and approaches – to have the opportunity to articulate my ideas and model the process in how we work together – a challenge to facilitate this as a team of trainers/facilitators. I knew that I would learn from the planning, doing and evaluating.

I had changed as a person from doing the original course and I knew that I wanted to continue that change. It is high risk work, and can get very emotionally charged as it is all about change and growth; it is not a comfortable space as the facilitator and highly skilled work.

I had some real challenges in completing the original course – two very small children, childcare problems and a commitment to a pre-school music group. The two trainers offered to go open the hall for the music group and welcomed my baby into the sessions – with that kind of support I had to continue! Having that level of investment in me meant that I can now invest the same in other women.

Delivering the programme

The programme was a mix of workshops, residential events, field visits, events and support sessions running over a 6–9 month period, depending upon the nature of the group. The IMPACT sessions ran on Saturdays as this was preferred by the participants – other courses in the past have run on weekdays. There were two field visits; to the English Parliament and to the European Parliament. In previous years we have held what is called 'round table' events, where women who are active in public and community life come to share their stories with other women. There were two weekend residentials where women were encouraged not to bring children but were given childcare costs instead (see Table 2).

Table 2 The IMPACT programme

	Saturday sessions	Weekend residential	Events and field trips	Assignments and support
Assistance with childcare and transport, accessible venues, small group work, support, safe environment for discussion and sharing. Encouraging a wide diversity of women to attend – with this mix being essential to sharing experiences and recognising common issues. There are between two and four tutors at all times to allow for small group and individual support.	Why Participate? What does citizenship mean for us?	Citizenship. Decision-making. Assertive communication. Capturing confidence.	*Participants are encouraged and supported to attend appropriate and relevant events taking place nationally. Wherever*	*Tutorials, assignment support, option for accreditation are offered. Women keep diary sheets.*
	Human rights. Power and powerlessness. Presentation skills.	Diversity, difference and citizenship. Leadership – skills and qualities.	*possible they are provided with opportunities to speak to influential*	Assignment: Citizenship and human rights.
	Democracy and decision-making. How laws are made in the UK. How to influence decisions. Consultation tools and techniques. Politics and everyday life. Meetings – how to make sure they work for you. Networking. Politics in Europe. Action planning.		*people – politicians, Ministers etc.* Visit to the House of Parliament – arrangements to meet women MPs. Visit to Brussels – European parliament – arrangements to meet women MEPs.	Assignment: Democracy and decision-making. Assignment: Participation and leadership. Assignment: Assertive communication.

Accreditation

The course was accredited with the Open College Network with four units:

• participation and leadership;

- citizenship and human rights;
- introduction to democracy and decision–making; and
- assertiveness.

There was also the option of a 'taster unit', which was a separate unit for those who had to miss out parts of the course. This unit covered elements of the four units above but with less detail.

All the units were available at Level 1, 2 and 3 and the assignments could be written or spoken – taped. We provided paper or electronic versions of the worksheets and questions and guidelines on what was needed in order to achieve the various levels.

There was the option of having tutorials and we offered two tutorials per participant. They were also asked to keep a course diary.

Outcomes and evaluation

... Nothing is impossible and if we try really hard we can attain any height!

IMPACT commissioned an external evaluation which focused on two aspects:

- the process of learning – what was it about the IMPACT programme which helped women to explore issues around power, participation and leadership; and
- the outcomes of learning – the range and breadth of what women gained, what they have gone on to do – how they feel and the impact they have had in terms of themselves, their families, communities, policies and services.

Some IMPACT participants undertook peer interviews – they were trained in interview techniques, introduced to the qualitative nature of the questions, provided with recording equipment and offered ongoing support from the external evaluator. Twenty two participants were interviewed by their peers or an external evaluator. They were first asked why they had wanted to be a part of the IMPACT programme, to determine if they had met – and perhaps exceeded – their expectations. Their responses are reflected below in quotations taken directly from a few of the interviews.

To get to know more people and to get out of the house.

To get out of the house after ten years of not leaving the house alone following an accident.

To learn more and become a better representative on the (Primary Care Trust) Forum.

To meet other women and learn a little more about politics.

I wanted to be involved in something.

To get confident as the 'powers that be' made me feel worthless, patronised – with no respect.

Subsequent interview questions asked about aspirations, levels of confidence, skills and knowledge; the benefits of working together with a group of diverse women, sharing experiences and the impact that this had on their own belief that they could change things. Questions were also asked about their levels of activity in community and public life, their understanding of systems and structures and how influential they now felt.

Responses were consistent and powerful; they demonstrate how women's initial expectations had been challenged and offer an impression of the much greater potential for IMPACT to encourage and support women to become more active in community and public life. The responses are illustrated here in a series of evaluative statements evidenced by quotes from participants.

Following the IMPACT learning programme participants have increased levels of confidence, skills and knowledge and are more politically aware.

I believe I can change things.

I have a thirst for knowledge now and the desire to do further research.

I am able to speak at forum meetings without feeling embarrassed.

It raised questions about democracy and the current voting system and arguments around 'first past the post' and 'proportional representation' systems.

I have the skills, understanding and confidence to feel that I can help people and have a new lease of life in retirement. Family life is much richer.

I am confident in the knowledge that I can make a valuable contribution and make a difference. I feel far more in control.

I have the self confidence to enable change in my own life – to stand on my own two feet.

Participants have learned more about themselves, their differences and collective experiences. They have surprised themselves, challenged the barriers of discrimination and have a better understanding of others.

The residentials and the trip to Brussels gave us a chance to break down barriers and get rid of preconceptions of women from other cultures.

Everyone boosted each other's confidence by telling their own experiences and listening to each other.

I was amazed that a woman of my age (73) can be of use to others.

It made me think about how some groups cannot access normal rights!

I am no longer frightened to ask questions of others on subjects I would have tip-toed around before e.g. culture, religion, family.

Participants have encouraged others to get involved in groups and forums. Participants recorded involvement in environmental groups, local area networks, community newsletters, disability networks and other groups. They have recognised the needs of their own communities, organised their political lives, become involved in different issues and made global links.

I've lived here for 21 years – it never dawned on me that we had nothing – 1,500 properties with no amenities, services – not even a post box.

I now help others to build their confidence and realise their potential. I am planning to set up a Women's Enterprise Development Agency.

I have been able to take my interest forward in housing, health, education, crime and neighbourhood safety, social welfare.

I have more interest in Europe and political structures.

Participants feel – and are – more influential:

Knowing how policies are put together and how the government works ... arms you with the information needed to target services.

We have provided input for national guidelines and made Council meetings more accessible by advising on processes to include deaf people.

I have influence on how my kids are looked after in school. I feel confident that I can get people involved – to challenge and change structures.

As a direct result of IMPACT, participants have become involved in:

- Borough Council structures – as community representative on a Scrutiny Committee and (separately) as a partner to organise an event;
- Women's Enterprise Development Agency – Board/Chair;
- Primary Care Trust – working in partnership to organise an event;
- community forum – as a member;
- school governing (and then elected as Vice-Chair);
- School Performance Management Committee;
- The Labour Party;
- a local housing estate management board – as Director;
- a local community association – as Director;
- Local Environmental Group – as Chair;
- a neighbourhood nursery;
- the Partnership Board of a Children's Centre;
- a Safety Partnership Board;
- an Estate Management Board – as Director;
- training as a union representative;
- Community Empowerment Network; and
- neighbourhood management – interviewed by evaluators.

And there have been wider impacts on family and friends.

My friends are really proud of me.

My daughter wants to be a politician!

I want to take my family to Brussels to share the same experience that I had and – in particular – to visit the European Parliament.

My husband is doing more volunteering and my grandchildren have more awareness of the world around them and the other people in it.

None of my children have stopped on at school except the younger one. After sitting and talking to her about what I have learnt and how it's made me feel – seeing me at my age learning – it helps her to feel responsible for herself – make her own decisions – and she decided to stay at school.

CHAPTER TWELVE

Enabling people with disabilities and other service users to 'speak up'; enabling public service providers to listen

PETER MANGAN WITH GABI RECKNAGEL AND LYNDY POOLEY

The session brought into sharp focus the impact of how we deliver services on the everyday life experience of people who use our services. I take so much for granted in my life; freedom to make my own choices, take control of my own life, do what I want when I want and this is not always supported by what we as service providers plan or do. I could feel that service users felt defined by their symptoms and diagnosis and not their personal qualities, values and beliefs. (Service provider responding to training received, early 2008, Devon)

Introduction

In the report launching ALAC it was explained that the programme had been initiated following a literature review and mapping exercise to identify relevant learning programmes in the voluntary and community sector, while at the same time recognising and valuing the knowledge, expertise and understanding of those directly involved in work at local levels (Woodward, 2004). At the time it was noted that, while this mapping exercise provided no more than a snapshot in a dynamic and constantly changing scene, this was sufficient to identify a wealth of approaches, working with a range of groups and communities (Mayo and Rooke, 2006). One challenge, therefore, for a national project which acknowledges from its inception the sheer diversity of what it reports on is to resist the lure of false homogeneity: what is reported on as the experience within one locale might, in fact, resist apparent comparison with that in another. ALAC's emphasis was upon partnership with the voluntary and community sectors, building upon existing research and expertise, in practice. Bringing together the partners in this way was key to ALAC's approach, based upon collaboration across sectors and stakeholders. Central to this was the creation of a system of 'hubs' and this chapter deals with the experiences within the South West hub, based in Exeter.

As Mayo and Rooke (ibid.) point out, the hubs were selected to reflect the experiences and approaches adopted in different regions, within different social and economic contexts, to facilitate comparisons and contrasts. And they were selected to encompass diversity in terms of the learners and learning priorities. There was a particular emphasis upon facilitating the participation of marginalised, disadvantaged and oppressed minority communities, including black and minority ethnic communities as well as white British communities, women from disadvantaged groups, people with disabilities including people with learning disabilities, migrant workers, refugees and asylum seekers. There was early recognition too that learning for active citizenship needed to be envisaged as not based upon a deficit model of citizenship education – 'pouring' knowledge into a minority of supposedly inadequate individuals and communities. From a national, co-ordinating perspective such a 'global view' lends itself to declarations that:

> *Professionals and policy-makers, in common with the rest of the population, stand to benefit from Active Learning for Active Citizenship, including learning how to develop strategies to promote social solidarity and social justice, challenging inequalities as well as learning how to listen to those whose voices have been less heard. (Ibid., p. 15)*

Listening to the voices less heard is one thing but what is done as a consequence is, of course, necessarily contingent and not least in policy development terms at local level.

The South West Hub

This hub was based in Exeter, led by Exeter Council for Voluntary Service (CVS) in partnership with local carers' groups, mental health advocacy groups and Devon Learning Disability Team. The South West hub had a particular focus on promoting civil renewal by empowering some of the most excluded people to speak up for themselves and voice their issues, to influence the planning and delivery of services in their communities and to take an active role in community development. Exeter CVS developed particular expertise in providing 'Speaking Up' courses to enable people with learning disabilities, physical disabilities and mental health issues to make their voices heard effectively, and this led on to the provision of courses for carers, as well as providing inputs to training programmes for professionals, including the police, enabling them to listen more effectively. The hub also included Cornwall Neighbourhoods for Change, the Plymouth Community Partnership, Plymouth Guild, and Students and Refugees Together supporting the integration and social inclusion of asylum seekers, refugees and black and minority ethnic groups through mentoring and cultural activity. Plymouth-based initiatives included training opportunities for social workers, placed with community organisations and groups.

Across the hub area activities were collectively grouped under a heading known as the 'Learning To Involve' (LTI) project (the 'project'); so, in following how this project evolved and effected change within the South West it becomes possible to chart the impact of ALAC within this area. (ALAC funding had 'pump-primed' activities across the area at the start of what later became known as the LTI project.)

The Learning to Involve project

Set-up details

The LTI project (LTI, 2006) took a dynamic approach to embedding effective and sustainable involvement through learning and development activities across the area by instigating innovative partnership working between the Public and Voluntary Sectors. This entailed developing workable and sustainable protocols for involvement across Health and Social Care. In turn, this resulted in developing and delivering training for service users and carers to help them be involved effectively in speaking up and having a say in their own futures. Underpinning this approach was the work done with carers and service users to embed active involvement in staff learning and development.

The partners

From within the Voluntary Sector these comprised the Devon Association of CVSs; Carers Link in Devon; Mental Health Carers and

Service Users projects; Learning Disabilities Support Workers and Projects, along with projects supporting older people, young carers, young parents and service users with physical disabilities. Devon County Council Adult Services and the Devon Partnership Trust were also involved, while from the Health arena the Royal Devon & Exeter (RDE) Foundation Trust and subsequently, the Devon PCT were involved. The University of Plymouth was represented on an 'associate' basis as well.

Staffing and funding

From the public sector one worker was seconded for the duration of the project, while from the voluntary sector the worker was based at Exeter CVS. This organisation had proved that it was well placed to offer a Devon-wide voluntary sector approach to training for those carers and service users who want to get involved, while supporting them effectively across the county to train staff in their own locality. Through a joint agency funding arrangement running up to March 2007 each contributor to the project gave the following: RDE – hosting a project worker; Devon County Council L & D – £45,000; Devon Partnership Trust – £15,000; County Carers Grant – £15,000, and ALAC (DACVS) – £10,000.

Project evolution

The project was developed over two main phases beginning from the inception of ALAC. (A third period which moves up to the present and looks to the future is considered later.)

- *LTI Project Phase 1 (2004–05).* In 2004 Exeter CVS began to train carers and service users to speak up and have a say in how their services are provided. This work was funded through ALAC until March 2006. This phase of the project resulted in best-practice guidelines and planned for the succeeding phase to focus on achieving these outcomes.

  1. Building on and sustaining the 'good involvement practice' that exists within health and social care learning and development function (L & D).
  2. Providing L & D staff with the resources and support that is needed to involve service users and carers to maximum effect.
  3. Sharing good practice, resources and ways of working between health and social care agencies.

4. Ensuring that service users and carers have access to an appropriate level of training, support and information to encourage and sustain involvement.

The model proposed to achieve these outcomes was the appointment of the two project workers: one joint health and social care officer (appointed November 2005) to support staff in involving users and carers within L & D, and one voluntary sector worker to train and support users and carers to become involved in staff L & D. These appointments were on a fixed-term basis until June 2007.
(From April 2006 all work continued through the funding provided by the LTI project.)

- *LTI Project Phase 2 (2005–07)*. From November 2005, the two project workers worked closely together on a number of initiatives which included 'Real Lives' a joint agency – carer awareness training programme; 'In my shoes' a Devon Partnership Trust (DPT) customer care training programme; ran a DPT Admin & Clerical conference; developed recruitment and selection policy, protocols and training; initiated networking Devon-wide among agencies and user/carer groups; worked with other multi-agency partners in developing a carers' training strategy and sustainable involvement L & D framework.

A selection of key activities is illustrated in Table 3 to give an idea of the breadth and impact of work undertaken across these main phases.

Table 3 Key activities

Activity	Outcome	Impact	Evaluation
Twenty-five accredited Speaking Up courses delivered to 225 learners Devon-wide.	Two hundred and twenty-five carers and service users (mental health, learning difficulties, young parents, deaf community) trained to speak up for themselves and their user group.	Personal empowerment and independence. Learners now involved in Health and Social Care activities, the police, self-help organisations and Forum representation.	This very successful course has been contextualised for different groups of service users. Demand is high. Delivery is Devon-wide.

Table 3 Key activities (*continued*)

Activity	Outcome	Impact	Evaluation
Development of a customer care course for mental health staff (Devon Partnership Trust).	Increased carer and service user involvement in both planning and delivery.	More effective training for staff to help them communicate effectively with carers and service users.	Established and effective involvement in mental health staff training.
Training for staff, carers and service users to help them be effective in recruitment and selection interview process.	Partnership working with HR departments from Health and Social Care, carers and service users to agree protocols. Design and delivery of interview skills training for carers and service users.	Multi-agency partnership working towards agreed protocols and interviewing process.	Sustainable and effective interview skills training delivered as a result of agreed protocols.
Support carers to design and deliver the Real Lives carer-awareness training for Health and Social Care staff.	Seven one-day courses delivered to 200 Health and Social Care staff in the East Devon area. Real Lives is currently being promoted throughout Devon.	A better understanding has been developed between carers and the staff who work with them. Locality carers are trained and supported to deliver effective training.	Two hundred Health and Social Care staff identified three ways they would work more effectively with carers, independent of budget or time constraints.
Speaking Up taster course developed and delivered Devon-wide to mental health carers and service users.	Carers and service users feel confident enough to design and deliver awareness training.	Personal empowerment through training, and an opportunity to use their skills and voice.	Quoted from a service user: 'Being able to train mental health staff to understand the issues helps my recovery.'

Table 3 Key activities (*continued*)

Activity	Outcome	Impact	Evaluation
Interactive work-shops designed and delivered by carers and service users at the DPT conferences on 'Communication'.	One hundred and sixty administra-tive and clerical staff worked with carers and service users to break down barriers.	Successful and well received training.	Quoted from a member of staff: 'The time spent with service users and carers at the Communication Conference was brilliant, very worthwhile, and helped to foster, for me, an even deeper under-standing of the problems people face.'

It is worth noting feedback from some of those involved in the project as training deliverers:

> For me, as a carer, it was the level of involvement that struck me – everyone really working hard and contributing, so much laughter, so much kindness. (Carer facilitating an 'In My Shoes' session for mental health staff)

> Because of the involvement I have had in the 'Real Lives' carer awareness training, my confidence has grown and this has helped me in other parts of my life. (Carer who facilitated 'Real Lives' training to Health and Social Care staff)

> Because of the work I have been doing on the 'In My Shoes' programme, I have now qualified as a trainer and can work with the professionals on an equal basis. (A mental health service user)

Interim evaluation

Throughout its life internal evaluations supported the view that the LTI project had been a success, while at the same time becoming concerned that the clear gains could be built upon in the future.

Responding to evaluation questionnaires, Devon County Council Disability Team were keen to draw attention to the government strategy for learning disabilities, Valuing People (2001), highlighting that it is based on the four principles of rights, independence, choice and inclusion. They pointed out that 'Speaking Up' course provision for people with learning disabilities or difficulties lies at the heart of changing practices and attitudes in statutory service providers, such as Social Services. They believed the course enhanced the confidence and skills of service users to self-advocate and to participate more effectively in service user representations. The funding from the Home Office allowed the Speaking Up course to be delivered county-wide, and it had been very successful in getting new users involved in advocacy and meetings, as well as developing the skills of existing forum members. Service users received support from both statutory and voluntary sector-based advocacy workers as required at meetings and other interventions, but many became able to operate without constant support.

This team saw that the key challenge was to obtain a change in attitude, both within service users' perception of themselves and within the attitudes of social services and health staff to their own perception of what people with learning disabilities can do. In supporting this assertion they focused on examples such as these: day centre staff were being trained in learning disability awareness by people *with* learning difficulties and this was seen to challenge some of the preconceptions, especially of staff who have been in place for some time. In addition, the Social Service LD manager who attended Service User forums for some time had learnt to adapt his language at meetings, so that interpretation became unnecessary for service users and, as a result of the queries put to him by them, he was able to push actions forward.

At county level, from Adult Services, the application of features of Active Citizenship was used to foreground the users' need to participate, as opposed to being excluded from decision-making. This was seen as ensuring that people with learning disabilities or any other disadvantaged people are enabled to have the same access to services as anybody else, and to control their lives. The impact on service users these respondents noted was that in users exercising more choice and control the planning of services would need to respond to a newly differentiated user base, rather than presenting them with ready-made solutions. The impact on carers and families was observed in these ways: for the older generation in particular, the changes in day care, for example, raised some anxiety, whereas some younger carers have different expectations (unspecified) on the increase in independence of the cared-for person. The implications for county-level staff were particularly telling with the respondents noting that they were having to learn how to listen and carry out person-centred work, not being the 'expert' any more. It was claimed they now had to 'understand citizenship' and would receive citizenship training.

Outside the project it was noted that the impact the training had on the public sector staff was reflected in the extremely positive training evaluation feedback, and the carers' effectiveness and motivation in making their voices heard in such an innovative way encouraged them to continue with further consultation and involvement activities (Mayo and Rooke, 2006). Indeed, all respondents were keen to cite the centrality of Exeter CVS as a key enabler and influencer in thinking of the future since it was independent from public service, thereby offering 'good inroads into engaging users and carers'.

Direction setting

The respondents' input to this thinking was based on the need to continue and refine the valued partnership with the voluntary sector in different ways and areas. Additionally, it was noted that the service user involvement approach enabled users with lesser learning disabilities to participate and develop impressively, to the extent of needing little support and encouragement to stay involved. The next step was to extend these principles to those service users with more severe learning disabilities, so that they too can make and state their choices. Underpinning this was an on-going and increased demand for training expressed by learners, for courses such as Speaking Up, Training the Trainer, meeting skills and financial numeracy. With difficulties in obtaining mainstream Learning and Skills Council funding, and the ending of ALAC funding by March 2006, the most likely route for sustainability would come through the government's modernisation agenda, as allocated by local social services. It was hoped that the 'undeniable success of ALAC activities in the area of Learning Disabilities' rendered it unlikely such activities would be discontinued in the foreseeable future.

For the LTI project staff themselves, the task was to build on what had been achieved, not just because of localised success but because the gains addressed some of the key government drivers and national and local performance directives, including: Section 11, Health & Social Care Act 2001

219

– planning and provision of services; Adult Social Care Performance Indicators – delivery improvement through engaging service users and carers using best practice; *Every Child Matters* – change for children; participation of children and young people in service development and delivery, and the proposed developments whereby service users and carers would be encouraged to participate fully in their community and know that their contribution is valued equally with other people's. The staff analysed the options open to them on completion which were abandoning the project's ethos in June 2007; reverting to agencies working independently and – the chosen option – to develop and expand the interagency model through a project jointly funded by Devon County Council, Devon Partnership Trust, RDE, Devon PCT and the voluntary sector. It was concluded that developing the interagency approach to involvement in L & D is the best way of ensuring true partnership between Health, Social Care, the voluntary sector and the wider community. This model reflects the 'joining up' emphasis prevalent in public services thus reducing the risk of duplication and increasing cost effectiveness. This option was best placed to carry forward the business outcomes of each partner in Health and Social Care. It would also ensure that through the project each agency will work together to achieve common objectives in areas such as involvement policy and protocols, workforce planning and the development of community services through local area agreements. In addition, the project would be able to concentrate on organisational drivers for each individual partner agency; for example, the Health and Social Care Act, Options for Excellence, Adult and Community Services and Children and Young Persons' indicators, while being mindful of how these objectives might impact across agencies thus creating a holistic approach to involvement in L & D.

Planning for the future

From the success of the project, any attempt to build for the future needed to be circumspect and acknowledge the existence of forces beyond the project boundaries which, if not militating against the project gains, could remain indifferent to them: the challenge for those involved was to take account of how they could remain 'locally' purposeful while observing how the policy landscape, nationally, can alter. In this respect, the strength of the position in the South West might be affirmed by the way in which the workers had overcome obstacles identified as silencing user involvement in debates over quality issues in personal social services (Beresford et al., 2000). These obstacles had been identified as, firstly, the overcoming of communication difficulties, given the unequal roles and relationships involved. Due to a lifetime without control over decisions affecting their lives, service users often need time 'to build confidence, decide what they want and make themselves heard. The source of such confidence is usually other service users' (Ibid., p. 191). Other possible obstacles were around the accommodating of differing values and competing discourses; and the degree of positive feedback on the success of the LTI project and related work demonstrated the capacity of this hub to get matters assessed accurately from the project's inception:

> Service agencies and service user discourses reflect totally different starting points, different value bases and different purposes .... a dialogue is not going to be easy; assumptions have to be questioned and some hard listening done on both sides if people are to understand each other's concerns. (Ibid., p. 193)

Concerns had been expressed within the hub that planning for the future needed to have an idea about which 'drivers' for involvement could be identified, not just from the realm of government policy, but also advocacy and Third Sector drivers, as well as those emanating from service users themselves. Attention would need to be paid to questions such as: who would be the 'stakeholders' and 'partners' of involvement? How would the processes of involvement actually be configured and what would constitute 'good practice' in the future?

It also was a concern that, in the light of resources post-ALAC having diminished, the capacity to maintain evaluation activities would be curtailed. Implicit in this was the commendable desire to base developments on the outcomes of research, to continue an essential *listening* function which had been critical to earlier success.

'Speaking Up' and 'Learning to Involve' as catalysts for change

At a deeper level of engagement with the work and outcomes of the hub's activities an ethical dimension was clearly expressed. This was put as a question about the extent of user involvement when driven by central government and local authorities: were they making use of people's voices for narrow purposes? What did the expression of 'citizenship' mean in the context of the hub's work compared with other radical forms of expression as embodied by 'community activism'? Was there some connection that could or should be established? The raising of such questions was consonant with the considered and practical engagement of the project participants in the ALAC work. As such, this question and the implications it raised meshed with those around the issue of 'empowerment', rescuing that term from its vacuous usage within political discourse: what precisely *are* the tangible benefits for service users and carers after they have been seen to grow in confidence after 'empowerment'? It was recognised that the issues emerging required contextualising within the government's emphasis on community development and consolidation.

Some of those working on the LTI project were concerned that the direct gains of the project could be diluted because of what they saw as a mis-match between the new working 'methodologies' it promulgated and the 'old ways of thinking and conceptualising' which were bound up within the policy setting framework at central level. These 'old ways' of thinking and conceptualising had the threat of isolating the successes gained in the micro-sphere of the South West. Critically, it was observed that the trainees and beneficiaries 'have not been told they are empowered, active citizens' and operate at a given level – simply that of the 'consulted' citizen. Such concerns cannot be resolved here but, positively, they may be arrayed in such a way that they transcend the predictable analyses of what is going on. What is taking place may be more interesting than the centre-periphery tensions which always come into play as localities mediate central policy. Perhaps the positioning of the voluntary services network within the project's life and aftermath has occasioned a shift in how it perceives itself and is perceived by others in the locality? This would accord with identified features of genuine community organisations which put citizens to the fore in terms of giving them a voice and making it count:

> ... *The ways in which community organisations help their members to be heard by society at large is often the key to their success. This ability derives from a curious feature: while most organisations tend to think they have two audiences, internal and external, for community organisations the audience is part of the organisation. As a result they can become especially adept at connecting what they do with what they think and say – an enviable quality when trust in most public institutions is in decline. (Skidmore and Craig, 2005, p.53)*

Indeed, as time has passed, it may well be that the shift at local level has been accompanied by one on the government's part as it moves away from a model of social care identified in the first New Labour administration as being concerned with top-down policy implementation which was essentially reactive (Baldwin, 2002) to one which is based on the user's entitlement and choice.

Conclusion

Recent feedback on the continuing training within the South West has been extremely positive. Respondents, commenting on workshops and training events in early 2008, stressed the direct benefits through comments such as these:

> The training was very powerful and it reminded me of why I wanted to work in mental health in the first place. I would like all staff to have an experience of this kind. To support this we need to review our learning priorities.

> We also need to help staff understand themselves and their reactions to the work they do. I believe if you understand yourself then you are much more able to understand others.

> Very good, particularly in terms of the relationship between staff and users/carers, it is a two-way approach in which staff and users/carers can talk through experiences and the impact our behaviour has on each other.

> I was surprised by how much more emotive the whole subject was by using direct users/carers experience and actually hearing that from them in person rather than just reading an account.

One of the workers involved with this training said that, 'this reaffirms to me the view that we are somehow just at the beginning of the process of professionals getting to meet with and understand the need to meet with service users and carers – quite significant though this is, in changing attitudes – rather than in increasing participation in decision and policy-making.' Understandable though such caution is when contextualised within the experience of delivering a project on the ground, there may also be grounds for optimism.

It is precisely this degree of meaningful reflexivity and the courage to connect the private with the professional which permits optimism in anticipating how service users and carers in the South West will interact with providers/enablers as the government's Independent Living Strategy (ILS) begins implementation in 2008 under the auspices of the Office for Disability Issues. The Strategy (ILS, 2008) with its challenging movement away from professional assessment to user-led support and advocacy needs a different measure of engagement on behalf of providers and agencies working with people with disabilities and other service users. For these people themselves, the successful management of their futures within such a new dispensation can realise an inclusive citizenship where they gain meaningful power over their lives, along the lines described by Hoffman (2004). When he speaks of 'emancipation' as a 'momentum concept' it is as an essential precursor to the realisation of an inclusive citizenship. As such, this contrasts powerfully with the static and divisive hierarchies of power within which people with disabilities have been locked for so long. The work in the South West has, commendably, done so much to prepare the necessary 'unlocking' before the strategy moves towards successful implementation across this region.

Acknowledgements

My thanks are due to Gabi Recknagel and Lyndy Pooley at Exeter CVS for assistance given in the writing of this chapter.

References

Baldwin, M. (2002) 'New Labour and social care: continuity or change?', in Powell, M. (ed.) *Evaluating New Labour's Welfare Reforms*. Bristol: The Policy Press

Beresford, P., Croft, S. and Harding, T. (2000) 'Quality in Personal Social Services: The developing role of user involvement in the UK', in Davies, C., Finlay, L. and Bullman, A. (eds), *Changing Practice in Health and Social Care*. London: Sage

Hoffman, J. (2004) *Citizenship Beyond The State*. London: Sage

ILS (2008) *The Independent Living Strategy*. www.officefordisability.gov.uk (Accessed 13 March 2008)

LTI (2006) *Learning to Involve: An integrated approach to full community engagement in service provision.* Project report. Exeter Council for Voluntary Service

Mayo, M. and Rooke, A. (2006) *Active Learning for Active Citizenship: Final report,* Centre for Urban and Community Research. London: Goldsmiths' College

Skidmore, P. and Craig, J. (2005) *Start with People: How community organisations put citizens in the driving seat.* London: Demos

Valuing People (2001) *Valuing People: Strategy for Learning Disability for the 21st Century, White Paper.* London: The Stationery Office

Woodward, V. (2004) *Active Learning for Active Citizenship.* London: Civil Renewal Unit, Home Office

CHAPTER THIRTEEN

Community leadership and active citizenship across the city

JOHN ANNETTE, HAMENT PATEL AND RAZIA SHARIFF

Community leadership and active citizenship

What is the role of local political participation in an education for democracy in the UK? According to J.S. Mill, local democratic government not only creates the opportunity for political participation but it also provides the basis for an education for citizenship. Gerry Stoker has written that, 'Local government should not be defined by its task of service delivery; rather it should be valued as a site for political activity.' (Stoker, 1996, p.194) While research has highlighted the problem of addressing the 'democratic deficit' in the UK nationally, there is also a growing literature which considers the 'crisis of local democracy' in the UK (King and Stoker, 1996; Pratchett and Wilson,1996; etc.) The Local Government White Paper, 'Modern Local Government: In Touch With the People' (DETR,1998) called for a democratic renewal which includes enhancing political participation and extending local author-ity and community leadership to promote the economic, social and environmental 'well-being' of local areas. (DETR, 1998 and cf. LGA, 1998) These ideas are embedded in the Local Government Act 2000 and the Local Government White Paper (Oct 2006) and currently local authorities are facing up to the challenge of developing new ways of involving communities in local governance. I would like to briefly explore how enhancing political participation in local and regional governance through community leadership can make a contribution to the renewal of democracy in the UK and provide a lifelong learning for active citizenship.

In the UK there are increasingly capacity building programmes for people in the voluntary and community sectors who participate in partnership working in local governance activities and public service delivery. There are also the 'Local Strategic Partnerships' for the development of local authority 'community strategies', which in key areas of deprivation are linked to neighbourhood renewal programmes. These capacity building programmes and the experiential learning involved in participating in regeneration activities offer an important opportunity for structuring non-formal lifelong learning for active citizenship. The learning theory and practice of community-based learning, with its emphasis on 'reflective practice' and the development of active citizenship through experiential learning can be adapted to provide a way of learning that best meets the needs of adult learners who are actively involved in their communities (cf. Mayo, Annette) In many of these cases the interest in lifelong learning for active citizenship may be more with building social capital (cf. Putnam, 2000) than with capacity building for democratic political participation (Annette, 2004 and Edwards *et al.*, 2001).

The main challenge facing such developments is whether local political authorities working with community leaders are willing and able to move beyond a politics of consumer satisfaction and public consultation to a more deliberative and participatory democratic politics. The model of community leadership developed by Clarke and Stewart is one where local councillors are seen as providing community leadership as part of the fabric of local governance and based on partnership working with local voluntary and community sector organisations and also tenant participation groups. (cf. Clarke and Stewart, 1998) Lawrence Pratchett has argued for 'a new democratic polity which not only improves the effectiveness of existing practices but also draws upon different components of direct, consultative, deliberative and representative democracy to create a new democratic order.' (Pratchett, 2000, p.9) This new democratic politics would include referendums, consultative activities and deliberative participation. There is an increasing interest in the activities of deliberative democracy which have been advocated by the Local Government Association and follow on from the work of the Commission for Local Democracy,1993–1995 and the ESRC research programme on 'Local Governance',1992–1997. The evidence indicates that local governance now includes a growing repertoire of approaches which can encourage public participation (Lowndes *et al.*, 1998).

Innovations in local democracy have included referendum, focus groups, citizens' juries, visioning, etc. (Barnes, 1999). As Pratchett notes, these activities in themselves cannot establish a more deliberative democracy but as part of a wider reform package they can provide the basis for the realisation of such a deliberative form of democratic politics (Pratchett, 2000; Stoker, 1996). As local authorities established 'local strategic partnerships' as part of the statutory obligation to involve the local communities in developing 'community strategies' and also for those areas which received neighbourhood renewal funding, there are an enormous variety of innovative approaches with which they are operating (Goss, 2001). This reflects a gradual shift from local government to governance and it includes the participation of a range of social networks that can generate both social capital and active citizenship (Newman, 2001).

One of the key issues underlying the development of a deliberative democratic politics is not only the problem of the levels and forms of participation but also the problem of social exclusion. To what extent do these new forms of deliberative democratic politics address the need to take into account an identity politics-based education, class, gender, race, ethnicity and disability? Another important question on the local level of governance is the question of how we define political participation and what should be the role of the voluntary and community sectors in local democratic politics? (Taylor, 2003).

The 'politics' of urban regeneration and the growing importance of the 'voluntary ' and 'community' sectors as well as residents' groups provide the context for the growth of ESF, SRB, NDC and now Neighbourhood Renewal-funded community development and partnership working in the UK. This provides another focus for studying 'political' participation in the UK and the creation of new opportunities for a lifelong learning for active citizenship (cf. Taylor, 2003). The concept of 'community leadership' from below is based on the partnership between local government and residents' associations as well as voluntary and community sector organisations (Purdue *et al.*, 2000; Taylor, 2003). This partnership working involves the creation of new forms of consulting and involving local people (Chanan, 2004) and the work of the Community Development Foundation. It is too soon to have any reliable information on the overall nature of the neighbourhood renewal programme and the success of local strategic partnerships as forms of democratic participation. We know, for example, that electoral turn-out for the election of NDC Boards in some areas has been greater than ward results for local elections. There seems to be some evidence of greater involvement beyond the usual suspects in area-based regeneration but there is no clear evidence base yet to support this view. We are only beginning to have a fuller understanding of the important role of black and minority ethnic voluntary and ethnic community organisations in urban regeneration and no full understanding of its wider 'political' implications. The role of faith-based community organisations in regeneration and their wider political significance is also an area where there is now some understanding but it still lacks a clear evidence base (Farnell, 2001 and 2003).

The Local Government White Paper (October 2006) embodies a central intention to empower local communities in order to improve public services, local democracy and the capacity of communities to have a greater influence over and involvement in the conditions of their lives; and The Governance of Britain (July 2007) Green Paper gives further substance to the vision of a truly participative society and the funda-mental role of empowerment in achieving a more equal, cohesive and productive society. More recently, the Local Government and Public Involvement in Health Bill received royal assent, thereby placing a cen-tral government requirement on local authorities to involve communities in decisions about health services.

The government recognises that there is already a good deal of work on empowerment taking place around the country, but of variable qual-ity, unstable provision and sometimes unclear impact. The Community Empowerment Division therefore commissioned the Community Development Foundation, CLG's specialist NDPB in this field, to set up a NEP, spanning the public and third sectors, and potentially the private sector, to improve the quality, co-ordination and evidence of empower-ment across England. The overall mission of the partnership is to improve the quality and functioning of relationships between citizens and government, in order to increase the ability of people to influence the decisions which affect their lives. This will be measured by National Indicator 4, under the new performance framework for local authorities. In addition a key focus for the NEP is the new Duty to Involve.

In addition to its national members, the NEP works through a network of regional consortia, supported by CDF, who carry forward much of the practical work, and develop relationships with local authorities and their partners. The London Civic Forum is the lead body for the London region and works to an agreed action plan for the region. The London Empowerment Partnership (LEP) draws members from key public bodies, voluntary and community sector networks and community development practitioners, and will link with its Regional Improvement and Efficiency Partnership and Government Office to ensure productive dialogue with local authorities. The LEP is tasked with setting up a framework to enable the statutory sector, Third Sector and communities at a regional and local level to share and maximise existing skills, expertise, knowledge and networks. It is a strategic initiative aiming to bring additional value to the many activities taking place, and to find ways to measure and then encourage effective empowerment of citizens in public services.

Community leadership and ALAC

In 2004 the Civil Renewal Unit of the Home Office, which was established under the influence of the then Home Secretary David Blunkett, enabled the development of the ALAC programme for adult learning in the community for citizenship education. As part of this programme the 'London Civic Forum' in partnership with the Faculty of Lifelong Learning' of Birkbeck College, University of London established a joint 'Community Leadership' course

The London Civic Forum was founded in 2003 and is now a network of 1,300 full member organisations and associate individual members, from the capital's private, public and not-for-profit sectors. It counts within its membership a wide range of community organisations, black, Asian and minority ethnic groups, faith groups, disabled people's organisations, young people's organisations, older people's groups, disabled and lesbian, gay, bisexual and transgender people's groups. Its members are based across all of Greater London in every London borough. Its members include colleges, hospitals, trade unions, chambers of commerce, large corporates, small consultancies, advice providers, campaign groups, big charities, local strategic partnerships, community policy consultative groups, training providers, helplines, museums, libraries, theatres, city farms, housing associations, social enterprises ...

The Civic Forum brings these together to strengthen civil society by which is meant the people and organisations outside of government and for-profit business that strengthen associational life, common values and a space for public debate. It works in partnership with other umbrella or second-tier organisations in London and closely with institutions that have responsibility for the governance of London. The Mayor and the London Assembly are, however, only a small body of elected representatives. For the administration to be truly effective, it needs to reflect and represent the views of the whole of society. The Civic Forum, along with a host of other stakeholders, is one key way of ensuring that the Mayor, the London Assembly and their functional bodies gain access to the widest range of views and expertise from within London's civil society.

The policy work of the London Civic Forum aims to build up a picture of what its members think about London and to develop a unique cross-sector contribution to debate on issues that affect Londoners. The priorities established also inform decisions on which consultations it will respond to. Civic participation is a key theme in this work and its policy perspectives are measured against the principles set out in its Civic Charter, namely civic literacy, civic space, civic co-operation and civic leadership and civic pride.

The foundation phase of policy work was through three Policy Commissions, which looked at public policy, democracy and community involvement. The commissions were cross-sectoral and involved members of the Civic Forum Council, as well as representatives of member organisations. Their findings have informed the structuring of Civic Forum policy work in the light of available resources.

Following the collaborative community leadership project between the London Civic Forum and Birkbeck, University of London a certificate of higher education award programme in 'community leadership was established. The Certificate of Higher Education in Community Leadership is for community practitioners at the sharp end who want to better understand the context in which they operate, to discuss common issues with colleagues from other organisations, and to take a step back and reflect on their work and its significance.

Community leadership work in London includes a wide range of roles in local strategic partnerships, neighbourhood management, New Deal for Communities, voluntary and community sector organisations, faith communities, local communities, and the various partnerships which have been set up for urban and civil renewal.

The first 'Community Leadership' module introduces key concepts of citizenship, community and community leadership in the context of urban regeneration policies in Britain today. Participants look at the development of civil society and the emergence of new forms of governance and community participation, with particular reference to London. The focus of the module lies in analysis of the forces acting upon communities, particularly disadvantaged ones, the responses in those communities and within the state to their situation and finally the ways in which these communities can gain greater voice. The module also examines the nature of community leadership in the modernisation of local politics in Britain, which will include understanding the ways in which community participation can be developed. The module allows students to reflect on the scope and purpose of community leadership and to review their own expectations. It also enables students to consider some of the best practices of community leadership. They are:

• democratic practice and the challenge of representation;
• inclusive practice and the recognition of diversity;
• effective practice through critical project management; and
• reflective practice through community action and experiential learning.

The second 'Community-Based Project Development and Management' module introduces important issues and principles to develop and manage community-based projects, using 'input sessions' incorporating action learning to deliver the essential content. It covers key areas for community activists and project co-ordinators and leaders, including project definition, business planning, partnerships, implementation, monitoring and evaluation, and fundraising strategies. The module is delivered using case studies and peer mentoring, by speakers with practical experience, and whenever possible in the community or through interactive learning.

The third 'Community Action' module is an 'action learning' module in which each participant undertakes some community activity – paid or voluntary. This can be their existing work or volunteer role, or part of it, or a special project or new initiative. This activity will be organised largely on an individual basis, usually with the partner organisation through which the community activity is being undertaken.

ALAC and participant learning approach, facilitation and assessment

The previous parts of this chapter have looked at the way in which the ALAC programme for the London Hub came about and was developed in association with Birkbeck, University of London, over two course participant cohorts: May 2005 and October 2005. In this part, a facilitator and former participant involved with the course at the time offer their perspective on the following: approach to learning, facilitation and assessment underpinning the community leadership course delivery, along with the course provision itself, and outcomes for the participants who attended. This latter aspect is undertaken by explaining general feedback from participants and also the former participant presenting an in-depth individual case study account of what this course meant both in terms of both her particular perception of her experience and also reflects on the position of other participants she worked with as part of the course. The chapter then considers the implications of the participant feedback and concludes on what have been responses to this.

The approach to participants learning, facilitation and assessment (optional) as part of the ALAC programme, was underpinned by a number of methods that operated within the context of a philosophy around participants learning about community leadership through their experiences and reflection on a range of issues they felt relevant, resulting from work that they undertook for or with different communities and groups. The methods involved formal lecturers delivered by established Birkbeck staff that was in-dispersed with follow-up activities which included small group work and role play workshop exercises lead by trained facilitators. The idea of learning through their experiences was based on the idea about the theory of experiential learning which was developed and published by David Kolb in 1984 (Kolb, 1984). This theory essentially asserted that one can view the learning process as involving a combination of participants grasping and transforming knowledge through experience(s) that emerges through a process of reflecting, understanding, testing acting and reviewing one's situation or position. An important part of participant's experiences was reflective practice, which was introduced in 1987 by Donald Schon as a critical process in refining one's own artistry or craft in a specific discipline. He then later defined within an educational and learning context as involving thoroughly considering one's own experiences in applying

233

knowledge to practice while being coached by professionals in the discipline (Schon, 1996).

In terms of how experiential learning and reflective practice translated into what were the strengths of the ALAC approach, was in the course provision allowing participants to situate and see how issues they face in their work could be understood and reframed by applying theoretical models.

One of the benefits was it helped participants look at what they could do differently and also provided some possibilities for thinking about how they might develop more effective practical longer term responses to issues they face. The small group workshop and role play exercises worked particularly well with respect to reinforcing and supporting this.

In turning to some of the challenges or weaknesses of such an approach was a difficulty in striking the correct balance between theory and practice in terms of both course provision content and delivery. This manifested in some participants (though not expressed in formal course feedback forms and evaluation report – see below) infor-mally suggesting that they felt there to be a gap and not a bridge between what they learnt in lectures which was more academic theoretical knowledge-based, which they could not always so easily take away and apply in workshops which sought to get participants to cultivate and apply experiential knowledge and reflect on practice. This did not, however, deviate from the fact that some participants found some of the lecturers to be helpful (see section below). It is nevertheless the case that the result of weaknesses discussed earlier in terms of the approach, it could be argued, did not help participants fully see what could be gained through praxis (bringing together theory and practice) in the course of their work.

In terms of participants who opted for the coursework assessment option this required the submission of three pieces of assignment which included a concept analysis, an essay and producing a learning log (portfolio of what participants learnt as part of their coming to the course and how had or would engaging with ALAC approach help them). While participants engaged quite well with the first two assignment pieces, it was the reflective learning log which was problematic for many, as this required quite deep introspection, and it could thus be debated the course wrongly assumed that through their work they would have been doing this.

Participant feedback

In the section to follow the general participant feedback is based on formal responses provided by participants in terms of quotes based on completion of end-of-course Birkbeck feedback forms, and also directly from the participant's final evaluation report for the London Hub (London Civic Forum, 2006).

In terms of general feedback from participants, mention was made of some of the reasons for joining the ALAC course programme, course delivery itself and also how they were able to take and use such knowledge from the ALAC course programme in their work as well as how it had helped them more specifically.

The motives for participants coming to the programme tended to be largely expressed in terms of gaining knowledge, understanding and skills which sets what they do within a broader context:

As one male participant explains:

> ... I need a good knowledge of the political structure of the country and how to use it to help the community.

For similar reasons another female participant added:

> I joined ALAC because I thought it would be a very good programme to equip myself with the skills and knowledge to better understand the decision-making institutions which govern London and also go through this programme with other like-minded individuals.

In terms of the formal lectures, while as mentioned in the previous section some participants informally expressed issues around course weakness in terms of the linkage and application of lecture content coverage to workshop exercises, other participants, focusing their experience more in terms of the specifics of a particular lecture, felt:

> The content of the lectures was very beneficial for me. I came also to know how my local government works and especially the roles of the cabinet and councillors.

In terms of the workshop exercises a female participant commented on what she gained from looking at the project management aspect of community leadership by stating:

> *I've learnt most from the case study to reach consensus with a group with such diversity was a nice opportunity to practice negotiation skills ... see the result later at the presentation, with a well planned work, which had the contribution of all the team, was absolutely meaningful.*

However, while there was another female participant who felt the lectures and workshops to be challenging, she saw this as positive:

> *...The lectures and workshops were a bit challenging because of my lack of background knowledge, but the novelty of most of the subject matter made it interesting.*

In turning to what, more specifically, participants felt that they had taken away from doing the course for them personally meant, as one female participant put it:

> *I work for a Latin American woman's organisation, providing information. Now I will use the information I learnt on the programme when I give people advice when they come to us.*

For another female student what the ALAC course programme did offer was important opportunities for individual networking and network development, which was also picked up in the sentiments of other participants who felt this be both useful and needed to evolve further as a critical part of any future such programmes:

> *In some ways, the main benefit of the course was in meeting so many people who were passionate about helping their community. I found this inspiring ... I have been inspired, with a friend I met on the ALAC course, to take steps towards setting up my own community mediation project. The networking skills learned on the course have been useful, as have the lectures about the government's policies on partnership between public bodies and citizens in meeting public needs.*

Finally, a male participant summed up what the ALAC course had encouraged him to go on to do:

> *While I have been engaged in work in my community the course has encouraged me to become more involved in the local education system, in that I have*

236

put myself forward to become a school governor and who knows I may in the future be interested in taking on the role of a local councillor.

Perspective from a former participant – a case study

I joined as a participant on the ALAC Community Leadership course programme in 2005 in order to widen and deepen my understanding of the theory and policy surrounding community leadership and civil renewal. I was then the Director of a London borough Community Empowerment Network (CEN) and was also a member of the National Community Forum (NCF) – a sounding board for the then Office of the Deputy Prime Minister and Neighbourhood Renewal Unit – now the Department for Communities and Local Government.

I started the course, returning to the world of academia after ten years, and the first lecture was quite a shock to the system! It highlighted the limitations of my knowledge of the 'bigger picture' and the different dimensions involved in current policy and contexts and the theoretical underpinnings involved. I was fascinated by this whole new world of knowledge that would inform my own work within the CEN and at the national level with the NCF. In addition to all this rich knowledge, I was meeting other like-minded community leaders from across London who also had a thirst to improve their understanding of the policy and theoretical contexts that informed their community work. For other participants however, it was too intense and too much and the numbers over the four weeks halved – maybe because the course was free, maybe because they had to submit a reflective log and a theoretical concept paper – and felt as a participant at the time that the programme wasn't designed for everyone – especially if they didn't have some prior experience of the world of academia and politics.

The course originally covered four key topics with lectures from guest speakers followed by practical workshops and this model has been maintained up to the present day, although the topics have changed. Originally there was civil renewal, community leadership, project management, governance structures, diversity practice and community media. Now there is community cohesion, civil renewal and empowerment, community development and multiculturalism, project management, partnership working and equalities, democracy and local governance, leadership and management.

All the topics covered in the course informed my work at the CEN and NCF, and although the initial concept of reflective practice was difficult to grasp – it has become a very useful tool in helping me develop my skills and expertise in applying new knowledge to the practical realities of my work. The first session on civil renewal put the government initiatives in a historical and theoretical context and explained the ethos behind the moves to re-position communities and the voluntary and community sector. This was very useful in the debates at the national level with NCF as it gave me a more detailed understanding of other issues beyond the community empowerment agenda.

The second session explored the distinction between leadership and management and more importantly the spectrum of styles – and best-practice models for a reflective and learning organisation – this really gave a backbone to my approach in my work at the CEN supporting self managed and self motivated teams, where mistakes were all part of the learning curve. The third session on governance structures opened up the inconsistencies between different local authorities and their engagement structures, giving my ideas on other systems and interpretations of government policy guidance. It also highlighted the disconnect between the different governance structure in London from the Mayor's London Assembly, to Westminster MPs to local councillors and local government and the obstacles faced by communities advocating for change. I suppose the biggest reality check was the session on diversity practice – not because of the message that it is the 'environment' that disables you but that the primary motive for all the equalities legislation was economic: to reintroduce sections of the population into the labour market so as the fund the Treasury for the ageing population in the UK! This has ever since heightened my sense of critical awareness on the rhetoric and spin used in promoting new policies which are part of the equalities agenda. The community media lecture on how to measure and market community engagement was another new area of interest, especially when having to negotiate indicators to define and measure success. The best part of the course was the workshop interactions where all the different experiences of participants came alive and the different ways in which participants had internalised the information given with their own understanding.

As a former participant of the first cohort I was asked to support the workshop facilitation of the second round of the ALAC programme and the same pattern of retention repeated itself. When Birkbeck took over the programme in Year 2 I was asked to support the course as a co-tutor on the Saturday Community Leadership course and together I and the other tutor designed a course programme that while having a theoretical grounding and policy context also provided a bridge with the real world of implementation through practical workshops and a much more facilitative and interactive approach in the learning environment. Although the starting numbers were less, as a fee had to be introduced since it was no longer a subsidised course, retention was improved, and over the past two years this model has been updated annually to keep up with the changes in policy and academic writings. One thing that has always struck me about the participants of the course is how diverse and multidisciplinary they are – I do not think there is any other forum where you get such a positive reflection of the communities of London, from all walks of life and all backgrounds.

I now lead on the Community Leadership course as a Birkbeck Sessional Lecturer, and I am completing my MSc in Conflict Resolution and Mediation studies at Birkbeck. Why do I still give up one Saturday each month to deliver the course? Because I learn so much from the reflective learning that goes on in the course with each cohort that joins the course, and on those Saturdays we are 'blue sky thinkers' who explore new possibilities based on our experiential knowledge. The free thinking gained in understanding the political and theoretical drivers to current policy initiatives inform how we can ensure that we lead the community in maximising the opportunities created in this brave new world of participatory democracy and citizens' empowerment.

Implications and conclusion from participants' feedback

The feedback from participants shows an overall positive experience gained from their engagement with the then ALAC course programme with such positive feedback being maintained in subsequent developments by Birkbeck taking over the management and running of the programme. The programme has since 2005 developed an infrastructure of delivering the course also on weekday evenings as part of both Cert HE Community Leadership and a new BSc in Community Development and Public Policy in both Central London and East London.

Birkbeck has also sought as part of developing its Widening Participation and Community Partnerships academic outreach policy and practices taken the course into different community-based learning settings by working with potential community partners to provide bespoke-based tailored learning along with taster opportunities, to encourage participants from diverse communities to take an interest in studying such topics more formally at Birkbeck (thus also linking the worlds of formal and non-formal learning).

References

Annette, J. (2003) 'Community, Politics and Citizenship Education', in Lockyer, A., Crick, B. and Annette, J. (eds), *Education for Democratic Citizenship*. Farnham: Ashgate

Barber, B. (1998) *A Passion for Democracy*. New Jersey: Princeton University Press

Barnes, M. (1999) *Building a Deliberative Democracy: An evaluation of two citizens' juries*. London: IPPR

Barnes, M. (2000) 'Researching Public Participation', in Pratchett, L. (ed.), *Renewing Local Democracy?* London: Frank Cass

Bochum, V., Pratten, B. and Wilding, K. (2005–09) *Civil Renewal and Active Citizenship*. London: NCVO

Burns, D. and Taylor, M. (2000) *Auditing Community Participation*. Bristol: Joseph Rowntree Foundation/Policy Press

Burns, D. *et al.* (2004) *Making Community Participation Meaningful*. York: Joseph Rowntree Foundation

Chanan, G. (2004) *Searching for Solid Foundations: Community involvement and urban policy*. London: ODPM

Chapman, R. and Lowndes, V. (2008) 'Faith in governance? The potential and pitfalls of involving faith groups in urban governance', in *Planning, Practice and Research (Special Issue on Race and Faith)*, Vol. 23, No. 1, pp. 57–75

Clarke, M. and Stewart, J. (1998) *Community Governance, Community Leadership and the New Local Government*. York: Joseph Rowntree Foundation

Commission for Local Democracy (1995) *Taking Charge: The rebirth of local democracy*. London: Municipal Journal Books

Dinham, A., Furbey, R. and Lowndes, V. (eds) (2008) *Faith in the Public Realm*. Bristol: Policy Press

Edwards, M. (2005) *Civil Society*. Cambridge: Polity Press

Farnell, R. (2001) 'Faith Communities, Regeneration and Social Exclusion: Developing a research agenda', in *Community Development Journal*, Vol. 36, No. 4, pp. 263–272

Farnell, R. *et al.* (2003) *'Faith' in Urban Regeneration?* Bristol: Joseph Rowntree Foundation/Policy Press

Fung, A. and Wright, E. O. (eds) (2003) *Deepening Democracy: Institutional innovations in empowered participatory governance.* London: Verso

Furbey, R., Dinham, A. and Finneron, D. (2006) *Faith as Social Capital: Connecting or dividing?* Bristol: Policy Press

Gastil, J. and Levine, P. (2005) *The Deliberative Democracy Handbook.* San Francisco: Jossey Bass

Goss, S. (2001) *Making Local Governance Work.* London: Palgrave

Imrie, R. and Raco, M. (eds) (2005) *Urban Renaissance? New Labour, community and urban policy.* Bristol: Policy Press

Joseph Rowntree Charitable Trust (2006) *Power to the People. The Report of Power: An Independent Inquiry into Britain's Democracy (also known as the 'Power Inquiry').* York: York Publishing Distribution

King, D. and Stoker, G. (1996) *Rethinking Local Democracy.* London: Macmillan

Kolb, D. (1984) *Experiential Learning: Experience as a source of learning and development.* Englewood Cliffs, New Jersey: Prentice-Hall Inc.

Local Government Association (1998) *Modernising Local Government.* London: LGA

Local Government Association (1999) *Community Leadership and Community Planning: Towards a Community Strategy for Well-Being.* London: LGA

Local Government Association (2002) *Faith and community: A good practice guide for local authorities.* London: LGA

London Civic Forum (2006) *Active Learning for Active Citizenship: Participants' report.* London: London Civic Forum

Lowndes, V. *et al.* (1998) *Enhancing Public Participation in Local Government: A research report.* London: DETR

McLeod, M. (2001) *Black and Minority Ethnic Voluntary and Community Sectors.* York: Joseph Rowntree Foundation

Newman, J. (2001) *Modernising Governance.* London: Sage

Newman, J. (2005) *Remaking Local Governance.* Bristol: Policy Press

Pattie, C., Seyd, P. and Whitely, P. (2004) *Citizenship in Britain: Values, participation and democracy.* Cambridge: Cambridge University Press

Pratchett, L. and Wilson, D. (eds) (1996) *Local Democracy and Local Government*. London: Macmillan.

Pratchett, L. (ed.) (2000) *Renewing Local Democracy?* London: Frank Cass

Purdue, D. *et al.* (2000) *Community leadership in area regeneration*. Bristol: Policy Press

Putnam, R. (2000) *Bowling Alone: Civic Disengagement in America*. New York: Simon & Schuster

Putnam, R. (ed.) (2002) *Democracies in Flux*. Oxford: Oxford University Press

Schon, D. (1996) *Educating the reflective practitioner: Towards a new design for teaching and learning in the professions*. San Francisco: Jossey Bass

Smith, G. (2005) *Beyond the Ballot: 57 democratic innovations from around the world*. London: The Power Inquiry
(cf. www.powerinquiry.com)

Stoker, G. (1996) 'Redefining Local Democracy', in Pratchett, L. and Wilson, D. (eds), *Local Democracy and Local Government*. London: Houndsmills, Macmillan

Taylor, M. (2003) *Public Policy in the Community*. London: Palgrave

CHAPTER FOURTEEN

Accrediting community-based active learning: building progression pathways

CAROL PACKHAM

This chapter draws on the experience of the Greater Manchester ALAC hub, which used the community-based delivery of accredited modules from Manchester Metropolitan University Youth and Community courses. Initially this involved the training of community teams in the carrying out of participatory research and evaluations (Community Audits), and the later development of modules in Conflict Resolution, Schools of Participation, and Community Education for Social Change (Training the Trainers), following their practical success in the community. The chapter sets out the principles and methods used and the requirements for effective group facilitation and partnership working. In addition the chapter discusses some of the issues and concerns raised by using empowering informal education methods within the increasingly restrictive requirements of social policy and the constraints of formal education contexts.

Thus the Greater Manchester hub has used the principles of informal education within the formal higher education sector. This was enabled by the host Community Audit and Evaluation Centre being part of the Youth and Community Work team at Manchester Metropolitan University, and using the principles and methods of Professional Youth and Community Work, those of informal education and community development, drawing on theoretical influence such as Paulo Freire (1972), Banks *et al.* (2003) hooks (1994), Ledwith (1997) and Popple (1995). What characterises this approach is the commitment and practice of dialogical education based on high levels of active participation of the learner, with a distinctive role for the worker as facilitator and enabler. These can be summarised into three characteristics, of making space, enabling voluntary, self directed and self help activities and using an inclusive critical perspective.

The aim of the Greater Manchester hub has therefore been to carry out the ALAC pilot using Youth and Community Work principles and methods through the following objectives:

- to deliver Manchester Metropolitan University (MMU) accredited modules in community settings;
- to work with community partners, particularly as co-trainers;
- to use experiential and dialogical learning methods in facilitated groups;
- to help identify and act upon community identified priorities;
- to make connections between communities, their members and higher education;
- to be able to identify and value the individual, civil and civic benefits;
- to facilitate the sharing of experience through the development of the hub community;
- to facilitate the progression of participants, for example to higher education; and/or
- to build the confidence and experience of participants so that they could progress into a variety of spheres including both employment and/or community action.

The challenge of the Hub has been to co-design and deliver programmes of work that were flexible enough to meet the aspirations of the community partners, meet the requirements of the ALAC pilots, meet the principles of informal education and community development while at the same time meeting the academic and quality assurance requirements of higher education.

The initial Greater Manchester hub activity, the Community Audit MMU accredited module consisted of ten two-hour sessions delivered alongside the community-based team carrying out research or evaluations. The content of the module plus the activities have involved working with groups through the three stages of the process of preparation, gathering information, and then analysing, report writing and dissemination. Sessions were a combination of theory and practice. During the

programme the groups explored principles, methodologies and appropriate methods and information gathering techniques, ethics and issues of
inclusion, exclusion and representation, predicting and avoiding blocks
and barriers, and planning and discussing their evaluations as they
progressed. The programmes have involved groups such as *Groundwork,*
who hosted a team of community volunteers in Tameside to research the
requirements for effective volunteering. In Manchester two teams of
women have been researching the barriers to employment for women
from marginalised communities.

Two other programmes have looked at health related areas with a
view to improving local services. The South Manchester Healthy Living
Network (HLN)'s programme involved the recruitment of a group of
volunteers from a team already working as volunteers and peer health
educators. These sessions were run at the HLN offices in the hospital.
The findings of the evaluation resulted in recommendations for the
effective support of the HLN's Discovery Team of volunteers, plus a
separate report for the HLN with recommendations for effective
working with community groups.

Another ALAC programme facilitated the National Health Service
Domestic Violence Unit, working jointly with the Women's Aid network
and the Pankhurst Women's Centre. Their team was recruited from
women who had experienced domestic violence; several were volunteers
within the refuges or at the Pankhurst Centre where the programme was
run. The team devised work to evaluate the access to NHS services of
those experiencing domestic violence. The report of their findings, alongside a screen saver and mouse mat with the pointers for effective working
with women experiencing domestic violence, were launched at a
Manchester-wide conference.

Approaches and methods

In line with the principles of informal education, although the programmes
were working to the framework of an accredited module, there were
high levels of participation and the courses were community based. The
focus for all of the programmes was identified by the community-based
organisations, and participants were recruited through their networks. The
participants in the HLN and the NHS Domestic Violence programmes
were familiar with the focus of the programmes and had experience as
volunteers or activists, for example. The teams were diverse in relation to

age, ethnicity, physical impairments, sexuality, class, geographical spread and levels of academic experience and educational ability.

The focus of each programme was loosely identified and teams were enabled to confirm for themselves what was to be done and how this involved the participants in planning their particular research or evaluation programme, identifying who should be involved and how; and in line with the principles of high levels of participation, they undertook the information gathering, analysis, report writing, feedback and dissemination.

For example, the HLN team first evaluated the role and effectiveness of the HLN volunteer team, the Discovery Team, through postal questionnaires to all Discovery team members. They then evaluated the impact of the HLN on the projects within the network. This involved carrying out interviews with project workers and running focus groups with project participants. The team involved in the Domestic Violence Project visited a range of NHS settings and undertook an environmental observation as well as interviewing key staff.

The role of the ALAC facilitator from MMU was to work alongside a co-facilitator from the agency, who carried out the support and link work with the individual team members while they undertook information gathering. In many cases the partner agency provided additional support with regard to child care and financial requirements. The facilitator has responsibility for facilitating the group process and ensuring the inclusion of all group members. A range of participatory methods were used to enable:

- the group to share experiences;
- best use of existing skills and knowledge; and
- networking.

The facilitator also ensured that the contents of the MMU module were being covered enabling the teams to make informed choices about how best to carry out their research and evaluation tasks. They also assisted team members in the analysis, drawing conclusions and making recommendations.

Outcomes from the work of the community-based programmes

Individuals who have participated in the programmes within the hub have developed a range of skills including research methods, communication (for example video recording), and built their confidence sufficiently to apply for courses and to pursue employment opportunities and to take action within their communities. They have learnt about policies, funding and strategies for service delivery and how different agencies work, how to work with them and how to access information and decision-making. The link between the university and the community-based programmes has been important for many participants who have been given the confidence to undertake further study, and to dispel the myths around the elitism of higher education.

> *I felt like I was a student again and yet practising what I was learning. I enjoyed this part of the training so much that I have now joined the university and (am) studying a degree part time in Health and Community Studies. (Participant in Tameside Community Audit team, Packham et al., 2004)*

Several participants subsequently registered to undertake professional Youth and Community Work Programmes at MMU, one at postgraduate level. They were to be given credit for the modules that they have already completed. Other participants have used their credits towards other programmes at the Open University and Salford University. The links with the University have also resulted in MMU hosting community conferences (for example National Ujima Conference, North West Community Development workers), seminars and 'away days', all enhancing the potential for future partnership work and 'widening participation' options for community members who may not have previously accessed higher education.

Participants have worked as diverse teams learning about each other and so about the wider community and world. They have formed new contacts and networked for the benefit of their group and their own community. Idea sharing has facilitated the development of community groups, and the networking that has taken place within teams and the wider hub has allowed people to share common concerns and identify ideas for action.

The work has directly impacted on the delivery of services, by showing gaps in provision and the need for greater inclusion: for example, making NHS services more responsive to women experiencing domestic violence; and in the case of the HLN work, valuing and developing the work of the network and particularly, the contribution of volunteers and peer educators. A team of community activists in

Hattersley, who were trained to carry out an evaluation of their Local Neighbourhood Partnership and its relation with community groups, for example, has been able to directly influence the future funding and support to local groups. They worked as a team to devise the evaluation questionnaire, carry out the research with group representatives and individual community members, analyse the findings and write the report and recommendations. This process taught them the power that external researchers and evaluators can hold, particularly in relation to the interpretation of data, and the identification of needs and future action. A member of the team has now gone on to present their work at the conference to launch the North West Regional Together We Can strategy, and to be a platform speaker with the then Secretary of State for Communities and Local Government, Hazel Blears.

One of the participants who has subsequently undertaken two of the ALAC hubs' MMU-accredited modules has registered to undertake the part time Youth and Community Work Diploma (starting with 30 of the total 120 credits required for the programme). Another participant in the team to identify barriers to employment for women from ethnic minorities, through her involvement with the University, has been able to ascertain that her degree and experience obtained in Africa would be sufficient to enable her to apply for the Post Graduate Diploma in Youth and Community Work, where she would be given credit for attendance and participation in the Community Audit Module and practice. Once on the course she would then be enabled to undertake the Community Audit assessment at postgraduate level.

Working with community partners

The hubs' approach has been to capacity-build at a local level, both with individual participants and local groups. Consequently all programmes were carried out with a co-facilitator from the community-based group. This meant that they could help facilitate the group's learning process based on their local knowledge and experience, and the process could also build the co-facilitators' capacity to be able to continue the work within the community after the end of the programme.

Delivering programmes in community settings has also meant that the participants have been typical of those who are usually involved in community activity, often as volunteers, and many have never been involved in further and higher education. In the Manchester ALAC pilot of 92 registered participants 75 per cent were women and 56 per cent were from 'ethnic minority' groups. For many of the participants their involvement in the programmes was a 'first step' or a return after a dormant period in relation to higher education. The opportunity for recognition of their learning and participation was therefore important. But progression could not always be assumed. Many participants used the programmes to improve their practice, and levels of confidence, and did not require or need the progression to further qualification or a professional career at this point.

Close work with community partners and participants has also led to the development of new accredited MMU modules in response to community-identified needs. For example a Conflict Resolution module was devised drawing on work undertaken with a group of women volunteers in East Manchester[1] who carried out intra-community work and anti-bullying programmes in local schools.

> We have all dealt with certain issues within the community, and learning mediation skills has helped us to resolve issues in the community, e.g. violence between people. We are now able to take a step back from a situation and look at things from different perspectives – being non-judgemental, staying calm and using positive body language. (Participant, East Manchester programme)

A Community-Based Active Learning module was developed drawing on the Freirian model of Schools of Participation (Freire, 1972), based on a Latin American model of popular education and community leadership training. 'The curriculum is approached through action learning where participants engage in an extended collective process where individual experiences are drawn upon and linked to theories and methodologies. This process facilitates the journey through the following elements and draws out links and relationships between:

- the individuals' experience and context;
- the group and community;
- the wider regional and national structures;
- the global situation.

---

[1] See www.resolutionsfirst.com.

The final part of the module 'allows participants to jointly identify a collective action that responds to the issues and learning through the module, or to reflect on individual action as a volunteer, or on practice placement' (Oteyza, 2005). The hub has facilitated Schools of Participation with a Refugee and Asylum Seeker Network who undertook a joint action to produce a Refugee Charter for good practice for service providers. Also, work with a group of deaf people in Manchester and Salford produced a video for use with service providers to raise their awareness of deaf culture and the requirements for effective work with deaf people.

The growing team of co-trainers has also produced a 'Training the Trainers': Community Education for Social Change (Theory and Practice) module designed to equip people to carry out experiential and dialogical training methods for enabling ALAC programmes, and other participatory training based on Freirian principles of popular education.

The Training the Trainers module worked on the same principles of open recruitment, and the offer of University Library registration and accreditation.

> *The course was designed and intended for community practitioners, adult educators, activists and community organisers with experience in community work and an on-going practice on which to draw. We hoped to attract committed people wanting to design engaging, effective workshops, extending experiential education into the domain of empowerment and transformation. (Oteyza, 2007, p. 6)*

The first cohort of the programme's fifteen participants included community activists, workers from the statutory and voluntary sector, and management committee members from disabled peoples and Asian organisations. They all commented on the importance of active learning within the sessions, both from the planned experiential content, but also from within the group. Group members stated in their on-going evaluations:

> *The size of the group, the good levels of attendance, and the activities/exercises created a friendly, safe and positive atmosphere. Having this developed from the first instance was really valuable foundation for all the other learning.*

Good mix of experience – the group is good ...

Felt that the session was very diverse and friendly, we were from different backgrounds and cultures but blended very well.

Members of the training programme have now gone on to utilise their learning both within work settings and within their private lives, an example of progression where learning is cascaded to those who you work and live with, as well as being of individual benefit to the participant.

Valuing achievement

In all of our programmes it has been important that participants could decide for themselves how much they wanted to be involved and what they wanted to get out of the programmes. It was also important that those looking for some form of accreditation should be able to work towards an outcome with both value and meaning.

For this reason, all participants in the teams were offered registration with MMU. At the end of each programme this was agreed through discussion with the participant, the agency partner (co-facilitator), and the facilitator, if the participant had undertaken the required module content and practice. The participant could then be awarded a certificate of accreditation of attendance for undertaking the MMU module. Those who had not been as fully involved received certificates of participation. Awards have been presented at large events to which all those involved have been invited and where the reports of the work were launched and findings discussed.

The award of higher education level credits was an important means of opening up progression routes and emphasising that a university education could and should be accessible to all learners. The approach piloted by the hub was that that the groups were mixed in relation to ability and experience and came together with a shared commitment to the focus of the project. The modules delivered have been accredited at Diploma of Higher Education, BA and Post Graduate Diploma levels. The participants do not have to decide at which level they are undertaking the module; this is only relevant when any assessment is undertaken. Participants, with the guidance of the module facilitator, can undertake the relevant assessment for the module at the appropriate level for their academic experience. Alternatively they can use their credits towards participating in MMU courses, such as the Youth and Community Work professionally qualifying programmes. The participants will then be asked to complete the associated assessment relevant for whichever route they have been admitted to, either Diploma of Higher Education, BA and Post Graduate Diploma/MA levels.

This approach has meant that the programmes have not recruited participants according to the level of the module, and this has resulted in diverse groups of participants who have stated, in their evaluations, that learning from each other has been an important part of the learning process. The Impact ALAC Programme in the West Midlands has also worked with participants from a variety of educational and experience backgrounds. Their evaluation also notes the importance of participants learning from each other:

> It is about offering women the opportunity to be part of a network that can offer encouragement, skill-sharing, information and support to each other. (Facilitator, Black Country Hub)

Other groups involved with the pilots have used a variety of ways of recognising achievement; these are reflected in the Take Part Learning framework.[2] Community-based groups have developed other means of supporting learning and recognising achievement. Proud City in Salford has developed an Individual Profile in Active Citizenship accredited and promoted nationally by City and Guilds, for example.[3] The profile allows individuals to work through a series of themes drawing on their ongoing experiences of community activity. Others such as the Black Country/ West Midlands hub women's Impact programme, and the Exeter Speaking Up programme for disabled adults offered Open College Network (OCN) credits as recognition of achievement and participation, and Tees Valley offered OCN and National Vocational Qualifications (NVQs) in Community Development.

Other hubs have had direct links with adult education providers such as the Workers' Educational Association in the South Yorkshire area, and linked with formal Education Institutions such as Fircroft College in the West Midlands, while the London Civic Forum worked with Birkbeck College, University of London to offer programmes of

---

[2] See www.takepart.org/framework-for-active-learning.
[3] See www.city-and-guilds.co.uk.

learning covering different aspects of governance. This hub offered accreditation and opportunities to learners to access higher education programmes, those successfully completing the programme exercises (which included a reflective learning log) received 30 credits towards a higher education certificate (74 from cohort one received accreditation).

The common themes in these pilots have been that accreditation and the level of courses should not be a barrier to participation, either in relation to selection by ability or by adding perceived formality. The programmes have all found and used a variety of ways of recognising achievements whether through celebration events, sharing achievements with others at an individual, community and national level, or by certification. A further characteristic has been that the programmes have been flexible enough to enable the participants and the trainer/facilitator to adapt the programmes to the requirements, interests and experience of each group.

The work of the ALAC programme has also highlighted the issue of 'what is meant by progression?', and made the case that it should not only be recognised as being development within the education and training sectors. As identified by the facilitators from the West Midlands hub

> *Accreditation is always viewed as an option, and for some women formal OCN accreditation is not important. One woman did not choose to gain OCN recognition but instead enrolled directly onto a Foundation Degree. For others, progression is to do with becoming more confident and more active in community and public life (Jill and Sue).*

The national pilot was able to show that progression was achieved for the participants on many levels. While individual progression to continuing education was facilitated, the hubs were aware that the progression achieved by the participants was also in relation to personal growth, community engagement and the impact on civic and civil life.

Issues and concerns

Although the work of the pilots has carried out and continues to carry out empowering and educative work with community members in a range of settings, using a variety of methods, the pilots have raised many issues and concerns that have implications for the possibility of the work being developed and utilised to its full potential.

Current English policy initiatives give little support for the notion of individual academic progression, particularly for those who are not unemployed and therefore unable to access Learning and Skills Council-funded courses. Several of our participants who have been involved in the ALAC programmes while volunteering have been unable to progress to fulltime education as benefits they have been receiving would be lost without equivalent replacement funding. Progression should be recognised as not only being within education; progression within the community and increased engagement with civic and civil activities may have a greater impact in relation to the development of social capital, and should be valued as such.

It is not usual practice in formal education settings to work in mixed ability groups. The growing emphasis in the community and voluntary sector on outcomes and the associated accreditation for learning has resulted in a reduction in mixed groups, with subsequent reductions in experiential learning from within the group. The Manchester hub pilot has obtained funding from the Greater Manchester Strategic Alliance to explore whether the model of community-based accredited modules can be developed with other providers, to facilitate wider progression and the recognition and transfer of credits. This would also explore whether other providers would adopt the model of working with mixed groups and initially accrediting the undertaking of the module and practice.

The dilemmas of providing informal education using formal structures and accreditation have been a challenge for the ALAC hubs. The role of the facilitator working with a self-selected group of willing participants has been crucial to the success of the pilots. It was important that hub co-ordinators and facilitators shared a common perspective on whether active citizenship can be empowering. We also came to a shared agreement that we were using a Freirian (1972) informal education approach, which put as centre place the notion of space for critical dialogue regarding ourselves and our relations with the world. The role of the programme facilitators has been crucial in each of the pilot hubs, not only in providing the informal education that has been central to our work, but also in relation to providing the necessary ongoing support to those involved. This has been on an individual and group level, where space for critical dialogue regarding the situational contexts and the exploration of issues was facilitated. Importantly we have not been 'teaching' active citizenship to isolated learners: they have been engaged

254

in groups and teams, learning and debating in an ongoing way, reflecting on the activities they chose to engage in. The association and voluntary nature of these programmes is essential if it is to contribute to the development of ALAC's approach.

The voluntary and self help nature of the work we were involved with was essential. But this has been controversial. Batsleer and Humphries (2000) recognised the restrictions of an imposed and set curriculum and noted the move 'away from the critical analysis of the social and political construction of knowledge towards the prescription and imposition of a narrowly defined curriculum based on approved pre-selections of knowledge and 'skills' (Ibid., p.6). Any moves to make community education programmes such as that of ALAC more rigid, with a pre-determined curriculum, would render them worthless in relation to ALAC's underlying principles, and in relation to the development of social capital. Specific and rigid outcomes could stifle rather than enable creativity and, as discussed by Batsleer and Humphries (Ibid.), this can lead to demoralisation among educators and participants alike.

The challenge for accrediting informal education, and for giving the opportunity for participants to use these credits for progression within education, is to be able to retain the principles and methods that guide the work. For example, these principles and methods involve facilitating organic development, and enabling participants to have high levels of control over the focus, content, process and methods of the work. The content of the ALAC modules was flexible enough to meet the requirements and experiences of the individual programmes and the participants, not being restricted by a preset curriculum.

The challenge of the ALAC programmes that have sought to offer recognition and the potential of progression within education has been to be able to provide the benefits and rigours of accreditation without perpetuating the constraints of formal education which might have stifled the potential for transformation and change which is inherent in informal education. David Blunkett (2003) in his introduction to the 'Active Citizens, Strong Communities – Progressing civil renewal' has appeared to support this approach. As he stated 'it is not just about better outcomes, crucial though they are. It is also about what happens to communities along the way, what they learn about themselves and each other, the way they develop and grow' (Ibid., p.1).

Summary

The work of the Greater Manchester hub and the work of the other pilots who used the option of accredited programmes have shown that accreditation of work, and the possible academic progression options this affords, is only beneficial if this enhances rather than constrains the principles and methods of ALAC, using an informal education framework. Informal education is usually referred to in the UK in relation to work with young people: the ALAC programme has firmly located this approach within the adult and community sectors as a method of reflective community learning (Packham, 2008). Our experiences have also shown that the opportunities for progression that can be afforded by such ALAC programmes must be recognised and supported in their broadest sense, giving equal value to the contributions that learning can make to improving practice in communities and in civic and civil society. This work is being taken forward through the Department for Communities and Local Government Take Part Pathfinder programme, which is working in 18 areas across England aiming to engage community members in active educational processes to support their involvement in decision-making at the civic and civil level.

References

Banks, S. *et al.* (eds) (2003) *Managing Community Practice: Principles, policies and programmes.* Bristol: Policy Press

Batsleer, J. and Humphries, B. (eds) (2000) *Welfare, exclusion and political agency.* London: Routledge

Blunkett, D. (2003) *Active Citizens, Strong Communities – Progressing civil renewal.* London: Home Office

Freire, P. (1972) *Pedagogy of the Oppressed.* London: Penguin Books

hooks, bell (1994) *Teaching to Transgress. Education as the practice of freedom.* London: Routledge

Ledwith, M. (1997) *Participating in Transformation: Towards a working model of community empowerment.* London: Venture Press

Oteyza, C. de (2005) *Community Based Active Learning* (School of Participation) Manchester: Module Descriptor, Manchester Metropolitan University.

Oteyza, C. de (2007) *Community Education for Social Change: Training the Trainer, report of the pilot course April–May 2007.* Manchester:

Community Audit and Evaluation Centre, Manchester Metropolitan University.

Packham. C. *et al.* (2004) *Delivering Effective Volunte*ering. Manchester: Community Audit and Evaluation Centre, Manchester Metropolitan University

Packham, C. *et al.* (2008) *Active Citizenship and Community Learning.* Exeter: Learning Matters

Popple, K. (1995) *Analysing Community Work. Its theory and practice.* Open University Press

SECTION THREE

THE WIDER CONTEXT

CHAPTER FIFTEEN

Putting the learning into citizenship

JULIET MERRIFIELD

In the current policy climate in England there is a great deal of talk both about learning and about citizenship. But too often it seems that the people talking about citizenship are not thinking about learning, and the people talking about learning are not thinking about citizenship.

At the very time when worries about the 'democratic deficit' – decreasing trust and increasing cynicism about the public arena – means that parts of the UK government are seeking to promote active citizenship, its adult education policy is being funnelled into a narrow skills and vocational agenda, turning its back on more than a century of learning for democracy. This chapter will review briefly some of the key policy initiatives in both learning and citizenship, and discuss ways that they might be linked to the benefit of both.

The policy agenda in learning

The Department for Innovation, Universities and Skills (DIUS) was formed in 2007 (splitting the previous Department for Education and Skills into two) with a mission:

> To drive forward delivery of the Government's long-term vision to make Britain one of the best places in the world for science, research and innovation, and to deliver the ambition of a world-class skills base. (HM Treasury, 2007, p.212)

261

DIUS became responsible for all post-compulsory education in England, funding further education (FE) and adult education (except higher education) through the Learning and Skills Council (LSC). Reviews of the various documents that govern the priorities of the LSC make it clear that learning for citizenship is not included.

The LSC Statement of Priorities, November 2007 – 'Better skills, better jobs, better lives' – makes a nod to the wider benefits of learning, but the main priorities are:

- creating demand for the qualifications and skills levels that the government has determined are essential for economic competitiveness (Skills for Life, Level 2 and Level 3);
- transforming the FE system to meet demand, and in particular to adapt to a more employer-led system of demand (through Train to Gain and other initiatives that enable employers to 'buy' certain kinds of publicly-funded training from FE providers); and
- delivering better skills, with targets for adult skills in literacy and numeracy, Level 2, Level 3 and progression to Level 4 (university level). (LSC, 2007b.)

The government and the LSC do recognise a connection between learning and social inclusion, and it appears in the 'better lives' part of its annual report title (LSC, 2007a), but the connection is an indirect one. In their policy analysis, better skills equals better chance of getting a job equals social inclusion:

> *We believe that raising skills levels and gaining new skills and qualifications is essential not only if we are to help more people to come off benefits and to enter and progress in work, but also if we are to reduce social and economic disadvantage and support greater social mobility. (LSC, 2007b, p.3)*

Similarly, the link between the LSC's priorities and other government targets (like tackling poverty and promoting greater independence and well-being in later life) is also via the skills agenda. The key task is seen as engaging 'priority groups' and convincing them to develop the skills and gain the qualifications that have been determined by government policy to meet their needs. These priority groups include young people who are not in education, employment or training (NEETs), lone parents, people on benefits, and people who live in deprived neighbourhoods. The LSC recognises that such people need 'the most support and encouragement both to engage with, and remain in, learning' (ibid., p.3).

While the 'world class skills agenda' was clearly dominant in DIUS, there was a small nod to the citizenship agenda in one of the DIUS Departmental Strategic Objectives:

> *Build social and community cohesion through improving social justice, civic*
> *participation, and economic opportunity by raising aspirations, and broadening*
> *participation, progression and achievement in learning and skills. (DIUS,*
> *2007b, p. 213)*

Again, the means of building community cohesion is not directly – through learning programmes that promote citizenship, civic participation and social justice, but indirectly – through the economic benefits of enhancing skills and employment. The challenge is defined not as active citizenship itself but supporting and encouraging excluded people to take part in the skills-based learning that is offered. The skills agenda is thus seen to 'contribute to social cohesion' through targeting public investment in recognised qualifications at foundation levels, Level 1 and Level 2 for priority groups of learners.

Off the radar – whether because it is seen as unproblematic or the responsibility of some other department – is any kind of learning that goes beyond getting people qualifications and jobs to promoting and supporting their engagement in civic life, involvement in their communities and participation in democracy. Only one very small element in the overall funding of adult education has any space at all for citizenship learning as such: the 'safeguarded' Personal and Community Development Learning (PCDL) funding stream. That funding is not only the smallest, but while 'safeguarded' is actually diminishing year on year because of inflation.

- 16–19 Further Education (FE) funding – £5,921 million in 2007–08 rising to £6,774 million in 2010–11.
- 19+ education (FE and adult) – £2,741 million in 2007–08 rising to £3,261 million in 2010–11, by which time almost half will be 'employer-responsive – i.e. providing courses to employed people that are determined by their employer – while the 'adult learner-responsive' funding decreases year on year.

- Included in the total adult education funding above, PCDL 'safe-guarded' learning – £210 million in 2007–08, remaining at the same amount through 2010–11. (LSC, 2007b, p.44.)

What's more, PCDL-funded provision has to meet a wide range of other government agendas including 'first steps' (engaging the most disadvantaged and socially excluded people in learning with a view to progressing them into the skills agenda) and informal learning (a 2008 consultation from DIUS seems to suggest that PCDL funding could be channelled into supporting 'informal learning', not clearly defined but encompassing self-directed learning as well as learning that does not lead to qualifications). Little space or support is left for learning citizenship.

The policy agenda in citizenship

The citizenship policy agenda currently has three main threads: citizens as consumers of public services, social cohesion and participatory governance. These three strands have different relationships with learning. Ruth Kelly, then Secretary of State for Communities and Local Government, wrote in the foreword to the ALAC evaluation report:

> *Citizenship is being able to influence the shape and design of our public services so that they are more responsive to their needs. (ALAC National Network, 2006, p.3)*

This is a 'customer' view of citizens as consumers of public services. It suggests little in the way of citizenship learning. A review of the DCLG website suggests that this view of citizenship as influencing public services is still significant, but there is a new concern about 'community cohesion'. One might expect that a community cohesion agenda would involve learning, at least about diversity, cultures and tolerance.

A recent Ipsos-Mori research report for CLG explores 'what works' in community cohesion through a series of case studies (Department for Communities and Local Government, 2007b). While learning does not appear as an explicit concept, it is apparent that the kind of learning activities developed as part of ALAC are very much part of the community cohesion agenda.

- Cohesion relates to encouraging positive relationships between different groups, respect for diversity and meaningful interaction.
- There is a clear emphasis on the role of participation and engagement.
- Building a sense of commonality around real life issues.
- Issues must be defined at local level (ibid, p.7).

The case studies indicate a range of different kinds of intervention, including drama or role play to provide opportunities to think in other people's shoes, and building the work around activities that provide a common goal (ibid., p.8).

The third strand of citizenship policy is about citizen engagement and empowerment. A recent international learning event, 'Champions of Participation: Engaging citizens in local governance', brought together participants from 15 countries who are active in making local government more participatory and engaged with communities. The project's report (Dunn et al., 2008) flags up the opportunity presented by two 2006 White Papers from the Departments of Internal Development (DFID) and Communities and Local Government (CLG).[1] Both focus on the value of civic participation for two reasons:

- instrumental – 'to show that participation contributes to poverty reduction' (ibid, p.5); and
- as an end in its own right – producing 'greater accountability and more inclusive forms of democracy' (ibid).

More recently, Hazel Blears, the former Secretary of State for Communities and Local Government, published an Action Plan for Community Empowerment (Department for Communities and Local Government, 2007a). This plan is intended to widen and deepen local empowerment opportunities, strengthen local representative democracy, and provide for a variety of actions to underpin and strengthen this work. The Action Plan defines community empowerment as 'the giving of confidence, skills and power to communities to shape and influence what public bodies do for or with them' (ibid, p.12). It acknowledges that empowerment done badly is worse than not at all.

---

[1] Department of Internal Development (2006) *Making Governance Work for the Poor*; and Department for Communities and Local Government (2006) *Strong and Prosperous Communities* (local government reform).

Scanning the Action Plan reveals a few references to specific learning activities. Learning to change neighbourhoods (the Guide Neighbour-hoods project), and active learning for active citizenship (the ALAC project) and other projects have been supported under the CLG empowerment banner. Information about tackling social issues is mentioned:

> *To help people find the way and know how to tackle an issue that concerns them locally, we will produce a 'menu' of the different opportunities that exist, and a series of 'how to' guides and information sources to help them get started and signpost people to further information sources as part of the development of the Together We Can section of the DirectGov website (www.direct.gov.uk/togetherwecan). (Department for Communities and Local Government, 2007a, p.39)*

The action plan also recognises that community participation is itself a learning experience. One of the case studies in the CLG action plan is the village of Gamblesby in Cumbria, which embarked on a project to take community ownership of its village hall from the local council and develop the funding to renovate it. As a result of these activities, the action plan says,

> *The whole process has enabled local people to develop skills and increased confidence that may open up future avenues for collective activity to benefit the village. (Ibid, p.41)*

Nevertheless, learning tends to be tangential and marginal in the government's policies around citizenship.

Learning and citizenship

The learning agenda embodied in DIUS policies focusing on skills seems to have a different world view from the learning agenda embodied in the ALAC experience focusing on citizenship (see Table 4).

While learning is not an explicit focus of either the local government White Paper nor the community empowerment action plan, it has long been recognised as an essential element of citizen engagement and empowerment. Adult education internationally has a long history as an agent for social change in society (see Merrifield, 2002). The roots of this

Table 4 Learning agenda

	Skills agenda*	**ALAC agenda****
Who participates?	'Target groups' of 'priority learners' – those without formal qualifications or with low level qualifications	Socially excluded groups but also others, bringing a wide range of people together to act on common concerns
Role of outreach and engagement?	Identifying priority learners and supporting them to take part in the skills learning and achieve the designated qualifications	Dialogue and negotiation about what learning is needed to respond to local issues
What is to be learned?	Defined ahead of time by government, focused on national qualifications at L2 and L3	Negotiated with participants, based on own experiences and concerns
How learning takes place	Led by professionally trained teachers, following set curriculum leading to qualification, usually in workplace or college environment	Flexible, variable, conducted in own spaces in the community by civil society groups, including learning from each other
Outcomes of learning	Qualifications, and progression into higher level qualifications and/or employment	Citizen action and involvement

* *Taken from DIUS (2007a) and LSC (2007a and 2007b).*
** *Taken from ALAC National Network, 2006.*

approach to adult education go back through the twentieth and into the nineteenth century. They include: Bishop Grundtvig and the Scandinavian folk high-school movement; the Antigonish movement in Canada; the Settlements, WEA and miners' libraries in the UK; Settlement Houses and the Highlander Folk School in the USA. Most of these combined explicit political values and education with work on economic and social conditions using a wide range of learning methods: mass meetings, study clubs, radio listening groups, short courses, kitchen meetings, conferences, leadership schools and training courses. In the study clubs or discussion groups everyday problems were discussed and ideas shared and solutions put forward.

Central to the history of adult education for citizenship have been the links between learning and experience, or action. The study circles and workshops involved people acting on the problems they faced, and supported them both in planning for and learning from those actions.

This view of learning as rooted in action is echoed in a review of the 'policy moment' for the Champions of Participation event (Zipfel and Gaventa, 2008). A summary of the policy lessons that these champions agreed includes, for example:

> *Lesson 4: Citizen engagement is not a quick win, easily reduced to targets and timetables. It must also be sustained over time through:*
>
> * *institutional and community-wide ownership, not only individual initiative;*
> * *a balance of immediate results and long-term commitment;*
> * **ongoing learning and improvement based on experience***; and*
> * *remembering previous promises and following-through on them. (Ibid, p. 7, added emphasis)*

Whatever we as educators (and governments) intend, people learn to be citizens. They learn what it means to be a citizen from growing up in a political culture that shapes what is seen as possible and as impossible. They learn from their experiences in civic participation. But what they learn from these experiences does not always make them more actively-involved citizens. As Dewey argued in the 1930s, some experiences are miseducative: people learn to be passive or resistant, to expect little of their political leaders or to actively collude in corruption, graft and anti-democratic practices (Dewey, 1938). When the political culture and everyday life experience send other messages, formal citizenship education efforts on their own cannot produce active citizens. But when there are opportunities and spaces to participate, citizenship learning activities can support and encourage their participation, enable people to learn the skills and knowledge needed and gain confidence to participate.

What adult education can offer citizenship

How has it happened that adult education has been so sidelined from the debates about civic participation and the 'democratic deficit'? The historical roots in education for social change and democracy seem to have been submerged by a generation of government-funded adult education for 'leisure' or 'skills for work'. The space for citizenship education, so familiar in the nineteenth century and even in the 1970s, seems to have disappeared. As adult educators we must take some of the blame for letting it disappear. I am principal of an independent adult education centre that, since its beginning more than 60 years ago, has had a focus on education for more than leisure and work skills:

> *Friends Centre is an independent adult education organisation where learners can develop their knowledge, skills, understanding and creativity. In a number of welcoming and supportive places across Brighton and Hove our learning programme aims to:*
>
> * *help learners achieve their aspirations and meet the challenges they face;*
> * *stimulate community interest and civic action; and*
> * *promote tolerance, social justice and international understanding (see www.friendscentre.org).*

The Friends Centre has grown and thrived through the last seven years, but we have not been able to find much space for the last two elements of our mission statement. The kinds of learning that support citizenship is indirect, at the margins, and through our partnerships with community organisations. We have been able to do a little:

* supporting formation of a local network of neighbourhood groups to promote internet access for disadvantaged people;
* working with a partner to provide training to community and voluntary sector groups;
* helping a local history group in a disadvantaged community to put memories and photos on the web;
* encouraging involvement of BME parents in primary schools in mainly white neighbourhoods through our ESOL classes; and
* convening a monthly gathering of local voluntary and community groups to discuss common themes.

Most of this has been done with other funding, not with LSC funds, and with volunteers. We would like to do more.

Friends Centre is not alone in finding the climate of recent years in adult education difficult to link with its social justice roots. NIACE is the lead representative organisation in adult education and it too has citizenship in its remit:

> *Through adult learning, we can create and maintain a more skilled and knowledgeable workforce while building learning communities in which people can explore shared enthusiasms and work together as active citizens.*

In recent years NIACE has been funded by and closely allied with government as a 'critical friend'. This makes it as difficult for NIACE to progress a citizenship learning policy agenda as it does for education providers to practice it.

Are we clear enough about what adult education can offer the citizen engagement and empowerment agendas of government? In an earlier review of learning citizenship for the Institute of Development Studies (Merrifield, 2002) I identified four main strands of learning activity that characterise much popular or transformative adult education:

- talk – providing a forum within which people can share ideas, discuss alternatives and reach decisions;
- cultural expression – using especially local cultural forms to give voice, pass on history and engender solidarity;
- knowledge – creating and accessing knowledge from which people are excluded, whether it is knowledge of the state, of specific issues or synthesising 'popular knowledge' (indigenous knowledge that has not been written down); and
- action – making a link between debate, knowledge and acting on decisions that affect people's lives, enabling learning from the experience of participating.

These strands suggest aspects of our own history as a field and of the range of work within it that could enhance a citizenship policy agenda. But the history is not widely known or celebrated, and the experience of those who have worked on this is increasingly marginalised.

The way ahead

There are opportunities now for new initiatives on civic engagement – 'the policy moment'. Adult educators need to be part of this – as learners (learning from international experience, learning from community organisations) and as educators (working more directly and explicitly to support citizen participation). The alternative is to remain stuck within a narrowly vocational skills agenda that offers disadvantaged people only one way out – to get a job. Not to be empowered citizens, not to be community leaders, not to be participants in important decision-making about public policy and the delivery of public services.

At the Friends Centre we are at the beginning of some exciting thinking about what we are calling 'one planet learning'. It is activated by our hope to be part of a new building being built in Brighton on 'one planet living' principles (www.oneplanetliving.com). It seems to us that one planet learning would take us back to our roots as well as forward into the future. We know that climate change and environmental sustainability are imperative for individuals, communities and governments to address. But we also think that 'one planet learning' is about more than climate change. It is also about learning to live together, on this one planet we have, with tolerance for difference. We think it's about getting involved in communities and in governance, at all levels from the local to the global to the virtual, and through that involvement to work with others to make a better world. Friends Centre's founders in 1945 called themselves 'starry eyed visionaries' who saw adult education as part of building a better world after the end of a horrific world war. The need for that better world is as great and as urgent as it ever was. We don't know how to fund one planet learning, any more than our founders knew how they would sustain their vision of adult education. But we are convinced there is both a need and a demand.

John Denham, former Secretary of State for Innovation, Universities and Skills may have needed no reminding that 'learning contributes to stronger communities and social justice' (in his foreword to *Adult Learning and Skills: Investing in the first steps*, DIUS, 2007a). Hazel Blears, former Secretary of State for Communities and Local Government, may recognise that empowering citizens is the 'best way to revitalise the local roots of our democracy and help build respect' (in her foreword to the *Action Plan for Community Empowerment: Building on success*, Department for Communities and Local Government, 2007a). But they are missing something by keeping the learning agenda so separate from the citizenship agenda. They are missing an opportunity to engage people in real learning, learning that matters to them, and to reach out particularly to people who are normally outside both the learning system and civic involvement activities.

References

ALAC National Network (2006) *Active Learning for Active Citizenship: An evaluation report by Professor Marjorie Mayo and Dr Alison Rooke.* London: Home Office

Department for Communities and Local Government (CLG) (2006) *Strong and Prosperous Communities.* London: HMSO

Department for Communities and Local Government (CLG) (2007a) *Action Plan for Community Empowerment: Building on success.* London: HMSO

Department for Communities and Local Government (CLG) (2007b) *'What Works' in Community Cohesion. Research Study conducted for Communities and Local Government and the Commission on Integration and Cohesion.* London: HMSO

DIUS (2007a) *Adult Learning and Skills: Investing in the first steps.* London: HMSO

DIUS (2007b) *Departmental Strategic Objectives.* London: HMSO

DIUS (2008) *Informal Adult Learning – Shaping the Way Ahead.* London: HMSO

Department for International Development (DFID) (2006) *Making Governance Work for the Poor.* London: HMSO

Dewey, J. (1938), *Experience and Education. The Kappa Delta Pi Lecture Series.* New York: Collier Books, Macmillan

Dunn, A. *et al.* (2008) *Champions of Participation: Engaging Citizens in Local Governance. International learning event report, 31 May–4 June 2007, UK.* Brighton: Development Research Centre on Citizenship, Participation and Accountability, Institute for Development Studies

HM Treasury (2007) *2007 Pre-Budget Report and Comprehensive Spending Review.* London: HMSO

LSC (2007a) *Better Skills, Better Jobs, Better Lives. Annual Report and Accounts for 2006–07.* London: The Stationery Office

LSC (2007b) *Our Statement of Priorities: Better skills, better jobs, better lives. The Learning and Skills Council's priorities and key actions for 2008/09 to 2010/11.* London: The Stationery Office

Merrifield, J. (2002) *Learning Citizenship. IDS working paper 158.* Brighton: Institute for Development Studies

Zipfel, T. and Gaventa, J. (2008) *Making the Most of the Policy Moment: New initiative for citizen engagement in the UK and lessons from international experience.* Brighton: Development Research Centre on Citizenship, Participation and Accountability, Institute for Development Studies

CHAPTER SIXTEEN

Reviewing the ALAC model

RENNIE JOHNSTON

This chapter aims to review the ALAC model in relation to key concepts within the discourse and practice of adult learning for citizenship. It seeks to explore how ALAC practice illustrates, illuminates and challenges the following key ideas:

- the role of civil society in promoting active democratic citizenship
- the use of spaces for learning and action in civil society;
- praxis, the inter-relationship between practice and theory in learning for citizenship; and
- the inter-relationship between equality and difference in the ALAC model of adult learning for citizenship.

This analysis will be based primarily on evidence from three ALAC publications: *Active Learning for Active Citizenship* by Val Woodward (2004), *Active Learning for Active Citizenship: An evaluation report* by Marjorie Mayo and Alison Rooke (2006) and Take Part, the national framework for active learning for active citizenship, compiled by ALAC participants and launched in December 2006. It will be supplemented by my own experience as a participant/observer at the ALAC cross-sector planning workshop in October 2003, the first ALAC conference in June 2004 and the launch of the ALAC evaluation in May 2006.

From the outset, the Active Citizenship model was developed on a focused collective level. As the ALAC evaluation puts it:

... ALAC (Active Learning for Active Citizenship) was based upon a community development approach. The emphasis was upon working democratically and learning collectively, through organizations and groups in the community. ALAC focused upon community empowerment through learning, enabling organizations and groups to enhance the effectiveness of their strategies for social change. Through increasing their knowledge and their critical understandings of power structures and decision-making processes, ALAC participants would be empowered to intervene and, where necessary, work towards changing these, in the pursuit of the values of equality and social justice. (Ibid., p.16)

One of the ALAC model's clear strengths was that it set out to build on good community practice, both in terms of existing partnerships and networks (the hubs), ideologies (avoiding deficit models and actively working with difference) and in terms of methodologies (a clear commitment to working democratically and learning collectively).

While ALAC was only a two-year funded project, by building on what already existed it was able to leave behind, after the funding period, considerable and continuing progress within the hubs and an *independent* national ALAC National Network (ANN) committed to: 'promote and sustain the development of active learning for active citizenship in communities'. Its work was also linked into the national government 'Together We Can' campaign to empower citizens and communities to work with public bodies to improve public services. A last and important development was its learning framework, 'Take Part', a collaborative effort on the part of a wide range of ALAC stakeholders with an aim to:

Inspire, inform and offer practical advice for individuals wanting to get involved in organizing, facilitating and supporting adult education for active citizenship (by providing) programmes of active learning that enable people to gain the skills, knowledge and confidence to become empowered citizens – citizens who are able to make an active contribution to their communities and influence public policies and services. (www.citizenshipfoundation.org.uk/main/news. php?n408)

It is in the interests of further developing community-based adult learning for active citizenship that the following key concepts are explored further.

The role of civil society in promoting active learning for active citizenship

A founding principle of ALAC was that active learning for active citizenship should be firmly rooted in civil society rather than being simply provided for citizens, as an instrument of public policy (Woodward, 2004, p.6; Mayo and Rooke, 2006, p.12). This ambition addresses the key historic question of the role of civil society in promoting active democratic citizenship. This is particularly important when the work of ALAC is considered in the context of the UK New Labour government's adoption of a 'Third Way' approach to economic and social policy. At one level, the virtues of neo-liberal market-led approaches are encouraged and extolled, with some previously public services being privatised or semi-privatised. Yet, at another, there has been a strongly expressed governmental concern to combat social exclusion and promote civil renewal and community development.

This raises questions about the nature of civil society and its ideological orientation. The UK Voluntary Sector Almanac understands civil society as encompassing 'all organizations operating in the space between the state and the market' (Wilding *et al.*, 2005) and sees it as a public sphere which provides spaces in which differences can be debated and taken forward. The UK New Labour Third Way approach certainly raises questions about the independence of civil society in relation to both the market and the state: As the National Council for Voluntary Organisations (NCVO) puts it:

> *The increased professionalisation of the sector and the resulting polarisation between large and small organisations are, to a great extent, linked to the influence of government and business. Target setting, performance management and monitoring are all part-and-parcel of the audit and funding culture that prevails today. Voluntary and community organisations have adopted a wide range of management techniques and tools originally designed for corporates or the public sector. (Ibid., p.5)*

Historically and ideologically, there have also been different understandings of and emphases in civil society between Right and Left. For example, those towards the Right are interested in civil society as it reflects a primarily apolitical arena to develop civic virtues like

276

self-sacrifice, duty and service for others, an arena separate from but still understood to be within the overall framework of a free market society (Green, 1993, p.ix). In contrast, the Left, drawing more directly from Gramsci, (1986) identifies civil society as a sector of public life outside of the directly regulated political and economic spheres where there is sufficient relative autonomy and subversive space to develop counter-hegemonic action.

In the context of the above two perspectives, a key contemporary development in the UK has been the process where some of the former regional and local responsibilities of the welfare state have been contracted out to voluntary and community organisations. While this can serve to bolster some of these groups and ensure, to some extent, a more regional or local voice in the delivery of civic services, there is a real danger that these organisations consequently lose their collective identity and independence, through becoming service providers and paid agents of the state. As Turner and Ridden (2001, p.39) argue:

> *The more voluntary associations become dependent on the state through tax benefits, cash payments or administrative services, the less they function as separate and independent forces in civil society ... state power is not diminished by a greater reliance on voluntary associations but is merely relocated.*

Public policy is increasingly being geared to incorporating citizens into the ambit of both the state and the market. With this in mind, it could even be argued that, despite the government rhetoric of 'double devolution' where power is devolved from the centre to local government and also devolved from local government to neighbourhoods and communities, in practice its view of civil society is not significantly different from that of the historic Right; that is, it 'reflects a primarily apolitical arena to develop civic virtues like self-sacrifice, duty and service for others, an arena separate from but still understood to be within the overall framework of a free market society' (op. cit.).

So clearly there are differing views about the nature of civil society and therefore the possibilities for adult and community development learning within it. Moves towards state co-option can create tensions at a regional and local level between learning for adaptation or compliance, learning for personal development and, more collective learning for social and economic change. In relation to adult learning, Finger and Asun (2001, p.132) make the point that:

> ...*The instrumental rationality which dominates the market and the organisation of labour has now also become adult education's dominant frame of reference. Knowledge and skills are now measured with respect to their practical usefulness to cope with the 'given' conditions of daily life.*

This has prompted community educators like Crowther (2001, p.3), following Gramsci, to characterise civil society as 'the bulwark of the established order and its Achilles' heel' (my underlining) where the "social glue" of hegemony which binds people to the dominant social order' is both created and undermined. Here, Shaw and Martin (2000), in relation to adult and community development learning make a very useful distinction between 'community as policy' and 'community as politics'. Whereas 'community as policy' is government and policy-led, for example as in the development of a range of regeneration schemes which are essentially top-down in their initiation and management and where community activists are drawn in to implement a government agenda and government targets, 'community as politics' is much more rooted in the local community and has the potential to be community-led. It affords greater scope for learner/citizens in communities to identify and promote their own interests and agendas. This ideological dichotomy is very useful for developing a critical analysis of policy and practice in the areas of community regeneration and development. However, it needs to be considered in relation to a world of practice which is much more messy, where there are real dangers of government co-option but where there are also opportunities to exploit government community rhetoric and hold it to account and even allow some space for more autonomous, even radical action, as has been the ambition of ALAC.

Early ALAC thinking was certainly well aware of this tension. As Bernard Crick, a key influence on early ALAC thinking, put it:

> *There is a real danger that voluntary bodies and charities, sometimes even more informal community groups, can end up tied by grants as virtual agents of the state. (Crick, 2001, p.7, cited in Mayo and Rooke, 2006, p.5)*

However, partly due to the early approach adopted by the ALAC project and perhaps partly due to the limited early funding commitment to

ALAC by government,[1] ALAC had a relatively free hand in conducting its initial mapping exercise and, most importantly, identifying existing experience of learning for active citizenship, most of which did not rely heavily on state sponsorship. At the same time, it was able to set out ruling principles which no left-leaning government could easily dispute, namely 'issues of equality, valuing diversity and strengthening co-operation, social cohesion and social solidarity, taking account of issues of gender, race and other aspects of marginalisation in the pursuit of participation for social justice', (Mayo and Rooke, 2006, p.12). Furthermore, its original governmental home, the Home Office, ensured that such a devolved, community-centred, relatively radical community development model could largely avoid being associated or influenced by a much more centralised, instrumental and targeted government approach to the funding of adult learning as promoted through the Learning and Skills Council (LSC) and the Department for Education and Skills (DfES).

With this fortuitous background, ALAC was able to develop a flexible 'community as politics' approach which was able to be both inclusive and radical at the same time, help individuals achieve accredited learning outcomes if they wanted without skewing the whole collective endeavour of ALAC and help groups engage critically with government policy without being 'owned' or sponsored by it. The UK government might well analyse and build on the devolved development model adopted by ALAC if it is serious that:

> *A central theme of the Government's 10-year vision for local government reform is the engagement of more people in making decisions and setting priorities in localities and neighbourhoods. (Civil Renewal Unit, Home Office, 2004)*

And their more recent commitment to:

- *better enable local people to hold service providers to account;*
- *place a duty on public bodies to involve local people in major decisions; and*
- *assess the merits of giving local communities the ability to apply for devolved or delegated budgets (Ministry of Justice, 2007, pp. 7–8).*

---

[1] On 7 June 2004, the *New Statesman* characterised this as 'Following the example of David and Goliath; it seems that the Home Office has pitted tiny resources, under the co-ordination of one part-time employee, against huge problems including voter apathy.'

The use of spaces for learning and action in civil society

A key aspect of ALAC's devolved development model has been the way it has identified and developed spaces for learning and action within civil society. In the interests of developing a citizenship that is both active and critical, it is important that 'horizontal involvement', for example, partic-ipation in community groups and networks, needs to be linked to 'vertical involvement', for example, critical and active involvement in wider local and regional forums and formal consultations with (local, regional and national) government. Certainly the ALAC hubs have been successful in the latter respect with, for example, their work with representatives and activists within the London Civic Forum, the wide-ranging political edu-cation work carried out by the Impact programme in the Black Country, the politicising processes and outcomes of the 'Speaking Up' courses in the South West, the development and support of the migrant workers' group in Lincolnshire and the creation of the Refugee Charter for Manchester. (Mayo and Rooke, 200, pp.17–38; Take Part, 2006, pp.70–91).

Some of the ALAC hubs have used as a theoretical baseline the American Westheimer and Kahne typology of the 'personally responsible citizen', the 'participatory citizen' and the 'justice-oriented citizen' which is not a million miles away from British models of liberal, community and radical adult education (see Johnston, 2003, pp.10–18). At one level, it can be seen that this underpinning typology has allowed the inclusion of different levels of involvement, while also identifying a possible progres-sion route towards more vertical and critical political involvement. However, in relation to progression, Westheimer and Kahne (2004, p.241) make the explicit point that:

> *Each vision of citizenship, therefore, reflects a relatively distinct set of theoretical and curricular goals. These visions are not cumulative.*

While the ALAC practice in connecting the 'horizontal' and the 'vertical' is impressive, it could be argued that, in their wider theorising, some clearer form of progression in moving from the individually active to the collectively active to the critically involved and collectively active citizen might be identified as a way of connecting the 'critical' and the 'active' and more explicitly linking 'horizontal' and 'vertical' involvement.

Spaces have been a central focus of ALAC work since its inception. In her interim report, Val Woodward looks to help groups 'tap into the creative space between the personal and political dimensions of their lives' (Woodward, 2004, p.4). And in the same report, the suggested framework for expansion highlights the need for 'deliberative space – opportunities for individual and group reflection' (ibid., p.18), a theme taken up at some length by the Take Part review of the role of the adult educator where both 'safe' spaces and 'spaces to challenge and be challenged' are stressed. This is no easy task as one ALAC facilitator readily identifies:

> *Working with such a diverse group of women has its rewards and difficulties. It can be hard to create 'safe' spaces to raise issues and has led us to look at how we develop safe spaces to talk about difference, diversity, assumptions, stereotypes, and working together. (Mayo and Rooke, 2006, p.11)*

This emphasis on spaces for critical, reflective and active citizenship accords with wider literature in this area. For example, Jones and Gaventa point to the need to look for and develop new 'spaces' or arenas in which citizens can participate as citizens, crucially moving from being 'users and choosers' (better informed consumers) to (more critical and collective) 'makers and shapers' of the policies that affect our lives. These spaces may be about extending the decision-making into:

- spaces where citizens spend everyday lives (for example Participatory Rural Appraisal, legislative theatre and citizens' juries);
- government spaces (for example, around participatory budgeting); and
- spaces related to the media (for example local radio, street theatre and citizen video to articulate messages and take them to public meetings to disseminate information. (Jones and Gaventa, cited in Warburton *et al.*, 2006, p.27)

A central part of this is to help local people explore, contest and turn 'invited spaces' and 'provided spaces' (usually government sponsored or provided) into 'claimed spaces' where community members and groups can enter into 'stakeholder dialogue' about identifying and (re)claiming oppositional spaces and so challenging dominant structures of power and discourse in the interests of a more democratic community and environment. (Cornwall, 2002). An important part of this is to hold local and national governments to account regarding the gaps between their rhetoric and their policies. As the ALAC evaluation puts it:

> *These spaces are not neutral, however. Spaces for citizen participation ... on the contrary, are 'permeated with relations of power.' (Cornwall, 2004, p. 9) within communities, between communities, between communities and states, and between states and communities internationally. (Mayo and Rooke 2006, p. 11).*

As a community-grounded and relatively autonomous part of the Together We Can project, 'the UK government's campaign to empower people', perhaps ALAC and the Take Part programme are well-placed to work 'both sides of the equation' to build a 'more active and engaged civil society and a more responsive and effective state that can deliver needed public services' (Gaventa, 2004, p.27, cited in Mayo and Rooke, 2006, p.6). However, a key part of this is the capacity to work towards a citizenship praxis which is active *and* critical.

The development of ALAC praxis

'Praxis', a term highlighted in the Take Part framework, embodies a range of tensions: between theory and practice, between critical reflection and action. Originally a Greek term meaning informed and reflective action guided by a moral disposition to act truly and justly (Carr and Kemmis, 1986, p.33), 'praxis' has been adopted and re-worked by, among others, Marx, to mean a unity of theory and practice (McLennan, 1976, p.92) and Gramsci, as the relationship between human will and economic structure (Gramsci, 1986, p.403). However, the most famous and meaningful reference for community educators is Paulo Freire's definition: 'reflection and action upon the world in order to transform it' (1972, p.28), which resonates strongly with the theoretical drift of Take Part.

Here, one aspect which is particularly interesting is the way ALAC, and especially Take Part, view 'praxis'. The original focus on experiential learning and good practice makes ALAC a very practice-centred approach. But here practice is not some kind of thoughtless behaviour. On the contrary, the ALAC development illustrates well that all educational practices have 'theory' embedded in them, that they are distinctive social activities conducted for distinctive purposes by means of specific procedures and skills and in the light of particular beliefs and values (Carr and Kemmis, 1986, p.113).

With this in mind, it can be seen that a cumulative process of ALAC praxis has developed where the interim report first draws on a range of practical experience and relevant literature to justify and underpin its key values and processes, then the evaluation report analyses ALAC practice in a wider critical theoretical context and, finally, Take Part includes a section on 'themes', 'educational theory and practice underpinning the Take That approach', which draws on Freire, Dewey, Kolb and other theorists. Take Part is primarily a manual for practitioners which, while acknowledging theoretical influences, develops a framework from which learner/citizens:

> ... Can collectively develop strategies ... through learning with other people, through practice rather than by absorbing theory ... with conversation and dialogue as key tools to facilitate learning ... .by enabling people to gain new skills, insights and understanding through tackling real-life challenges in the community. (Take Part, 2006, p.8)

In the context of education, Usher (1989, pp.80–81) suggests that we can conceptualise 'theory' in terms of two dimensions: a formal-informal dimension and a framework-products dimension. The first makes a distinction between formal 'academic' theory which is founded upon codified bodies of knowledge most commonly embodied in academic disciplines and the 'informal' theory which is not formally organised or sometimes even identified but is closely bound up with action. ALAC has been mainly concerned with the latter but still informed by the former. Usher's second distinction points to a difference between 'theory' in the sense of a framework of understandings, concepts, beliefs and values which underlie any activity, be it theoretical or practical, and particular theories which are rooted in these wider frameworks and are held and developed by different participants, 'theory as product'. Here, it is noticeable that Take Part has moved away from the original idea of a core curriculum for citizenship learning to developing a more flexible and inclusive *framework* which in turn has been able to move towards its own theory as *product*, namely its integration of theoretical themes, adult and experiential learning, community development, community engagement, commitment to lifelong (and lifewide) learning and perhaps its most original contribution, the addition and development of 'constructed conversations', as introduced and pioneered by the Lincolnshire/East Midlands hub (Take Part, 2006, pp.93–100). Interestingly, this idea of 'constructed conversations':

> *A systematic process of engaging with local groups and individuals who have*
> *already demonstrated an interest in citizenship issues, encouraging them to*
> *reflect on activities, concerns and resources, and so helping them to resolve*
> *community problems. (Take Part, 2006, p.79)*

is an educational/political process which has some similarities to the more
structured popular education practice of 'systematisation' which has been
developed in South America and which involves a more systematic and
reflective engagement with the experience of learners in social
movements and a more dialectical understanding of the relationship
between theory and practice (Kane, 2001).

In relation to praxis, Usher, Bryant and Johnston (1997, p.137–8)
discuss how an element of theorising can involve making informal
theory (which is always present in practice) more open and explicit, so
enabling practitioners to identify and surface their ruling frameworks,
change their understandings and hopefully, their practice. This allows
practice to become 'praxis' which is both reflective and reflexive. While
the developing praxis of ALAC is certainly reflective, sometimes its
reflexivity is limited. It would have been interesting to know more about
wrong assumptions, different understandings between activists, community workers and academics, methods that did not work, approaches that
needed to be revised as a way of being more reflexive and more self-
critical about ALAC praxis, but, of course this process of self-critical
reflexivity is often reduced and influenced by the imperative in practice
to tell 'success stories' which justify government and other funding.
Still, there was a much more reflexive approach in ALAC's approach to
working with equalities and difference.

Linking equalities and difference in the ALAC model of citizenship

From the outset, ALAC foregrounded equality and diversity as being
core values. And the way this was taken forward in a critical, reflexive and
active way may have been one of its most important contributions to
debates about adult learning for citizenship. In the interim report, Val
Woodward (2004, p.10) nails the ALAC colours to the mast when she
identifies the ALAC focus as being 'citizenship as a capacity within people
rather than citizenship as something people do or do not possess at any one
time, in any one place'. Such an approach explicitly rejects any kind of

deficit model of citizenship, very much in contrast to New Labour's over-instrumental, sometimes even dangerous, obsession with deficits and specific target groups, 'raising basic skills levels among the seven million people who cannot read properly and are not comfortable with numbers' (Hodge, 2002). Woodward takes this process further in asserting that:

> *Providing education for and encouraging active citizenship needs to actively challenge exclusionary attitudes and practices, not just guard against excluding groups of people. (Woodward, 2004, p.13)*

From this important starting point, a critical and reflexive learning from each other developed among the hubs. Indeed a gradual progression can be seen from the work of the hubs, through the in-depth analysis of the ALAC evaluation, right into the Take Part 'values in action' which, from a starting point that:

> *Take Part approach is underpinned by the recognition that our society is not equal in terms of money, capital, education, prospects, environments, employment, health and so on.*

It then goes on to advocate:

- *supporting people to challenge attitudes and behaviours of individuals and practices of institutions that discriminate against and marginalise people;*
- *making sure that barriers to attending and taking part are reduced as much as possible – so that learning opportunities are open and inclusive to those who want to take part; and*
- *bringing diverse groups of people together and facilitating authentic dialogue around differences and commonalities to try to reduce the perceived barriers between them.* (Take Part, 2006, p.19)

From South Yorkshire hub's active and critical engagement with members of Sheffield's Somali community and with Gypsy and Travellers' groups, through the Black Country Impact multifaceted work with women, through the South West's work helping disabled people to speak up, through the Tees Valley's work with isolated individuals, through Asian women's participatory research in Manchester, through Lincolnshire's 'constructed conversations' with migrant agricultural workers to London's courses for, among others, black and ethnic minority groups, faith communities, older people and members of lesbian, gay, bisexual and transgender communities, a recurring ALAC theme has been an assertion and exploration of social cohesion and solidarity in the context of diversity and multiculturalism. And this has been facilitated by the critical analysis of the ALAC evaluation and the developing Take Part framework which takes an unequivocally 'liberating' rather than 'liberal' view of diversity and equality (Johnston, 2003, p.13).

So, it looks like ALAC has succeeded in practice in developing what Fiona Williams has called:

> ... *Solidarities based upon respect for difference: not the solidarity of the lowest common denominator, nor the solidarity that presumes all will forgo their particularities in aiming for a common goal: rather it is the pursuit of unity in dialogues of difference. (Williams, 2000, p.350)*

ALAC's pursuit of common purposes out of a recognition of difference is a clear contrast to some ideas of citizenship which focus on more top-down, prescriptive and consensual ideas of the 'good citizen' (Coare, 2003, pp. 41–52) and the 'common good'. In exploring the interface between equality and difference, ALAC praxis gives the lie to more assimilationist ideas of citizenship. Therefore, it is perhaps ironic that at the ALAC Dissemination Conference, the government minister who introduced the project also seized the opportunity to launch his new personal drive for a focus on 'British values' in education: 'freedom, fairness, tolerance and democracy', which are rooted in British history. While these values appear to be both liberal and universal, their re-assertion by a government minister also raises questions about the whole idea of plurality, difference and integration. In the face of the ALAC project and model's explicit endorsement of social cohesion and solidarity in the context of *diversity and multiculturalism*, the ministerial focus on 'British values' introduces the dangers of adopting unitary communitarian models of community which take insufficient account of diversity and difference. Indeed, this approach was soon after re-emphasised by another minister, at the time directly responsible for Communities and Local Government (and the Together We Can initiative) in initiating a new government-led debate:

> *We have moved from a period of uniform consensus on the value of multicul-turalism, to one where we can encourage that debate by questioning whether it is encouraging separateness ... In our attempt to avoid imposing a single*

British identity and culture, have we ended up with some communities living in isolation of each other, with no common bonds between them? (Kelly, 24 August 2006)

This is an important question which raises the longstanding issue of developing meaningful 'cultural citizenship', described by Turner and Ridden (2001, p.34) as 'cultural empowerment, that is, the capacity to participate effectively, creatively and successfully within a national culture, and also the capacity to participate in one's own culture'. As they also point out:

Adult education, as both a field of interest and an institutional space, constitutes an important arena for debate about what citizenship involves, how it is related to the nation-state, and how marginalized groups can be active in the process of debating and shaping change. (Ibid., p.55)

While the UK government is actively promoting a debate on the exact nature of 'Britishness', it may be necessary to take greater account of the vital contribution adult education can make in the development of a cultural citizenship which is both active and critical. At the same time, while it extols the virtues of 'evidence-based practice' it may also be salutary for it to learn from the evidence and practice on equality and diversity from a pioneering project like ALAC.

References

Carr, W. and Kemmis, S. (1986) *Becoming Critical: Education, knowledge and action research.* London: Falmer.

Civil Renewal Unit, Home Office (2004) *Review Findings: Building Civil Renewal: Government review of support for community capacity building.* London: Home Office

Coare, P. (2003) 'Shaping the Good Citizen: Politics and Policy' in Coare, P. and Johnston, R. (eds) (2003) *Adult Learning, Citizenship and Community Voices: Exploring community-based practice.* Leicester: NIACE, pp. 41–52

Cornwall, A. (2002) *Leading Citizen Participation.* IDS Bulletin, Vol. 33, No. 2. Brighton: Institute of Development Studies

Crowther, J. (2001) *Participation in Popular Struggles: Towards a reconciliation of the learning iceberg,* unpublished PhD thesis, University of Edinburgh

Finger, M. and Asun, J. M. (2001) *Adult Education at the Crossroads: Learning our way out.* Leicester: NIACE

Freire, P. (1972) *Pedagogy of the Oppressed.* London: Penguin

Gramsci, A. (1986) *Selections from Prison Notebooks,* edited and translated by Hoare, Q. and Nowell Smith, G. London: Lawrence and Wishart

Green, D. G. (1993) *Reinventing Civil Society.* London: IEA

Hodge, M. (2002) 'Labour Plans for Lifelong Learning in the Second Term', speech to the Social Market Foundation, 11 April

Johnston, R. (2003) 'Adult Learning and Citizenship: A framework for understanding and practice', in Coare, P. and Johnston, R. (eds) (2003) *Adult Learning, Citizenship and Community Voices: Exploring community-based practice.* Leicester: NIACE, pp. 3–21

Kane, L. (2001) *Popular Education and Social Change in Latin America.* London: Latin America Bureau

Kelly, R. (2006) Speech to the Commission on Integration and Cohesion, 24 August

Mayo, M. and Rooke A. (2006) *Active Learning for Active Citizenship: An evaluation report.* London: Goldsmiths, University of London

McLennan, D. (1974) *Karl Marx: His life and thought.* Frogmore: Paladin

Ministry of Justice (2007) *The Governance of Britain.* London: HMSO

Shaw, M. and Martin, I. (2000) 'Community work, citizenship and democracy: Re-making the connections' in *Community Development Journal,* Vol. 35, No. 4, pp. 401–404

Take Part (2006) *The national framework for active learning for active citizenship.* (See www.takepart.org)

Turner, B. and Ridden, J. (2001) 'Balancing universalism and diversity' in Bron, A. and Schemann, M. (eds) *Civil Society, Citizenship and Learning.* Muenster: Litverlag, pp. 29–59

Usher, R. (1989) 'Locating Adult Education in the Practical' in Bright, B. (ed.) *Theory and Practice in the Study of Adult Education: The epistemological debate.* London: Routledge

Usher, R, Bryant, I. and Johnston, R. (1997) *Adult Education and the Postmodern Challenge: Learning beyond the limits.* London: Routledge

Warburton, D. *et al.* (2006) *Community learning and action for sustainable living.* Goldalming, Surrey: World Wildlife Fund UK

Westheimer, J. and Kahne, J. (2004) 'What Kind of Citizen: The politics of educating for democracy' in *American Educational Research Journal,* Vol. 41, p. 240

Wilding, K. *et al.* (2004) *The UK Voluntary Sector Almanac.* London: NCVO

Williams, F. (2000) 'Principles of recognition and respect in welfare' in Lewis, G, Gewirz, S. and Clarke, J. (eds), *Rethinking Social Policy*. London: Sage, in association with Open University, pp. 338–352

Woodward, V. (2004) *Active Learning Active Citizenship: A report by the Civil Renewal Unit*. London: Home Office

CHAPTER SEVENTEEN

Looking backwards, looking forwards – and looking outwards, in the context of globalisation

Marjorie Mayo

Citizenship has emerged centre stage, as Chapter Two argued, both in Britain and more widely too (Kabeer, 2005). It is not only that relationships between citizens and the institutions of governance have been characterised by a growing crisis of legitimacy – although these relationships have indeed been the subject of widespread concern. Significantly too, in the global era, as Giddens (Giddens, 2000) among others has argued, citizens need to engage with international processes of structural change, processes that impact upon citizens in very different national contexts, albeit in widely varying ways. Active citizens committed to social justice agendas need to engage with these processes of structural change then, (Giddens, 2000), building links between the local, the national and the global.

The case for addressing these interconnections has emerged already, in previous chapters. A range of ALAC strategies has been providing illustrations here, including ALAC strategies to promote active citizenship through working with refugees and asylum seekers, as well as with more established communities, working together to tackle racism and xenophobia. These interconnections emerged too, for example, in the context of ALAC strategies to enable migrant workers from the EU accession states to claim their rights, as active citizens. Active learning for active citizenship has included visits to Brussels as well as to Westminster, to enable women to engage with the structures of governance at European as well as at national level. And active learning for active citizenship has included strategies to empower citizens of differing faiths and hybrid identities in the global city of London.

This chapter starts by illustrating some of the ways in which participatory approaches to learning for active citizenship have been shared across national boundaries, with a particular focus upon examples of learning from the global South. These Southern experiences have been formative in the development of participatory approaches to learning for active citizenship, stretching back over the past three decades. While South/North learning has been significant in the past, however, the current context poses additional challenges too – how to build two-way connections between active citizenship locally, nationally and globally? This chapter concludes by exploring examples of active citizenship to illustrate the potential for developing future notions of citizenship with global as well as with more local and national dimensions.

Sharing learning from the global South

There has been growing interest in sharing learning from the South, in general, in recent years, challenging previous assumptions rooted in cultural forms of imperialism, assumptions about the supposedly superior benefits of learning from the global North. This pattern has been particularly marked in relation to participative approaches to development including participative action research and adult education for active citizenship. As Gaventa and Merrifield have so clearly demonstrated, over the past decade a great body of literature has developed about the theory and practice of participatory approaches. 'Much of it has its roots in experiences in developing countries, and has been labelled and promoted as a concept by persons involved in networks of adult education and development' (Gaventa and Merrifield, 2005.122). The experiences themselves are far from new – the novelty lies rather in our increasing recognition of the value of sharing the learning from these, recognising the extent of the debts that current debates on learning for active citizenship owe to theories and practices developed in the global South from Latin America to Asia, building upon the work of Paulo Freire (Freire, 1972) Rajesh Tandon (Tandon, 1980) Budd Hall (Hall, 1982), Fals Borda and Rahman (Fals Borda and Rahman, 1991), John Gaventa and Juliet Merrifield (Gaventa, 1991) and others, through the seventies and the eighties onwards. These participative approaches continued to be developed even through those challenging Thatcher/Reagan years of rampant neo-liberalism, described as the 'lost decade', in terms of development, including, more generally, community development.

This past history sets the context for the discussion of particular illustrations of more current approaches and practices, with a focus on an emerging world power with a long tradition of democratic participation, the example of India – together with examples of other significant cases in point. While these examples can in no way claim to be representative of the range and depth of experiences, they do offer opportunities for exploring the possibilities for shared learning across North/South divides, opening up the discussion of two-way processes of learning for active citizenship, globally as well as locally.

The background to active learning in the global South: illustrations from India

India has a particular history of learning for active citizenship, as one of the oldest democracies in the global South, as well as having a history of cross fertilisation between Indian approaches and those being developed in Latin America and elsewhere. Imperial education strategies in pre-independent India could, perhaps, be described as the precise opposite of education for active citizenship – ' "education" to persuade people to defer to the priorities of powerful interests abroad policy' it has been argued (Bordia, 1973, p.11). The reality, however, was far more complex and far more contradictory. One effect was precisely the opposite of that intended, the creation of a Western-educated section of the population, many of whom became deeply frustrated and antagonistic to the colonial administration. This educated middle class provided one of the key elements in the development of the movement for national independence, finally achieved in 1947. In summary then, as Steele and Taylor have argued (Steele and Taylor, 1995), colonial educational policies and provision, including adult education policies and provision were deeply contested. So India has a long history of learning for citizenship – whether or not this was quite what her former colonial masters had in mind.

Post-independence, citizen participation was to be promoted with policies for decentralisation via the institutions of 'Panchayati Raj' (local district and village councils) and via programmes to promote community development. Education, including adult education, came to be seen as a key component in these processes of democratisation, with the

emphasis upon social education and social consciousness, including awareness of civic rights and leadership as well as more practical knowledge
and skills for development – 'general education to enable every Indian
to participate effectively in the new social order' (Bordia, 1973, p.24).
Resources were scarcely adequate to support such wide-ranging aims, it
has been pointed out. But even the limited resources that were provided
(through the National Adult Education Programme from the late 1970s)
enabled what has been described as a rising generation of adult educators
to develop participatory programmes based upon principles with direct
parallels and connections with those developed by Paulo Freire in Brazil
and elsewhere, emancipatory approaches to learning for social transformation, focusing upon learners' needs, with priority being given to
working with women and members of scheduled groups (among the
most deprived and excluded groups of citizens in the case of the new
democracy of India) (Steele and Taylor, 1995).

There are direct links here with the values and approaches developed
within ALAC. As Rajesh Tandon, one of the key figures in the development of these approaches, both in India and internationally, has explained,
participatory approaches start:

> From the assumption that ordinary people already possess some knowledge.
> Some elements of this knowledge may be distorted, and some may be
> authentic. This, in fact, is also the starting point of adult education. Adults
> already have some knowledge and information. They do not start with a
> clean slate ... it is the synthesis of popular knowledge with existing scientific
> knowledge (that) strengthens the educational experience of the people. (Tandon,
> 2005, p.43)

Through participatory approaches, relatively powerless people can build
the knowledge and skills to challenge dominant knowledge and power
structures, developing and systematising their own knowledge in the
process (Gaventa and Merrifield, 2005).

As Tandon has gone on to point out, this type of approach may be
relatively new to some Northern academics but for those in the field this
'has been an ongoing process' with its own history in India. This history
has included a range of examples of women's empowerment (Kanhere,
2005) and the empowerment of disadvantaged minority groups including 'tribals' (Madiath, 2005) and 'dalits' – disadvantaged castes, groups who
have been increasingly engaged in active citizenship through participatory

learning and participatory research, over the past three decades. There would seem to be powerful parallels here, with key implications for active learning for active citizenship in Britain and elsewhere.

Supporting the civic participation of women and disadvantaged minorities

Women and disadvantaged minorities in India have been offered new constitutional opportunities for active citizenship, over the past decade, while continuing to face the most extraordinary challenges in practice. In summary, India, in common with so many states in the global South, focused upon developing policies for decentralisation in the nineties, as part of wider strategies for restructuring and democratic renewal. In India the structures of Panchayati Raj, introduced after Independence, were seen as being in need of revitalisation, if decentralisation policies were to be effective.[1]

In addition to attempting to strengthen the three-tier Panchayati Raj system at village, block (groupings of villages) and district level in general, for rural India and for the municipalities of urban India, this restructuring provided that a third of the seats were to be reserved for women and seats were to be reserved for other disadvantaged groups, scheduled castes and tribes, seats that were to be directly elected, with regular elections at each tier. Through this reservation of seats, it was argued, democracy would be strengthened as the voices of all sections would be enabled to be heard. This was ambitious to say the least, for any society, given how much is known already about the barriers to participation in Britain and elsewhere, structural barriers of access and resources as well as motivational barriers, not to mention barriers arising from lack of information, background knowledge and skills.

In India, there have been particular challenges, including specific challenges for the participation of women and other disadvantaged groups. Indian society has been embedded 'in patriarchal, traditional values that set restrictive conditions on women' it has been argued (Sharma, undated. 4). As a study of women's participation in six Indian states demonstrated, 'women elected to their local bodies were not acquainted with the process

---

[1] This revitalisation was to be facilitated via the 73rd and 74th Constitutional Amendments which were enacted in 1992, coming into force in 1993.

and procedures of these bodies. Governance was new to them, they were not equipped with the knowledge and skills required for the elected representatives in these bodies' which meant that in so many cases their husbands (or in some cases other male family members) 'guided them' (ibid., p.4). Effectively what was happening, in many cases, was that the men who had previously been elected, when they found that they were ineligible, because the seats in question had been reserved, decided to put forward their women folk, to stand in their place. This would enable them to retain power and influence, their women folk becoming known as 'dummy' representatives, proxies acting on their behalf. As research from Uttar Pradesh illustrated, for example:

> In Ittaunjha Nagar Panchayat … (T)he present chairman is a lady but her husband looks after the work. He was the previous chairman and because the constituency was declared reserved for women his wife contested the election. The husband chairman is even present in the monthly meetings and no one is allowed to meet the wife … the work of the municipality is not going on smoothly and the monthly meeting is not yielding fruitful results. (PRIA, 2002, p.10)

This effective dependency was compounded by so many of the women's low levels of formal education (typically lower than the men's, (Sharma, 30) as well as by more practical barriers such as the cost and difficulties of transport to and from meetings, especially in rural areas.

This was the situation, then, for so many women who were elected for the first term, following the passing of the Constitutional Amendments. There were similarly disturbing findings about the limitations experienced by other disadvantaged groups, strongly entrenched notions of caste compounding those of gender while women from poor economic backgrounds were further disadvantaged, in terms of their opportunities for independent decision-making.

The Society for Participatory Research in Asia (PRIA) has played a key role, in response to these challenges. PRIA describes itself as 'an international centre for learning and promotion of participation and democratic governance. It is a non-profit voluntary organisation, promoting initiatives for the empowerment and development of the poor, marginalized and weaker sections of society' (Tandon, 2005, p.328). For a quarter of a century PRIA has been promoting participatory research and learning for active citizenship in India and elsewhere in Asia and beyond, internationally. And this has included a focus upon strengthening institutions of local self-governance, in the Indian case to make Panchayati Raj Institutions more effective institutions of local self-governance and democratic citizen participation.

From 1995 PRIA has been working together with the Network of Collaborating Regional Support Organisations on a joint action pro-gramme of strategic multi-sectoral interventions to strengthen Panchayati Raj Institutions. This programme has included orientation and training, backed by educational materials prepared for the purpose, bottom–up planning and research. In the second phase, from 1997 to 2000, the programme has also included promotional interventions as well as research and advocacy and networking, working with a range of partners includ-ing voluntary and community-based organisations as well as government agencies and officials and the elected representatives themselves. By 1999 more than 15,000 elected representatives had been covered and the number of partner organisations was expanding, enabling the work to be further increased. Support for women's active participation fitted into this wider picture of strategic support for strengthening local democracy and participatory planning from the bottom–up (PRIA, 2000).

One particular feature of the joint action programme was the inclu-sion of the Pre-Election Voters' Awareness Campaign. This campaign enabled voters to develop clearer and more critical understandings of the nature of elections and the whole election process. As a result there were instances of women questioning candidates who were seeking their votes, asking candidates how they planned to take up issues of concern to women. Women candidates who found difficulty replying, or who implied that they would simply ask their husbands for their views were exposed to challenge.

Assessing the impact of these strategic interventions the evaluation report recognised that the numbers of those affected were still relatively small. Reaching 15,000 elected representatives might seem impressive indeed, in the British context – but this has to be set in the context of the vastness of the scale of institutions and representatives in India. The inter-ventions could be seen as 'addressing only the tip of an iceberg, in a sense' the report reflected, pointing out that 'the large mass underneath (in terms of local level inertia, institutional indifference and Civil Society apathy) could help sink the whole intent of the 73rd and 74th Constitutional Amendments. Limitations of scale notwithstanding' the Report concluded (ibid., pp.14–15), much had been achieved, providing opportunities for learning from hands-on engagement with issues of self-governance, helping to synthesise the lessons and systematise knowledge through research, building support networks and enabling appropriate policy responses from the institutional framework.

Overall, then, the evaluation report pointed to increasing participation by masses of people whose interface with institutionalised governance had been 'so discouraging and exclusionary' in the past. Political space for participation had been widened, in particular, for women and for other socially marginalised sections of society. The change for women was staggering, it was argued, 'given the limited opportunities available in a patriarchal social system' (ibid., p.16), as were the changes with new leadership emerging at the grass roots, breaking traditional caste barriers. The ripple effects could be expected to widen further. As Tandon reflected, writing in 2003, 'Over the years there has been a shift from proxy candidature and submissiveness to a situation where there are increasing number of cases where women have started handling the panchayat affairs confidently and efficiently' (Tandon, 2003.5). There were similar reflections on the strengthening of the dalit community (PRIA, 2003b). As a more recent research paper commented, dalits have been asserting themselves politically, so that political parties 'can no longer take the support of dalits or marginalized sections of society for granted'. One can say, this paper concluded 'that this warning signal is a view from below of the process of deepening democracy in Indian politics'. (Shukla, 2006, p.8).

Since then PRIA has continued to work to spread these ripple effects. As the 2005 Annual Report pointed out, reflecting upon the past year's work:

> *Our coverage now spreads to 12 states, 26 districts and 25,000 Panchayats and 37 municipalities; nearly 25,329 women leaders were actively supported; capacities of 5,140 citizen leaders were strengthened; 1,496 intermediary civil society organisations were oriented and enabled to engage with issues of governance.*

The website report concluded that still more needed to be done, with others, however, in order to make a sustainable impact on these issues (www.pria.org).

In summary then, these experiences illustrate the potential contribution that can be made by participatory learning, backed by participatory research. Even in societies where women and disadvantaged groups face the challenges that they have been facing in parts of India, they can be supported in ways that are empowering, enabling them to be more effective in taking up the issues of concern to them as active citizens. There are potential parallels to be drawn more widely here, sharing the lessons from these Southern experiences elsewhere, including Britain, putting gender higher on the devolution agenda, alongside more general equalities issues. There are examples where this learning has been directly transferred already over the years, just as there have been examples involving ALAC professionals who have gained experience from Southern contexts, experiences with direct relevance for their subsequent practices back in Britain.

Linking the local and the global

This chapter started with a focus on the learning that has already been shared internationally, over the past three decades or so, emphasising the importance of the learning that has been and continues to be transferred from South to North. These exchanges have already provided evidence of the potential for going further still, moving on to develop joint actions of international solidarity. This was illustrated, for example, through the learning and the participatory research that was developed back in the 1980s, building solidarity between US trade unionists working for Union Carbide and the Indians who were facing the results of Union Carbide's failure to ensure health and safety – leading to the tragedies of mass deaths and injuries in Bhopal, India in 1984 with an estimated 10,000 killed and thousands more maimed (Gaventa, 1999). Through joint research and shared learning (Agarwal, Merrifield and Tandon, 1985) Union Carbide's attempts to shift the blame onto the Indian management were challenged, strengthening negotiations for compensation and for improved health and safety for the future.

With increasing globalisation, such links are potentially more significant than ever. And here too there are Indian examples to draw from, as well as examples from other contexts in the global South, including more contemporary experiences. Two-way interconnections have been developing, involving mobilisations around environmental issues and trade justice issues, for instance, just as they have been developing around issues of health, education and poverty reduction, to name just some of the most evident examples.

In recent years, in summary, a number of changes in globalisation and global governance have challenged assumptions about where power resides, and how and where civil society can best engage to bring about significant policy changes. These changes have been the subject of continuing debate. Globalisation has opened up new spaces for citizen engagement, it has been argued, offering increased transparency, with enhanced opportunities for participation and democratic accountability. The World Bank Inspection Panel has been cited, for example, as a case in point (Clarke and Fox *et al.*, 2003), along with World Bank structures for consultation with NGOs. Conversely, however, critics have pointed to the limitations of such spaces, in terms of their remit. How far is the discourse effectively remaining limited within the neo-liberal paradigm and to what extent can citizen engagement make a difference? (Fiorini, 2000). 'Global civil society exists,' according to Lipschutz, for instance, but 'it is too fragmented and diverse to wield significant structural power' or to develop significant challenges to the dominant development discourse (Lipschutz, 2004, p.231).

Others disagree, however, focusing more positively on the potential opportunities for global civil society to strengthen citizens' voices, help claim rights, and develop strategies to challenge policies that fail to address unequal power relations globally as well as more locally. To do this, though, '[T]ransnational civil society cannot float free in a global ether.' It has been argued. 'It must be firmly connected to local reality' (Fiorini 2000, p.217). That connection to local reality can give international campaigns legitimacy, and it can provide them with a representative base. Grassroots local groups can also benefit from the vertical links to global campaigns, finding solidarity with others fighting for the same issues. With international and outsider support, they can benefit from added weight in their efforts to pressurise their own governments (Gaventa and Mayo, 2009).

Tarrow has reached similar conclusions about the importance of understanding these continuing links between local and global activism – while taking due account of the challenges to internationalism from what he has described as 'the orgy of national chauvinism that followed September 11' (Tarrow, 2005, p.217). Tarrow's research raises further questions too, questions about the learning that civil society activists and civil society organisations do or do not take with them, from one experience of activism, from one episode to another. The future of transnational activism, Tarrow suggests, may well be episodic and contradictory, but like a series of waves that 'lap on an international beach, retreating repeatedly into domestic seas' these mobilisations may be 'leaving incremental changes on the shore' (Tarrow, 2005, p.219). Social movements have long been identified as sites for learning, both learning about the issues in question and wider learning about civil society and active citizenship. Getting involved, as ALAC's experiences have already demonstrated in previous chapters, has the potential to change actors' own perceptions about active citizenship and themselves as active citizens (Foley, 1999; Merrifield, 2002; Newell and Wheeler, 2006).

There are major challenges for learning here, then, how to facilitate learning for active citizenship globally as well as locally, taking the learning from one experience to the next. Evaluations of the global campaign to 'Make Poverty History' (the Global Campaign Against Poverty or GCAP as the campaign has been known internationally) have demonstrated a number of the tensions that are inherent in global campaigning, including some of the tensions involved in balancing the demands for rapid responses, to keep pace with a rapidly moving international campaign, and the requirements for maintaining democratic accountability, with firm roots locally. As the Make Poverty History 2005 Campaign Evaluation Report pointed out, 2005 was a significant moment, 'a unique opportunity to make progress in the campaign against global poverty' (Firetail, 2006, p.5). While the evaluation report celebrated the campaign's achievements, however, concerns were expressed about a number of issues, including the extent to which the coalition was genuinely representative and democratically accountable, internationally (ibid., 2006). Issues have to be framed in ways that relate to local priorities, it has been emphasised, while presenting unified demands internationally. Lessons are being drawn, then, with a view to ensuring that global campaigning brings genuine benefits locally, as well as gaining legitimacy and strength from its local roots. The following case study is based upon joint research with John Gaventa, part of a wider international study of citizen engagement in a globalising world (based at the Institute of Development Studies at the University of Sussex).

The Global Campaign for Education (GCE) offers a particularly valuable case through which to explore some of these challenges. The Millennium Development Goal (MDG) of 'Education for All' is centrally important in its own right, as well as for its impact on other MDGs including the promotion of gender equality via increasing girls' access to schooling. Free basic education was declared to be the right of every child as long ago as 1948, yet so many of the world's children, over 77 million, well over half of whom are girls, are still out of school. 'Education for All remains an aspiration to be achieved', as the GCE explains, 'which is why the MDGs include the target of transforming this long agreed right into reality by 2015, backed by the pledge that no country seriously committed to education for all would be thwarted by a lack of resources'. (GCE, 2005b). Without education people lack the capability, 'the actual ability to achieve valuable functionings as a part of living' in the words of Amartya Sen (Sen, 1993, p.30) – without the capacity to become effective as active citizens.

The Global Campaign for Education describes itself as a 'unique coalition of actors who have come together to demand that future generations should not have to suffer the scourge of illiteracy and ignorance'. GCE is made up of a coalition of civil society organisations, linked national coalitions of NGOs, child rights activists and teachers, including their unions, supported by Education International, UN agencies and most importantly, parents and school children in over 100 countries.

The GCE mobilises over seven and a half million campaigners in more than 120 countries during the Global Week of Action in April each year. With 37 million fewer children out of school, over the past five years, much has been achieved – in part at least, in response to these mobilisations of active citizens through the campaign. As the GCE president, Kailash Satyarthi has reflected, however, addressing the high-level Group on Education for All in Cairo on 22 November 2006, huge challenges remain. Building coalitions vertically, linking local coalitions together, at national and international levels is particularly problematic, for a number of reasons, not least of which may be the problems associated with ensuring effective representation and democratic accountability, at every level. Despite these inherent and continuing challenges, though, the GCE clearly has contributed to the MDGs and has done so through mobilisation at every level, raising important implications for the study of active citizenship and learning for active citizenship, globally as well as locally.

As part of a wider programme of research into Local-Global Citizen Engagement (one of the themes of the Development Research Centre programme on Citizenship, Participation and Accountability, based at the Institute of Development Studies at the University of Sussex) the authors explored the GCE, as an illustration of these possibilities and challenges, selecting the GCE as an example of citizen engagement that has been making a difference – building a democratically representative coalition

AND impacting on people's sense of themselves as active citizens, globally as well as locally. This research included interviews with international NGOs and trade union organisations involved in the campaign, as well as interviews with participants at national and local levels, right down to village level committees. These more local interviews took place in India and Nigeria, selected because both countries illustrate active civil society engagement, working towards the achievement of Education for All, addressing the problems associated with having significant numbers of children (especially girls) out of school. In addition, researchers participated in the mobilisations for the Global Week of Action in Birmingham, April 2007, to gain more direct evidence of the impact of involvement in the Global Campaign on young people back in UK.

Although the research evidence was insufficient to reach definitive conclusions, there were clear indications that involvement in global campaigning was not only making a difference in terms of the campaign itself, with citizen action at different levels providing mutual re-enforcement, each potentially strengthening the other. Engagement in global as well as local activism was also impacting upon participants' perceptions of themselves, as active citizens. Reflecting on her experiences of becoming involved in global advocacy, for example, an Indian summarised her feelings about international advocacy, contrasting these with her previous experiences, working for a multi-national company. 'Before (this) I worked for a multi-national ... I was connected with a global network but didn't feel very good about it. This (that is global advocacy) has given me another way to be connected, where I feel much better about what I am doing.' 'You feel part of all this – you could influence this. That's very empowering.' A Nigerian activist reflected in similar terms: participating in a global campaign 'increases my confidence that there are people somewhere struggling with the same issues'. This was about 'solidarity ...recognising that part of the solution lies outside my shore'.

While many international NGOs and trade union organisations had long histories of advocacy and campaigning, there was also powerful evidence to illustrate the impact of engagement in some of the more recent local/global campaigns. Getting involved in campaigning does itself build 'interest, understanding and commitment among activists' it was suggested. 'Campaigning does provide ways of mobilising and involving people in ways that formal representation and accountability structures simply cannot do' a trade unionist reflected and the:

> *...Very fact of being involved in GCE joint endeavours does change perceptions and increases members' sense of involvement. You do get a sense that you are actually part of something. This activity helps produce the 'glue' that builds the representation and accountability structures – this builds solidarity – giving the role of agency ... active engagement to activists.*

Being involved in global campaigns such as the GCE can have powerful effects, then. One NGO professional reflected that 'I've changed,' going on to comment that 'I've completely changed my sense of global community'. A lot of people, in this professional's view had 'learned a sense of global citizenship. We experienced a particular kind of feeling when we were all around the world talking together on the global teleconferences.' Others made similar comments. When people see others engaging and themselves engaging 'they get a sense of community and find it very empowering'. These campaigns were creating 'genuine educational experiences which have changed people's understanding of power and of themselves as actors. It will also change their understandings of North and South'. Through this, it was argued people begin to see themselves as part of a global community.

While there was evidence for a growing sense of connection globally by those involved in global campaigns, this was not necessarily separate from their local identities, however. In Nigeria, for example, GCE activists were emphatic that 'yes, ok, we are global citizens,' but 'we are global citizens who act locally'. 'We've run global campaigns in Nigeria ... and we've contributed to global decisions, but I still see myself as very local', reflected another. It was important not to lose one's local roots.

At the Global Week of Action in Birmingham, 2007, similar themes were heard. A local councillor observed that as a very diverse city, people in Birmingham were already 'linked to so many parts of the world'. So he felt that there was 'a duty to influence those with power and resources', so that people elsewhere could have the same opportunities. For him, 'citizenship is global': demonstrating solidarity with others was also the basis for building greater social cohesion locally.

Some twenty years ago, an NGO professional reflected, international issues had been 'a bit of a turn-off' for many young people, whereas now the opposite was true. A number of influences were identified as potential causes, factors such as the ripple effects of the 'Battle of Seattle', the World Social Forums, the Make Poverty History campaign and most significantly the Stop the War campaign against the war in Iraq (which was described as a watershed in terms of young people's consciousness). There was increasing scope for the development of global citizenship and international solidarity within the next generation. There would seem to be important implications here for citizenship education and development education in the global North, more generally, building on young people's increasing consciousness of themselves as global citizens, for the longer term.

There were, however, some potentially disturbing comments on global citizenship from the South. Although involvement in global campaigning was described as being about solidarity, as people elsewhere struggle with the same issues, there were contrasting comments that raised questions about the very notion of global citizenship. 'I can't say that I feel like a global citizen' reflected one participant, echoing concerns that have already been raised more generally (Bandy and Smith, 2005; Batliwala, 2002; Giffen and Wright-Revolledo, 2007). Despite having extensive experience of international campaigning, this Nigerian participant explained that 'I feel like a second-class citizen outside Nigeria … we are made to feel that if you come from a developing country' a feeling compounded perhaps by some of the negative stereotypes that had been associated with Nigeria under military rule. Global citizenship based upon notions of solidarity, equality and respect still seemed a long way off here, implying important challenges for activists and for those concerned with development education and citizenship education more generally in the global North campaigning for the global goal of Education for All.

Looking outwards as well as forwards

Active citizens develop such understandings through their own involvement in activism. Like any kind of learning, though, this learning can be facilitated. Educators can and do stimulate the process 'respecting the knowledge of those directly involved as well as the knowledge to be acquired' (Tandon, 2005, p.29). There are parallels here with some of the learning described in the chapter on the work of the Workers' Educational Association and others in ALAC South Yorkshire hub, exploring the interconnections between the arms trade and civil disturbances in one country and the flows of refugees reaching South Yorkshire, for example, or the interconnections between the loss of call centre jobs relocated from one area (in the UK for example) and the issues associated with wages and conditions, health and safety and child labour in the other (in India for example). Active learning for active citizenship in Britain is already exploring these connections.

As ALAC hubs have already demonstrated, this type of learning is centrally important for the development of global citizenship in the North as well as in the South. Without such critical understanding North/South relationships with their roots in the colonial past may be perpetuated – relationships that have been tainted by regressive Northern attitudes. Agendas to promote community cohesion in Britain can be expected to be at risk, as long as Southern activists feel labelled as second-class citizens – as recipients of Northern charity, rather than as global citizens, acting in mutual solidarity.

References

Agarwal, A., Merrifield, J. and Tandon, R. (1985) *No Place to Run: Local realities and global issues of the Bhopal disaster.* Tennessee, TN: Highlander Center

Bandy, J. and Smith, J. (2005) *Coalitions Across Borders: Transnational protest and the neoliberal order.* Lanham, MD: Rowman and Littlefield

Batliwala, S. (2002) 'Grassroots Movements as Transnational Actors: Implications for Global Civil Society' in *Voluntas,* Vol. 13, No. 4, pp. 393–409

Bordia, A. (1973) 'Adult Education During the British Period and After Independence' in Bordia, A., Kidd, J. and Draper, J. (eds) (1973) *Adult Education in India.* Bombay: Nachiketa Publications, pp. 11–41

Clarke, D. and Fox, J. *et al.* (eds) (2003) *Demanding Accountability: Civil-society claims and the World Bank inspection panel.* Lanham, MD: Rowman and Littlefield

Fals Borda, O. and Rahman, M. (1991) *Action and Knowledge.* London: ITDG Publishing

Fiorini, A. (2000) *The Third Force: The rise of transnational civil society.* Washington DC: Carnegie Endowment for International Peace

Firetail (2006) *Make Poverty History: 2005 Campaign Evaluation.* London: Firetail Limited

Foley, G. (1999) *Learning in Social Action.* Leicester: NIACE

Freire, P. (1972) *Pedagogy of the* Oppressed. London: Penguin

Gaventa, J. (1991) 'Toward a Knowledge Democracy' in *Action and Knowledge,* pp. 121–131

Gaventa, J. (1999) 'Crossing the Great Divide: Building links and learning between NGOs and community-based organizations in North and South' in Lewis, D. (ed.) (1999) *International Perspectives on Voluntary Action: Reshaping the Third Sector.* London: Intermediate Technology Publications, pp. 153–166

Gaventa, J. and Mayo, M. (2009) *Spanning Citizenship Spaces Through Transnational Coalitions (Research Summary). IDS Research Summary 327.* Brighton: Institute of Development Studies

Gaventa, J. and Merrifield, J. (2005) 'Participatory Research in North America and India' in Tandon, R. (ed.) (2005) *Participatory Research: Revisiting the roots.* New Delhi: Mosaic Books, pp. 122–137

Giddens, A. (2000) 'Citizenship education in the global era' in Pierce, N. and Hillgarten, J. (eds) (2000) *Tomorrow's Citizens.* London: IPPR

Giffen, J. and Wright-Revolledo, K. (2007) *Global Civil Society Organisations: Location North or South?* Oxford: Intrac

GCE (2005) *Missing the Mark: A school report on rich countries' contributions to universal primary education by 2015.* Brussels: GCE

GCE (2005b) *Contradicting Commitments.* Brussels: Global Campaign for Education, ActionAid International

Hall, B. (1982) 'Breaking the Monopoly of Knowledge: Research methods, participation and development' in Hall, B., Gillette, A. and Tandon, R. (eds) (1982) *Creating Knowledge: A monopoly? Participatory Research in Development.* New Delhi: PRIA, pp. 13–25

Kabeer, N. (2005) 'Introduction' in Kabeer, N. (ed.) *Inclusive citizenship.* London: Zed, pp. 1–27

Kanhere, V. (2005) 'The Struggle in Dhulia: A women's movement in India' in Tandon, R. (ed.) (2005) *Participatory Research: Revisiting the roots.* New Delhi: Mosaic Books, pp. 163–171

Lipschutz, R. (2004) 'Global civil society and global governmentability' in Barnett, M. and Duvall, R. (eds) *Power and Governance.* Cambridge: Cambridge University Press, pp. 229–248

Madiath, A. (2005) 'Tribals and Land Alienation in Tandon, R. (ed.) (2005) *Participatory Research: Revisiting the roots.* New Delhi: Mosaic Books, pp. 143–153

Merrifield, J. (2002) *Learning Citizenship. IDS Working Paper 158.* Brighton: Institute of Development Studies

Newell, P. and Wheeler, J. (eds) (2006) *Rights, Resources and the Politics of Accountability.* London: Zed

PRIA (2000) *Annual Report 1999–2000 'Strengthening Panchayati Raj Institutions in India.* New Delhi: PRIA

PRIA (2002) *Gender Paradigm in Local Governance: An Indian experience.* New Delhi: PRIA

PRIA (2003a) *Women Leaders in Panchayats.* New Delhi: PRIA

PRIA (2003b) *Civil Society and Panchayats.* New Delhi: PRIA

Rogers, A. (1992) *Adults Learning for Development.* London: Cassell

Sen, A. (1993) 'Capability and Well-being' in Nussbaum, M. and Sen, A. (eds) *The Quality of Life.* Clarendon Press, pp. 30–53

Sharma, D. (undated) *A Study of Women's Leadership: Towards gender mainstreaming governance in the Karuli District of Rajasthan.* New Delhi: PRIA

Shukla, S. (2006) 'Deepening Democracy and the Subaltern Citizen – A view from below', paper delivered to the Fourth International Conference on Citizenship and Governance 1–3 March 2006, Jaipur, India

Steele, T. and Taylor, R. (1995) *Learning Independence.* Leicester: NIACE

Tandon, R. (1980) *Participatory Research in Asia.* Canberra: ASPBAE

Tandon, R. (2005a) 'Participatory Research: Main Concepts and Issues' in Tandon, R. (ed.) (2005) *Participatory Research: Revisiting the roots.* New Delhi: Mosaic Books, pp. 22–39

Tandon, R. (2005b) 'Knowledge as Power; Participatory Research as the Alternative' in Tandon, R. (ed.) (2005) *Participatory Research: Revisiting the roots.* New Delhi: Mosaic Books, pp. 40–53

Tarrow, S. (2005) *The New Transnational Activism.* Cambridge: Cambridge University Press

Author biographies

John Annette is Professor of Citizenship and Lifelong Learning, the Pro-Vice Master at Birkbeck College, University of London. He has published articles on citizenship and service learning, community development and community leadership and his publications include *Education for Democratic Citizenship* co-edited with Sir Bernard Crick and Professor Andrew Lockyer, published by Ashgate in December 2003. He has been an advisor to the British government on citizenship education in schools and also adult learning for citizenship through civic engagement.

Jill Bedford, Sue Gorbing, and *Sal Hampson* have all worked together in the last ten years to develop ideas and courses around women becoming more active and influential in community and public life: active in their own lives, in the life of communities and in the public domain. Jill Bedford and Sue Gorbing now work as part of Changes partnership and have been working on the Women Take Part research around what needs to happen for more women to become involved and influential in public life.

Tony Breslin has been Chief Executive at the Citizenship Foundation since September 2001. He sits on a range of national policy bodies, forums and advisory groups. Tony has published widely on educational issues and is an occasional contributor to the press and to TV and radio broadcasts. He is co-editor (with Barry Dufour) of *Developing Citizens* (2006).

John Grayson was senior tutor for research at the Northern College until October 2006. He is now a partner in a not-for-profit social enterprise, the AdEd Knowledge Company, which is dedicated to 'changing the world through popular adult education'; and teaches at Sheffield Hallam University. He is involved in anti-racist campaigning, researching and adult education work with migrant workers, Roma, and refugees and asylum seekers.

Ted Hartley is secretary of the Take Part Network and engaged regionally in promoting active learning for active citizenship, especially around the theme of migration and its impact on local communities.

Rebecca Herron is Head of the Community Operational Research Unit at Lincoln University.

Rennie Johnston is a freelance researcher and practitioner in lifelong learning and community development. He is co-author and editor, with Pam Coare, of *Adult Learning, Citizenship and Community Voices*, NIACE, 2003, and has written widely on adult learning for citizenship, community education and experiential learning.

Peter Mangan works as an educational consultant specialising in communication and learning in diverse settings such as prisons, NHS clinical practice and higher education. One particular focus is upon enabling agency in and through people who have been dispossessed.

Marjorie Mayo is Professor in Community Development and Joint Head of the Centre for Lifelong Learning and Community Engagement at Goldsmiths, University of London. With Alison Rooke, she evaluated the ALAC programme. Other publications include *Imagining Tomorrow: Adult Education for Transformation* (1997) and *Global Citizens* (2005).

Zoraida Mendiwelso-Bendek is Senior Research Fellow in Citizenship at Lincoln University and is leading the Take Part East Midlands Network.

Juliet Merrifield is Principal of the Friends Centre, an independent adult education centre in Brighton. She has worked as an adult educator and researcher for the last 25 years, in the USA, England and Ireland. She was Director of the Learning from Experience Trust in London, and of the Center for Literacy Studies at the University of Tennessee, USA.

Carol Packham was the co-ordinator of the Greater Manchester ALAC pilot hub. She is course leader of the BA in Youth and Community Work at Manchester Metropolitan University, Director of the Community Audit and Evaluation Centre and an active member of her local community, as vice-chair of the community Forum and Treasurer of the Whalley Range Youth Opportunities Association. Her recent book, *Active Citizens and Community Learning* (2008), draws on practice and learning from the ALAC programme.

Hament Patel is a Sessional Lecturer in Community Development at Birkbeck, University of London.

Lyndy Pooley and *Gabi Recknagel* have promoted active citizenship and user involvement at Exeter Council of Voluntary Service. Lyndy has been instrumental in establishing and expanding Speaking Up training to a range of service users groups in the Devon area, developing user involvement partnerships with local health and care authorities. Gabi's work has included active citizenship for refugees and migrants. She represents Take Part Network on the South West Regional Empowerment Consortium.

John Potter is a consultant in citizenship education. He has worked as Director of CSV Education for Citizenship during the period when citizenship education was being developed for schools and colleges. Subsequently, he has worked as a freelance consultant. His projects have included heading up the impetus values programme at the Institute for Global Ethics UK Trust, a period with the Take Part National Network and the South East Regional Empowerment Network. He is currently the leader of the Salisbury RSA

Fellows Big Project, a partnership between schools, local government and communities, and is the Hon Vice-Chair of the Salisbury City Community Area Partnership. He has written extensively on community service learning and is the author of *Active Citizenship in Schools: A Good Practice Guide to Developing a Whole School Policy* (Kogan Page, 2002) and Co-editor (with Titus Alexander) of *Education for a Change: Transforming the way we teach our children* (Routledge, 2004).

Alison Rooke carried out the evaluation of the ALAC project together with Marjorie Mayo. Alison is a researcher and lecturer at the Centre for Urban and Community Research, Goldsmiths, University of London. She is particularly interested in visual and participatory research and evaluation.

Razia Shariff is a Sessional Lecturer in Community Development at Birkbeck, University of London.

Henry Tam is a specialist in the development of democratic citizenship. Currently in charge of Community Empowerment Delivery at the Government's Department for Communities and Local Government, he was previously Head of Civil Renewal at the Home Office where he devised the cross-government Together We Can action plan. His publications include *Communitarianism: A New Agenda for Politics and Citizenship*, and he is a visiting professor at Birkbeck College, University of London.

Val Woodward was author of the Active Learning for Active Citizenship (ALAC) report published by the Civil Renewal Unit in 2004, and subsequently coordinator of the ALAC project that grew out of that report. Val is now a self-employed consultant offering training and support services to community, voluntary sector and statutory agencies that use and participate in community engagement processes to promote community empowerment.

Acronyms

ACT	Association for Citizenship Teaching
ALAC	Active Learning for Active Citizenship
ANN	ALAC National Network
ASB	Anti-social behaviour
BME	Black and Minority Ethnic
CEN	Community Empowerment Network
CLG	Communities and Local Government
CPD	Continuing Professional Development
CVS	Council for Voluntary Service
DCSF	Department for Children, Schools and families
DfES	Department for Education and Skills
DfID	Department of Internal Development
DIUS	Department for Innovation, Universities and Skills
DPT	Devon Partnership Trust
EMDA	East Midlands Development Agency
EU	European Union
FE	Further education
GCAP	Global Campaign Against Poverty
GCE	Global Campaign for Education
GEM	Gender and Community Engagement
HLN	Healthy Living Network
ICLEI	Local Governments for Sustainability
ILS	Independent Living Strategy
IPPR	Institute for Public Policy Research
L & D	Learning and development
LEP	London Empowerment Partnership
LSC	Learning and Skills Council
LSDA	Learning and Skills Development Agency
LSN	Learning and Skills Network
LSP	Local Strategic Partnership
LTI	Learning to Involve
MDG	Millennium Development Goals

MMU	Manchester Metropolitan University
NCF	National Community Forum
NCVO	National Council for Voluntary Organisations
NEET	Not in education, employment or training
NEP	National Empowerment Partnership
NFER	National Foundation for Educational Research
NSEP	National Strategic Empowerment Partnership
NVQ	National Vocational Qualification
OCN	Open College Network
OTS	Office of the Third Sector
PACE	Professional Adult and Community Education
PCDL	Personal and Community Development Learning
PLEAS	Public Legal Education and Advisory Support
PRIA	Society of Participatory Research in Asia
PSA	Public Service Agreement
PSHE	Personal, Social and Health Education
QIA	Quality Improvement Agency
RACATEL	Raising Civil Awareness Through English Language
RCO	Refugee Community Organisation
SEF	School Self Evaluation Form
SPACE	Social Politics and Citizen Education
TBL	Triple bottom line
TDA	Teacher Development Agency
VOCAL	Voluntary Organisation Community Action Lincolnshire
WEA	Workers' Educational Association

Index